# New Directions for Elementary School Mathematics

*1989 Yearbook*

**Paul R. Trafton**
1989 Yearbook Editor
National College of Education

**Albert P. Shulte**
General Yearbook Editor
Oakland Schools, Pontiac, Michigan

**National Council of
Teachers of Mathematics**

*Copyright © 1989 by*
THE NATIONAL COUNCIL OF TEACHERS OF MATHEMATICS, INC.
*1906 Association Drive, Reston, Virginia 22091*
*All rights reserved*

ISSN: 0077-4103
ISBN: 0-87353-272-4

Third printing 1990

Printed in the United States of America

# Contents

Preface ..................................................... vii

## PART 1: PERSPECTIVE ON CHANGE IN ELEMENTARY SCHOOL MATHEMATICS

1. It's Time to Change ........................................ 1
   *Mary Montgomery Lindquist,* Columbus College, Columbus, Georgia

2. Communication and Reasoning: Critical Dimensions of Sense
   Making in Mathematics ..................................... 14
   *Glenda Lappan,* Michigan State University, East Lansing, Michigan
   *Pamela W. Schram,* Michigan State University, East Lansing, Michigan

3. Developing Understanding in Mathematics via Problem Solving .. 31
   *Thomas L. Schroeder,* University of Calgary, Calgary, Alberta
   *Frank K. Lester, Jr.,* Indiana University, Bloomington, Indiana

4. The Role of Computation in the Changing Mathematics
   Curriculum ............................................... 43
   *Terrence G. Coburn,* Oakland Schools, Pontiac, Michigan

## PART 2: CHILDREN'S REASONING AND STRATEGIES: IMPLICATIONS FOR TEACHING

5. Assessing and Building Thinking Strategies: Necessary Bases for
   Instruction .............................................. 59
   *Harriett C. Bebout,* University of Cincinnati, Cincinnati, Ohio
   *Thomas P. Carpenter,* University of Wisconsin—Madison, Madison, Wisconsin

6. Thinking Strategies: Teaching Arithmetic through Problem
   Solving .................................................. 70
   *Paul Cobb,* Purdue University, West Lafayette, Indiana
   *Graceann Merkel,* Klondike Elementary School, Lafayette, Indiana

## PART 3:  NEW DIRECTIONS IN TEACHING THE CONTENT OF THE CURRICULUM

7. Language Experiences:  A Base for Problem Solving .......... 85
*Rosemary Reuille Irons, Brisbane College of Advanced Education, Brisbane, Australia*
*Calvin J. Irons, Brisbane College of Advanced Education, Brisbane, Australia*

8. Using "Part-Whole" Language to Help Children Represent and Solve Word Problems ...................................... 99
*Edward C. Rathmell, University of Northern Iowa, Cedar Falls, Iowa*
*DeAnn M. Huinker, University of Michigan, Ann Arbor, Michigan*

9. Making Sense of Numbers ................................. 111
*Larry P. Leutzinger, Area Education Agency 7, Cedar Falls, Iowa*
*Myrna Bertheau, Shell Rock Elementary School, Shell Rock, Iowa*

10. Teaching for Understanding:  A Focus on Multiplication ....... 123
*Marilyn Burns, Marilyn Burns Education Associates, Sausalito, California*

11. Collecting and Analyzing Real Data in the Elementary School Classroom ................................................ 134
*Susan Jo Russell, Technical Education Research Centers, Cambridge, Massachusetts*
*Susan N. Friel, Lesley College, Cambridge, Massachusetts*

12. Developing Measurement Sense .......................... 149
*Jean M. Shaw, University of Mississippi, University, Mississippi*
*Mary Jo Puckett Cliatt, University of Mississippi, University, Mississippi*

13. Teaching about Fractions:  What, When, and How? .......... 156
*Nadine Bezuk, San Diego State University, San Diego, California*
*Kathleen Cramer, University of Wisconsin—River Falls, River Falls, Wisconsin*

14. The Calculator as a Tool for Instruction and Learning ........ 168
*Barbara J. Reys, University of Missouri—Columbia, Columbia, Missouri*

## PART 4:  IN THE CLASSROOM

15. Making Mathematics Come Alive through a Statistics Project .. 177
*Alison S. Claus, Sprague School, Lincolnshire, Illinois*

16. The Power of Mathematical Investigations ................... 183
*David J. Whitin, University of South Carolina, Columbia, South Carolina*

17. Hidden Mathematics Lessons ........................... 191
       *Anita S. VanBrackle*, Virginia Polytechnic Institute and State University,
       Blacksburg, Virginia

## PART 5:  PERSPECTIVES AND NEW DIRECTIONS IN TEACHING AND LEARNING

18. Connections between Psychological Learning Theories
       and the Elementary Mathematics Curriculum ................ 199
       *Diana Lambdin Kroll*, Indiana University, Bloomington, Indiana

19. Mathematics Teaching and Learning:  Meeting the Needs of
       Special Learners ........................................ 212
       *Barbara Wilmot*, Illinois State University, Normal, Illinois
       *Carol A. Thornton*, Illinois State University, Normal, Illinois

20. Staff Development:  Directions and Realities ................. 223
       *Arthur A. Hyde*, National College of Education, Evanston, Illinois

21. Cooperative Learning in Mathematics Education ............. 234
       *David W. Johnson*, University of Minnesota, Minneapolis, Minnesota
       *Roger T. Johnson*, University of Minnesota, Minneapolis, Minnesota

# Preface

These are exciting times for school mathematics. For the first time in almost three decades, there is strong support for substantial change in the content and emphasis of the curriculum. The publication of this 1989 Yearbook coincides with the publication of the NCTM's *Curriculum and Evaluation Standards for School Mathematics*. The *Standards* presents a coherent vision of what it means to know and do mathematics, of the content of the curriculum in the age of information, and of the roles of teachers and students in the teaching and learning of mathematics. This yearbook shares the vision of the *Standards* and offers additional insights into the meaning of the standards for K–6 mathematics programs.

In this time of curricular reform, it is most appropriate to have a yearbook devoted to K–6 mathematics, since the early years of school mathematics establish the foundation for future study of the subject. The extent to which children acquire important mathematical knowledge, processes, and insights during these years greatly affects how well the secondary school curriculum will attain its goals. During the early years children also form beliefs both about mathematics and about themselves as learners of mathematics. These beliefs influence how they approach the study of mathematics and decisions they make to pursue it further. Creating programs that are appropriate for elementary school students is a challenge that must be met if they are to develop the mathematical competence they will need in future, if they are to see that mathematics makes sense, and if they are to retain their mathematical curiosity and interest.

This yearbook consists of five sections, with samples of children's work appearing between sections. These examples reinforce the active, dynamic approaches to learning mathematics that are portrayed in the articles.

Part 1 (chapters 1–4) describes and discusses broad components of change in elementary school mathematics. The central roles of problem solving, communication, and reasoning are highlighted, as is the need for revising our thinking about computation.

Part 2 (chapters 5–6) addresses knowledge about children's thinking and reasoning, how they construct ideas, and the importance of incorporating their mathematical understandings into instruction. The articles reflect the extensive efforts in recent years to gain insight into how children develop mathematical ideas.

Part 3 (chapters 7–14) presents new approaches to developing the content of the curriculum. These articles strongly reflect the ideas presented in the previous two sections and offer practical guidance for teachers and curriculum developers.

Part 4 (chapters 15–17) captures the spirit of mathematical exploration and the active involvement of students through descriptions of classroom investigations.

The yearbook concludes with part 5 (chapters 18–21), which focuses on important factors that influence the way mathematics is taught and learned and that must be considered in implementing change.

The 1989 Yearbook reflects the hard work and commitment of many people. The editorial panel developed guidelines, reviewed and selected manuscripts, made valuable suggestions for improving manuscripts, and shaped its overall direction. The panel included the general editor, Albert Shulte, and five individuals with great insight into elementary school mathematics and programs. My sincere thanks and deep appreciation go to these individuals:

| | |
|---|---|
| Donald Chambers | Department of Public Instruction, Madison, Wisconsin |
| Alison Claus | Sprague School, Lincolnshire, Illinois |
| Cathy Cook | National College of Education, Evanston, Illinois, and Corridor Partnership for Excellence in Education, Naperville, Illinois |
| Frank Lester | Indiana University, Bloomington, Indiana |
| Barbara Reys | University of Missouri, Columbia, Missouri |
| Albert Shulte | Oakland Schools, Pontiac, Michigan |

I gratefully acknowledge the assistance of Cynthia Rosso, Charles Clements, and the able NCTM production staff—Drake Byrum, Jean Carpenter, and Lynn Westenberg—whose efforts contributed greatly to this yearbook. Finally, the thoughtful contributions of the authors are deeply appreciated—their time, commitment, and involvement in developing articles made editing this yearbook a satisfying and enjoyable experience.

This yearbook conveys an exciting message about teaching and learning mathematics in the elementary school, and thus it supports and complements the *Standards*. It helps us all better understand the possibilities for K–6 school mathematics and suggests a direction for translating potential change into classroom reality.

PAUL R. TRAFTON
*1989 Yearbook Editor*

# FIRST GRADERS EXPLORE GEOMETRIC PATTERNS

Submitted by Pamela Carter and Ruth Pearlman

# 1

# It's Time to Change

## Mary Montgomery Lindquist

R ECENTLY, there have been many calls for reform of schooling, and in
particular there has been major rethinking of school mathematics. The
initial thrust for change in school mathematics was the poor achievement of
students, but there are even more compelling reasons for change. Today's
technological society requires a different mathematical preparation for its
citizens—and for a greater proportion of its citizens—from that of the past.
Astute teachers and researchers, aware that mathematics did not make sense
to many students, have found different and successful approaches to teaching and learning mathematics. Thus, exemplars on which to base change
already exist. Additionally, newly articulated recommendations for school
mathematics have been made by the *Curriculum and Evaluation Standards
for School Mathematics* (NCTM 1989). These standards, endorsed by many
groups, provide direction from the professional organization most closely
involved in mathematics education for students. Interwoven in this article is
my interpretation of the *Standards* as I discuss five areas of needed change in
the elementary school: the view of mathematics and mathematics learning,
curriculum, instruction, evaluation, and support.

### A VIEW OF MATHEMATICS AND MATHEMATICS LEARNING

Underlying the *Standards* is a view of mathematics and the learning of

1

mathematics that is quite different from that presently held by many people. My logical side says that the first step in implementing the recommendations is to change people's perception of mathematics and mathematics learning to make it consistent with this vision. My practical side says that the acceptance of this view will come incrementally as students, teachers, and others begin to see results of some of the changes. Common to both my logical and practical sides is the need for everyone to be aware of this view.

*Mathematics is a changing body of knowledge.* Some say that in five to seven years there will be twice as much mathematics as there is today. Although much of this new mathematics will not be appropriate for students in elementary school, the magnitude of change will have an impact on how we teach mathematics at this level. At present, students perceive mathematics as a set of rules to be learned and practiced. Yet children come to school with a sense of mathematics, for they have been using it to solve problems they understood. We have failed to capitalize and build on this understanding as we teach more abstract procedures. We must help children construct meaning and sense by approaching mathematics as problem solving. They must see that mathematics is created by us and that it can make sense.

This view of mathematics as a dynamic subject must be begun as soon as children enter school. It does not take long for students to adopt the opposite view as they become receivers of procedures: "Tell me what to do, not why." The short-term payoff for students' knowing "what to do" is great, because that is what we reward. The long-term payoff is a disaster, as shown by the present state of mathematical learning.

Technology has made possible many of the new creations in mathematics, and we must be responsive to technology. Students have often been seduced by the power of a paper-and-pencil algorithm; they know it will do something and they know how to do it, but they do not know what it really does or why. Thus, they perform mathematical antics with little thought as to the reasonableness of answers. Technology is even more powerful, and we need to know how to use it skillfully, just as in the past we needed speed and accuracy with paper-and-pencil algorithms. Without a strong conceptual base, the ability to use technology will be severely limited.

As the amount of mathematics content increases, so does the amount and type of applications. There are new applications of geometry, of measurement, of statistics, and even of sophisticated counting. We need to broaden the curriculum so that our young, beginning students do not have a narrow view of mathematics and so that they will be prepared to study a wide variety of mathematical topics.

Thus, viewing mathematics as a changing body of knowledge forces us to look again at what we are doing with mathematics for the elementary child.

*Mathematics is useful and powerful.* Everyone agrees that mathematics is useful, but often our opinion appears to be that it is useful for someone else. This attitude is well ingrained by the seventh grade (Lindquist et al. forthcoming). At one time this may have been a valid opinion, but it is not one today, for every career is becoming more dependent on mathematics. Do you realize that over 60 percent of college career choices are closed if one has not taken advanced mathematics in high school? Similarly, our technical schools also require a strong background in mathematics for a diversity of career options. Even to function well outside the workplace we need more mathematics and more sophisticated reasoning related to mathematics.

Mathematics, even in elementary school, is often approached on an abstract level as students learn to manipulate symbols. Little attempt is made to have the mathematics grow out of, or be tied to, problems children have solved in other ways. For example, when being taught subtraction, children might wonder why they would *subtract* to find out how much longer a rod of nine cubes is than a rod of five cubes when they have been counting or thinking about how many more cubes would have to be *added* to the shorter rod. Even if one is imagining taking away some cubes, it is not the five cubes. With situations like this, it does not take children very long to think of mathematics as a different world from the one that once made sense.

Any mathematics is powerful if one has control over it, and one can gain control by understanding how it works. In the example described in the last paragraph, if children trying to solve the problem understand that subtraction has many meanings including the comparative meaning, then they will have power. They will understand why subtraction can replace their more primitive method of counting and how subtraction is related to addition. The *Standards* calls for developing the language of mathematics so that students can see its power. The symbolic language of mathematics is powerful, but it is abstract; consequently, it takes time for students to develop the meanings of these symbols.

A goal of the *Standards* is for children to view mathematics as a useful subject that gives them power to solve problems. Our challenge is to create classrooms in which this will happen.

*Mathematics is learned by doing mathematics.* An underlying assumption of the *Standards* is that learning mathematics is a constructive rather than a passive activity. When students are using prior knowledge to construct new mathematical knowledge, they are learning mathematics. Otherwise, they are receiving a body of knowledge, and often in unrelated and unorganized pieces, which makes it difficult to retrieve and use.

This does not mean that the *Standards* advocates that students not be taught. It does mean a new view of teaching for many of us. The teacher must make decisions about what mathematics students are ready to learn and what experiences will help them construct meaning for this mathematics.

This approach is success oriented. Children will be learning that which they can learn and thus will develop the sense that they can *do* mathematics. Developing this self-confidence in students is critical, so that they will continue to use, study, and enjoy mathematics.

*Mathematics can be learned by all.* Mathematics is often viewed as a subject that can be learned only by a few. One often hears, "Either you have or you don't have what it takes to learn math." Of course abilities differ, but often all students do not have a true opportunity to learn mathematics.

We cannot afford to neglect any student or any segment of our population. Evidence from NAEP (Dossey et al. 1988) shows that since 1978 the differences in performance between some subgroups have been narrowing. Black and Hispanic students have made progress in closing the performance gap relative to their white peers. Students in the Southeast improved significantly during this period with comparatively larger and more consistent gains than their counterparts in other parts of the country. Differences between the performance of females and males were not significant at ages nine and thirteen, but small, significant differences in favor of males were present at age seventeen. Overall, these results are encouraging, but substantial gaps in performance still exist between many subgroups and between many individuals. Moreover, much of the gain has been made in computational skills, not in higher-level arithmetic or in other areas of the curriculum.

Not only do we need to close the gap between these subpopulations, but we also need to look at our low-ability students. Any change must take into account this group. One of the most striking differences between American and Asian schooling is that the latter expect hard work. "If a child's rate of learning is slower than that of other children, it means only that the child must study even harder" (Stevenson 1988, p. 8). We need to set realistic goals for low-ability students and then expect them to reach them. One crucial goal, often not expected of these students, is that they should make sense out of mathematics. At present, we are overloading them—as well as many other students—with a preponderance of isolated nonsensical procedures.

Mathematically talented youth also need special attention, for they, with proper encouragement and background, will be the ones who discover new applications of mathematics. But the masses of students in the middle also must be given the chance to learn mathematics in a way that makes sense. They will be the users of much mathematics in their careers and in their daily lives.

## CURRICULUM

*The Underachieving Curriculum* (McKnight et al. 1987) focused attention on the need to make changes in the mathematics curriculum, and the *Standards* proposes many changes. The elementary school has the greatest responsibility for their success, since it will be difficult or nearly impossible to make significant changes in the secondary curriculum without first making changes in the elementary curriculum.

Four aspects of the curriculum—the emphasis, placement, integration, and treatment of topics—need careful consideration in making these changes consistent with the direction set forth by the *Standards*.

*Emphasis of topics.* In the past ten years, interest and progress in including more than paper-and-pencil computation in elementary schools have increased. Textbooks have increased the number of story problems, included problem-solving strategies, and made suggestions for mental math and calculator activities. Statewide tests have increased their emphasis on geometry, measurement, probability, and statistics. Teachers are attending in-service sessions on these topics. Yet elementary students still perceive that mathematics is computation and that the goal is to get the correct answer as quickly as possible. It is evident, although we have made a beginning, that we have not overcome the preoccupation on computation.

Seven changes in the presently implemented curriculum can take us another step forward. If the two recommended decreases are made, there would be time for increased emphasis in the five areas described below. In fact, by implementing the seven proposals below, we can ensure that our students will reach the same level of achievement they now have but without spending the time they do now on computation and repetition.

1. *Increase the emphasis on building an understanding of numbers.* Central to much of mathematics is a firm understanding of numbers, yet children have a narrow understanding of numeration and little understanding of fractions or decimals. On the fourth NAEP mathematics assessment, fewer than half of the seventh- and eleventh-grade students knew that 5 1/4 was the same as 5 + 1/4 (Lindquist et al. forthcoming). The *Standards* refers to this understanding of numbers as number sense. This includes such meanings as knowing that 8 is 6 and 2, or 7 and 1 more, or 2 less than 10; that 23 is small compared to 3856; and that the sum of 57 and 71 is more than 100. This number sense permits a child to mentally add 8 and 4 by thinking 8 and 2 is 10 and 2 more is 12, or to mentally find the sum of 56 and 7 by thinking 56, 60, 63. It is the sense that permits people to make reasonable estimates, not wild guesses.

2. *Increase the emphasis on the meanings of the four operations.* Until recently, any discussion of operations usually focused only on how to develop meaning for computation. One of the greatest contributions of the *Standards* is the highlighting of operations as a separate standard, putting the proper emphasis on *concepts* of operations rather than only on computation.

This missing emphasis on operations is a prime cause of students' difficulty with word problems and with a lack of understanding of computational procedures.

3. *Increase the emphasis on the variety of ways to compute and to make estimates.* In a recent national survey (Weiss 1987, p. 44), 72 percent of teachers of grades K–6 indicated that they placed a heavy emphasis on having their students perform computations with speed and accuracy. Only 2 percent of these teachers had students use calculators "in the previous day's lesson." Although the two percentages are not directly comparable, they do indicate the status of computation in schools today. It is time to educate youth in how to use the tools of today—including their minds, paper and pencil, calculators, and computers. They also must know when it is appropriate to use each tool. For too long our students have needed pencil and paper to find the sum of 56 and 7, which indicates that this problem is not a new one surfacing only because of calculators.

4. *Increase the emphasis on geometry, measurement, probability, statistics, and algebra.* The new applications of mathematics in all aspects of society give us an impetus for reexamining the need for a broader curriculum. Just as we have laid the foundation of arithmetic in the elementary grades, so we need to lay the foundation of the other topics listed above not only for the further study of mathematics but also for use in everyday life.

5. *Increase the emphasis on appropriate, individual segments of the curriculum at each grade level.* When we try to cover everything at each grade level, we end up not covering many things in enough depth to enable children to retain the concepts and skills. A recent study (Porter et al. 1988, p. 4) found that "teachers devoted less than 30 minutes of instructional time across the full year to 70 percent or more of the topics they covered." For example, in many texts *each year* there is one lesson on *each* of these topics: pounds, quarts, liters, and kilograms. The curriculum needs restructuring so that fewer bits and pieces are included each year, thus allowing time for children to internalize the new material. Then in succeeding years we should use, not reteach, this material.

6. *Decrease the emphasis on paper-and-pencil computation.* This recommendation is not a call for doing away with all paper-and-pencil computational work. Much can be learned about numbers and the operations through such work. It does call for a reevaluation of the amount of time now spent on paper-and-pencil computation and ways to free the curriculum for other mathematics. The *Standards* gives direction to this change.

7. *Decrease the repetition from year to year.* The amount of repetition is well documented in the literature or by a look at the scope and sequence in textbooks. This repetition is partially due to the premature introduction of some topics into the curriculum. It may also be due to students' perceptions

of what is important—they soon learn that it is not necessary to learn many things, since they will be retaught in time for the test the next year. It is also due to not staying with a topic long enough for students to build meanings. Certainly old topics will be revisited, but there are many ways to use previously taught material in new settings or with new twists so that students do not think it is the same old stuff. Our motto should be, Use previously learned mathematics yes, but reteach no.

*Placement of topics.* A careful consideration of the placement of topics may alleviate some problems with time. It is clear, for example, that if enough time is spent on two-digit subtraction in the second grade, many children will become at least mechanically proficient. But what is sacrificed? At present, much of this skill must be relearned in third grade because students lack the foundation. Valuable time is lost that could be used for other topics, not to mention the frustration for those second-grade students who were unsuccessful and the third-grade students who had mastered two-digit subtraction earlier and must sit through it again. In general, our computational strand needs to be slowed down so that ample time can be spent developing number sense and meanings of operations as well as applying learned computational skills.

Some people question whether this slowing down of the paper-and-pencil computation strand is weakening the curriculum. I see it as just the opposite; it is opening time in the curriculum for more problem solving, more communicating about mathematics, and more reasoning. These are higher-level skills that demand much more of students.

If number sense is to be well developed, then neither the large numbers nor the small numbers (decimals) can be rushed. I am convinced that time spent on these topics will make time later; if not, at least more students will have a better understanding of the basis of much mathematics.

Appropriate segments of all other topics should be placed in each grade. As with number work, the development should be done carefully so that it is not necessary to repeat the same topic as new work the next year. This, of course, does not mean that there is no need for maintenance or review. It does mean that new topics should be clearly marked and treated differently from those needing only to be reviewed.

*Integration of topics.* There are many reasons why topics should be integrated. First, the integration of topics keeps concepts, vocabulary, and skills alive. It provides a natural way to review these aspects of learning. Second, integrating topics also helps children to make connections between mathematical content. For example, they can see how geometry can help them visualize an arithmetic problem. Third, the compartmentalization of content encourages children to think that once they have passed a test, they can forget the material. Thus, integration would set expectations of having to know, use, and remember the different topics in mathematics.

*Treatment of topics.* It does not matter what we emphasize or how we place or integrate topics if the topics themselves are not treated in a way consistent with what we want children to learn. In the *Standards,* each of the usual content topics is addressed separately to indicate what children should be able to do as a result of instruction in that content area. The reader is referred to the *Standards* for further discussion and to the other articles in this book for examples of content treatment.

## INSTRUCTION

It also makes little difference what we teach if we do not change how we teach. If we wish children to make sense out of mathematics and to develop confidence in their ability, then we must find a better fit between teaching children and teaching mathematics. Although the standards focus on curriculum, they imply a great deal about instruction.

*Problem solving, reasoning, and communicating.* Three of the standards are common across all the grade levels (K–4, 5–8, and 9–12) and address problem solving, reasoning, and communicating. These three standards, crucial to the overall view of mathematics being presented in the *Standards,* are discussed in the next two articles, but let me make one point about each.

If problem solving is to become the focus of the curriculum, then it must be central to the way we teach. We cannot expect children to solve problems unless we help them build mathematics from problems rather than teach them procedures that later can be applied to problems.

Children can reason in mathematics. That is, they can make sense of it if we give them the chance. The atmosphere of our classes should be one of both teachers and students wanting to know why and not being satisfied with knowing only how.

A classroom that encourages communicating will be one in which there is a lot of talking, listening, writing, and reading. Students can more readily communicate about something concrete. Herein lies another reason to provide physical materials that model mathematical ideas.

*Building connections.* We need to help students build several connections. One is the connection between conceptual and procedural knowledge. Learning rules and procedures without understanding eventually causes difficulty because there are too many isolated rules to learn and remember, too many rules from which to select, and too little chance of transfer to new situations (Hiebert and Lindquist forthcoming).

Similarly, we need to connect the concrete with the abstract. Manipulatives are of little use unless the bridge is made to the symbolic aspects of mathematics. Again, communicating is central as we help children make the connection between something that makes sense to them (the concrete) and something that makes sense to mathematicians (the abstract).

Another connection that needs to be made is between topics in mathematics. The integration of topics in the curriculum will help children make some of these connections, but we must also do it as we teach. For example, how is rounding a number like measuring to the nearest centimeter? How is finding an average like making equal groups? How is dividing by 3 like dividing by 2/3?

Still another connection to make is that of connecting mathematics with other areas of the curriculum. It is this connection that may help children see the usefulness of mathematics from the very beginning of their long school career.

*Role of students.* Listen to the verbs used in the *Standards: investigate, explore, describe, develop, use, apply, invent, relate, model, explain, represent, validate. . . .* This list alone should indicate what students ought to be doing.

*Role of teachers.* Obviously, the teacher is the central figure in the instruction of children, but we often seem to forget this when recommendations are pronounced. The *Standards,* during its development and during the year of hearings on the draft version, had much input from teachers. Yet, without the acceptance of change by this group, no real and meaningful change will occur.

Those of you who are elementary teachers have a great challenge. The reward will be seeing children make sense of mathematics as you become less of a dispenser of knowledge and more of a facilitator of learning. How can students be actively involved in doing mathematics if they are taught by the rule-example method? How can they communicate if mathematics classes consist mainly of individuals doing paper-and-pencil worksheets? How can they learn to solve problems and reason unless they have the opportunity?

## EVALUATION

*Evaluation* is a critical word in the title of the *Standards,* for if evaluation is not changed, then there is little reason to change curriculum or instruction. Several aspects of evaluation need to be addressed; among these are the view of evaluation, the role of evaluation in the classroom, and standardized tests.

*The view of evaluation.* Changing one's view of evaluation must accompany changing one's view of mathematics and mathematics learning. Evaluation is considered a driving force of curriculum and instruction; if this idea is correct, then we must use evaluation to help make changes that will improve students' learning of mathematics.

Evaluation must be a partner, not an adversary. When assessments of students are used to provide the appropriate curriculum and instruction, then the partnership is sound. Inherent in the previous statement is the need to assess students' learning of the mathematics that is deemed important. That is, if we value reasoning and communicating, then we must include these skills in our evaluation. Thus, there is a need for new approaches and techniques to assessing. When we use evaluation to help determine the overall worth of our mathematics program, then the partnership becomes profitable. We can no longer afford to have mathematics programs that do not enhance the future of all our citizens.

*Evaluation in the classroom.* Assessment must be an integral part of instruction if it is to be useful in providing appropriate curriculum and instruction for students. It is an ongoing process of finding out what students are doing, thinking, and feeling. This is not an easy process, but one that must accompany the changes suggested by the *Standards.* Here are a few questions that you might ask yourself to begin this process of assessment:

1. *Written tests.* Do they include a balance of concepts and procedures? Do they include problems that make the students think rather than problems that are exact replicas of the text's problems? Do they include questions calling for a written response? Do they include questions that ask why? Do you permit calculators to be used?

2. *Use of questions.* Do you use questions as you explain something to see what the students are thinking? How often do you encourage students' questions? How often do your questions probe or require higher-level thinking skills? How often do you ask students why they think this topic is useful?

3. *Observations.* How often do you make a judgment by watching children working alone or in a group? Do you use this as part of the assignment of a grade?

4. *Interviews.* Do you ask individual children to explain just to you how they are doing something or what they are thinking?

5. *Listening.* Do you listen to children as they explain to others what they are doing or thinking? Do you really listen to what they are saying as they explain to you or as they ask you questions?

6. *Understanding.* Do you *really* understand the concepts and the procedures and how children learn them?

*Standardized tests.* Standardized tests have become the villain in the minds of many. They can be a positive force in moving toward implementing the recommendations of the *Standards* if they change and if our use of, and attitude toward, them change. These tests must become more responsive to the need to assess in a variety of ways, must include calculator use, must assess how children do mathematics rather than only the end product, and must respond more quickly to the changing curriculum. In its turn, the education community must clearly understand the purpose of each test and use the results appropriately, realize that good instruction will produce better long-term results than teaching the test, demand tests that are consistent with our goals, and realize that there are no easy, quick solutions to low test scores.

## SUPPORT

Both the quality and the quantity of support for teachers and students need to change if we are to reach toward the goals set by the *Standards*. Although support is needed on all fronts, I have chosen four areas—time, textbooks and other teaching materials, teacher preparation, and the public—to discuss here.

*Time.* One of the most striking characteristics of Asian teaching is the amount of time teachers have to prepare for teaching. Few elementary school teachers here have a planning period or even any time to themselves during the day. If changes are to occur, then elementary teachers must have time to prepare to teach each day as well as time to reflect on their teaching. They also need time to observe and work with other teachers. They need time for further study of mathematics and mathematical instruction.

Students also need time to learn mathematics. Many questions about students' time need answering. First, is enough time each day or week devoted to mathematics? Second, is that time used constructively? Third, what time of day does mathematics instruction occur? Fourth, how much time do we expect students to spend outside of school working with mathematics?

*Textbooks and other teaching materials.* Over 90 percent of the teachers in grades K–6 use a published textbook in their classes (Weiss 1987). The textbook undoubtedly has great influence on what is taught. It is easy to be critical of textbooks, and publishing companies must accept some of this criticism, but it is a two-way street. Textbooks cannot do everything—as they are sometimes expected to do—and textbooks will change if teachers ask and are ready for change. Both sides, teachers and publishers, must be willing to take some risks and accept change.

The *Standards* makes clear that a textbook alone is not sufficient for teaching and learning mathematics. Classrooms must be equipped with calculators, computers, physical materials, and the associated "software" to support these. Teachers must learn how to use these materials to help children learn mathematics.

*Teacher preparation.* Teachers are the key to effective change, and they deserve everyone's support, particularly in their preparation, whether it be initial, preservice preparation, help as a beginning teacher, or in-service programs. As initial preparation, we must provide the mathematics background they will need to teach in a changing world of mathematics. Along with this preparation they need to learn mathematics as they will be expected to teach it. They need to leave this preservice experience knowing that mathematics makes sense, so that they can impart this sense to their students. Preservice teachers also need to maintain or develop their self-confidence about mathematics so they can help children develop theirs. We must provide them with ways to help children learn mathematics and let them experience children learning mathematics.

During their first years of teaching, teachers need to continue this learning process in a more systematic way. Of course they learn by doing, but there are other ways that could help them during these first years. In addition, after the first years we need to provide for ongoing, meaningful in-service programs.

It is time to take seriously the need for mathematics specialists in elementary schools, at least after grade 3. It is unrealistic to expect a teacher at these grades to have the in-depth background needed to teach eight subjects. It is even more unrealistic to expect them to find the time to prepare daily to teach each of these areas.

*The public.* The support of the public is needed in many ways. The public needs to be aware of the changing view of mathematics and the implications for schooling. As parents, we must be open to reasonable changes in the curriculum. Just because we or Sue's older sister learned the multiplication tables in the third grade does not mean that it is better for Sue if she learns them in the second grade—or perhaps even in the third grade. Just because we did not use a calculator in elemementary school does not mean that our children should not use one.

We must encourage our students to study mathematics; it can be fun and rewarding, but it takes hard work. We often do not like to see our children struggling, and there is, of course, a limit. But when children give up on a problem after a minute, then they have not developed the perseverance necessary to become mathematically powerful. As I have discussed, changes must be made in the classroom, but few gains will be made without the support from home.

## IN CLOSING

At the beginning of this century, Dewey (1901) implied that a change in curriculum is more than it appears. This is probably even more true today as we end the century. The task ahead is great, but so are our resources. Teachers, textbook publishers, testing companies, administrators, public, and students—together we can do it. It is time.

### REFERENCES

Dewey, John. "The Situation as Regards the Course of Study." *Journal of Proceedings and Addresses of the National Education Association* 40 (1901): 332–38.

Dossey, John A., Ina V. S. Mullis, Mary M. Lindquist, and Donald L. Chambers. *The Mathematics Report Card: Are We Measuring Up?* Princeton, N.J.: Educational Testing Service, 1988.

Hiebert, James, and Mary M. Lindquist. "Developmental Learning and Teaching." In *Teaching and Learning Mathematics for the Young Child,* edited by Joseph Payne. Reston, Va.: National Council of Teachers of Mathematics, forthcoming.

Lindquist, Mary M., Catherine A. Brown, Thomas P. Carpenter, Vicky L. Kouba, Edward A. Silver, and Jane O. Swafford. *Results of the Fourth Mathematics Assessment of the NAEP.* Reston, Va.: National Council of Teachers of Mathematics, forthcoming.

McKnight, Curtis C., F. Joe Crosswhite, John A. Dossey, Edward Kifer, Jane O. Swafford, Kenneth J. Travers, and Thomas J. Cooney. *The Underachieving Curriculum: Assessing U.S. School Mathematics from an International Perspective.* Champaign, Ill.: Stipes, 1987.

National Council of Teachers of Mathematics. *Curriculum and Evaluation Standards for School Mathematics.* Reston, Va.: NCTM, 1989.

Porter, Andrew, Robert Floden, Donald Freeman, William Schmidt, Jack Schwille, Linda Alford, Susan Irwin, Janet Vredevoogd, and Frank Jenkins. "Elementary Math Curriculum Out of Balance." *IRT Communication Quarterly* (Winter 1988): 3–4.

Stevenson, Harold W. "America's Math Problems." *Educational Leadership* (October 1987): 4–10.

Weiss, Iris R. *Report of the 1985–86 National Survey of Science and Mathematics Education.* Research Triangle Park, N.C.: Research Triangle Institute, 1987.

# 2

# Communication and Reasoning: Critical Dimensions of Sense Making in Mathematics

Glenda Lappan
Pamela W. Schram

A S THE twentieth century enters its last decade, many professional groups are examining the mathematics education that our young people will need to become the citizens, workers, and leaders of the twenty-first century. Technological advances have put remarkable computational and graphing capabilities into the hands of anyone with access to a computer. In fact, technology has influenced the very nature of the discipline of mathematics, not only as a source of many new problems but also as a tool for investigating these problems. These modern shifts in the way that mathematics is both created and used in our society have been behind many of the pervasive calls for reform in the school mathematics curriculum.

In 1986 the National Council of Teachers of Mathematics established the Commission on Standards for School Mathematics. Writing groups have created an articulated vision of a school mathematics curriculum, K–12, that would help students become mathematically powerful in our modern technological world. As defined in the working draft of the *Curriculum and Evaluation Standards for School Mathematics* (NCTM 1987), *mathematical power*

> denotes an individual's abilities to explore, conjecture, and reason logically, as well as the ability to use a variety of mathematical methods effectively to solve nonroutine problems. This notion is based on recognition of mathematics as more than a collection of concepts and skills to be mastered; it includes methods of investigating and reasoning, means of communication, and notions of context. In addition, for each individual, mathematical power involves the development of personal self-confidence. (P. iv)

Such a curriculum would certainly include new content as well as a refocusing of old content. But the *Standards* is much more than a list of content. The purposes for learning the content and the uses to which it will be put were used to judge any content recommended in the *Standards*. The content included in a curriculum must make a contribution to the development of individuals who are mathematically powerful. Major goals of mathematical power are seeing connections and relationships, making sense of mathematical situations, reasoning and conjecturing, and having confidence in discussing one's ideas. These goals imply action by students. The vision of how children learn that pervades the *Standards* is in stark contrast to the picture of typical mathematics classrooms across the country. The following description drawn from NSF case studies (Welch 1978) illustrates well the consensus of many recent studies of mathematics classes:

> In all math classes I visited, the sequence of activities was the same. First, answers were given for the previous day's assignment. The more difficult problems were worked by the teacher or a student at the chalkboard. A brief explanation, sometimes none at all, was given of the new material, and problems were assigned for the next day. The remainder of the class was devoted to working on the homework while the teacher moved about the room answering questions. The most noticeable thing about math classes was the repetition of this routine. (P. 6)

The introduction to the K–4 Standards gives a summary of a different vision:

> Young children are active individuals who construct and modify ideas, and integrate existing knowledge through interacting with the physical world, materials, and other children. Thus, the learning of mathematics must be an active process. Throughout the standards, verbs such as *explore, validate, represent, solve, construct, discuss, use, investigate, describe, develop,* and *predict* are used to convey this active physical and mental involvement by children.
>
> Active learning by children has implications for the way mathematics is taught. Teachers need to create an environment that encourages children to explore, develop, test, discuss, and apply ideas. They need to listen to children and guide the development of their ideas. They need to make extensive and thoughtful use of physical materials to foster the learning of abstract ideas. (NCTM 1987, p. 20)

Active physical and mental involvement by children in making sense of mathematics pervades the *Standards*. This theme is highlighted in the two standards entitled "Mathematics as Communication" and "Mathematics as Reasoning." This paper focuses on these two critical dimensions of sense making and addresses two questions:

- Why are learning to communicate mathematically and learning to reason mathematically important goals for K–6 students?

- What kinds of experiences should occur in mathematics classrooms to provide opportunities for students to learn to communicate and reason in mathematical situations?

## SIGNIFICANCE OF COMMUNICATION

Discussing, listening, writing, reading—these are all important aspects of learning to communicate mathematically. Teacher-pupil as well as pupil-pupil interactions are important aspects of discussion (i.e., talking and listening) during a mathematics class. Celia Hoyles (1985), a strong proponent of classroom discussion, suggests that different aspects of pupil-pupil discussion can "facilitate a pupil's integration of her fragmented knowledge" (p. 206). She delineates two functions of "talk": the "communicative" and the "cognitive" functions. She describes the communicative function as forcing the communicator to

> frame thought in language which has to be recognized and accepted by others as a conveyor of meanings. This compels the communicator therefore, to identify those parts of a mathematical situation seen as important for meaning and those that are not, and how the former relate to one another. (P. 206)

She describes the cognitive function in this way: "Language facilitates reflection and internal regulation since difficulties in formulating the language to describe a situation may lead the speaker to modify her analysis of that situation" (p. 206). Hoyles argues that listening is also important and requires active participation during discussion. "The ideas of others can suggest modifications to one's own thoughts, clarify half-worked out predictions or explain half-understood processes" (p. 207). This suggests that children's problem-solving strategies can be enhanced by discussing ideas and fine-tuning their explanations. Children learn from one another as they talk and listen.

Classroom discussion can give teachers an excellent assessment of how the students are thinking and what they know. All teachers have experienced students moaning, "But I understood it when *you* did it in class yesterday!" Receiving information is very different from transmitting it. Students may think they understand an idea, but inconsistencies in thinking may become apparent when they are asked to explain their thinking or to tell why they think their answer is correct.

Another powerful means of communicating that is seldom used is writing about mathematics. Writing helps students clarify their ideas about a specific topic or problem and also helps them develop a better conception of mathematics. Having students write about how they tackled a problem and how the members of a group thought about aspects of the problem can help them realize that the teacher values their thinking and reasoning about a problem.

Learning to think can then be seen as a part of doing mathematics. Marilyn Burns documents many wonderful examples of young children writing about mathematics problems. Here are two group reports from a lesson (Burns 1987, p. 127):

> Our job was to draw a foot in which the area was 260 square cm. We thought it would be EASY. HA! Our first try we figured out we should make a rectangle 130 by 20. We thought that would equal 260 cm. We taped six sheets of paper together. Mrs. Scheafer [their teacher] didn't know what we were doing. Neither did we. Our second try we did 30 × 8. We tried to make it look like a foot. We didn't try hard enough. Our third try was more successful. We just enlarged Amanda's foot 4 sqs out. It actually looked like a foot. We counted the sqs and they equaled exactly 260 cm.
>
> Other students began drawing a foot and adjusting it. Lisa, Marcie, and Karine reported their method: We taped two pieces of paper together to make the rectangle of 300 square cm fit. Then we drew a foot inside. After that we colored all the wholes green and the fractions yellow. Then we counted whole squares and added the fractions. We found out the answer was 250 altogether so we added to the toes and got 257, so we added to the heel and finally got 260.

Such experiences are valuable to children's mathematical development and to the building of confidence in doing mathematics. They are equally valuable to teachers in assessing students' thinking.

We highly value reading because of the power it gives students to interact with the huge portion of human knowledge recorded in books and papers. This is equally valid in mathematics. Learning to read mathematics allows one to learn from the written record of mathematical knowledge. Think of the difference between having to be told everything and being able to find out things for yourself by reading. Most mathematics classes are organized around the material in a textbook, which students are seldom encouraged to read and make sense of. For the most part, the text becomes a source of homework problems rather than a source of information and ideas, leaving knowledge in the hands of the teacher to be transmitted to students rather than empowering students to seek information for themselves.

There is also a rich mathematical literature appropriate for children, including books and pamphlets of mathematical explorations, interesting problems, and stories about mathematics and mathematicians in our culture and history. Resources such as *Mathematics Libraries—Elementary and Junior High School,* published by NCTM, can help build a library for students.

Language evolved as humans developed the need to communicate. Mathematics has been described as a language that consists of ordinary language, technical vocabulary, definitions, symbols, notations, models, charts, graphs, diagrams, and accepted rules and procedures. For children this can be a puzzling mix of the familiar and unfamiliar.

The ability to communicate well in a given language requires more than a surface understanding. It is necessary, but not sufficient, to learn vocabulary and grammatical rules and structures. Additionally, one needs to become immersed in the language. Frequent opportunities to be an active participant are necessary to enable a person to communicate well—for example, conversations using the language, thought in the language as opposed to literal translations, considerations for the cultural and historical perspectives, and acquiring new vocabulary. Similar opportunities are equally important for appropriate understanding and communication in the language of mathematics.

The grades 5–8 portion of the *Standards* (NCTM 1987) argues: "Unless students discuss the relationships between concepts and symbols frequently and explicitly, they are likely to deal with symbols as unrelated objects to be memorized" (p. 56). This is analogous to attempts to learn a second language. Simply memorizing vocabulary, grammatical rules, and structure does not result in fluent communication. One comes to "speak" the language of mathematics fluently by using concepts and their related symbols to model situations, to express ideas, and to convince others.

## SIGNIFICANCE OF REASONING

For most children, mathematics classes are places where authority resides totally with the teacher and the answer key. Reasoning about situations and seeking ways to validate their own thinking are seldom what children associate with doing mathematics. Conventional instruction seems to lead them to believe that mathematics consists of doing a computation to get the answer in the book. Yet the problem students will encounter in their jobs or in their private lives that have mathematical aspects do not come with an answer key or a teacher to say "Yes, that's right" or "No, that's wrong." To enable students to use mathematics, we must free them from overdependence on authority. We must give them the freedom to explore, to conjecture, to seek ways to validate, and to convince others that their thinking is correct. We must give children opportunities to observe regularities and patterns and encourage them to describe what they observe in words, in mathematical statements, in pictures, or in models. "Why?" "What will happen if . . . ?" "Give an example. . . ." "Can you find one that does not work?" These questions imply that mathematics involves thinking, conjecturing, modeling, and describing—all aspects of reasoning about situations. Changing children's beliefs about the nature of mathematics and the doing of mathematics is a crucial aspect of building mathematical power.

Thinking and reasoning have received very little attention in elementary mathematics classrooms. The prevalent notion that facts and skills must be mastered *before* they can be applied to reasoning and problem solving has denied many students the opportunity to engage in interesting mathematical problem solving. A balance among teaching facts, teaching processes, and teaching thinking has not been satisfactorily achieved. We know from research on cognition that there is an intimate relationship between knowledge and reasoning. Both are important to the development of mathematical power; students must have something to reason with and about. However, facts and procedures acquired out of context, with no reasoning or problem solving as part of the process, are often meaningless to students. Rather than a linear progression from the acquisition of facts to reasoning to problem solving, there should be a constant interplay among the three. A problem situation may provide the motivation for learning a skill or technique. Thinking about why the skill or technique works may lead to new insights that can now be explored. Hence, reasoning is what makes it all meaningful.

For children in the elementary grades, reasoning in mathematics should be the informal thinking, conjecturing, and validating that makes the mathematics make sense. Although young children can make chains of deductions that could be formalized, excessive formalization is likely to move students and teachers away from the real heart of the matter, which is to establish a spirit of inquiry as students tackle problem situations. A mathematics classroom environment that encourages students to communicate and to reason about situations is likely to be characterized by children asking questions and posing problems. An example of this occurred in a sixth-grade class in a lesson on rounding. The teacher said, "I am thinking of a number. When rounded to the nearest tenth my number is 2.1. What could it be?" After several students gave possible answers, one student asked, "What is the smallest the number could be?" After several minutes of conjecturing and arguing, the students decided that it was 2.05. Then another student asked, "What is the largest?" which led to an even more interesting discussion. After five minutes the teacher had recorded these numbers as students made conjectures and gave arguments to support their answers:

$$2.14$$
$$2.149$$
$$2.1499$$
$$2.1499999$$

Then a student said, "I know! It's 2.149 with a bar over the 9, which means it goes on forever!" The class seemed duly impressed until another student said, "But isn't that supposed to be dead equal to 2.15, and that rounds to 2.2!" Another five minutes of discussion led those sixth graders to conclude that there was no largest. In their language they said, "You can have as many nines as you want, but you have to stop somewhere." What a powerful lesson on what children can do with mathematical ideas when we give them the time to puzzle through a situation, to go down wrong alleys, in an environment where asking questions, making conjectures, listening to others' arguments, and helping to evaluate their reasoning is a part of doing mathematics.

This is, in fact, how mathematicians do mathematics. Unfortunately, students see only the final record of a mathematician's thoughts formalized according to the precise rules of evidence within the discipline. They do not get to see the playing around with ideas that finally leads to a "proof" of a new piece of mathematics. As Alan Schoenfeld (1987) puts it, "In real mathematical thinking formal and informal reasoning are, as the phrase has it, deeply intertwined."

The coin of the realm in the twenty-first century will be ideas. It will no longer be sufficient for students to enter the working world with only disconnected rules, theorems, and techniques stored in their mathematical heads. What will be valued in business and industry is being able to think and reason mathematically and to bring the power of mathematics to bear on a problem that needs a solution. The computational aspects of the solution can often be done by a computer, but a human must reason through the situation to decide what techniques need to be applied to solve the problem. Romberg (1983) talks about mathematical inventions as a part of knowing and doing mathematics:

> There are two aspects to all mathematical inventions: the conjecture (or guess) about a relationship, followed by the demonstration of the logical validity of that assertion. (P. 126)

This is the essence of mathematics—conjecturing and reasoning about those conjectures. In order to convince others of your conjectures, you have to marshal the facts at your disposal into a coherent argument. High school geometry has traditionally carried the whole load of teaching students to construct valid arguments. In order to give more students the opportunity to develop their mathematical reasoning abilities, we must incorporate reasoning as part of everyday life in mathematics classrooms. Making sense of things, perceiving structures, seeing relationships, and analyzing them in order to explain why something is as it seems is what mathematical thinking and reasoning mean. Relying on rules and repetition may develop competence in skills and procedures, but of what use are they when students cannot reason about the situations in which these very skills and procedures are needed to solve problems? To give our students mathematical power, all mathematical knowledge must be acquired in situations where thinking is necessary.

If we accept as a goal that the mathematics education of our students should empower them to use their mathematics to think, reason, and communicate about problems that arise in real-world contexts, then we must also accept that this goal cannot be relegated to "higher mathematics." The investigative, inquiring approach must pervade all mathematics classes.

Behaviors and dispositions are very difficult to change. Once children have established a "facts to be memorized" approach to mathematics, their expectations become a very great constraint to change. Task completion—getting the answer—becomes the goal, and thought goes out the window. The elementary school years should be a time when students have many opportunities to explore mathematical situations with a real sense of inquiry—asking questions, talking about ideas, looking for patterns, making conjectures, and reasoning about what makes sense.

## ACTIVITIES TO FOSTER COMMUNICATION AND REASONING

Children are given few opportunities to think about geometry and the special way geometry describes the world in which they live. Thus, we have selected geometric situations to illustrate activities that can help children learn to appreciate the power of mathematics to communicate ideas.

### I.  Can You Build My Structure?

The goal of this activity is communicating precise information. Pairs of students should (*a*) face each other with a barrier between them so that they cannot see what is on the other's desk and (*b*) have identical sets of Cuisenaire rods (or blocks). Three to six rods is a good beginning set (fig. 2.1).

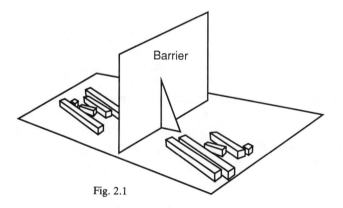

Barrier

Fig. 2.1

Student A builds a structure using all the rods. Then he or she gives verbal directions to Student B about how it is constructed. Student B attempts to follow the directions by constructing with his or her rods. The barrier is removed and the students compare buildings. Now the students switch roles.

*Discussion.* This is an excellent activity to help the students playing each role (the giver and the receiver of information) in understanding the complexity of giving precise descriptions. It opens the door to students wanting ways to talk about orientation. Such concepts as vertical, horizontal, parallel, perpendicular, slanted, over, under, and beside can arise naturally. Some students use measurement ideas such as, "Place the purple rod across the green rod exactly one red rod from the end." Others try to locate the exact spot on the desk top where the building is to be made, leading to a rich discussion of locating points on a plane.

## II. Sending a Message

Show one student a structure like that shown in the two views in figure 2.2:

> Here is a building made of cubes. Your friend is in another room with a supply of cubes. You can send a piece of paper to help your friend know how to construct a building like this one. Be as creative as you wish.

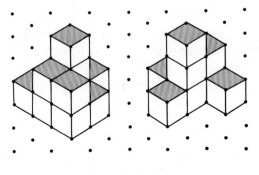

Fig. 2.2

*Discussion.* When children communicate about such situations in writing, the responses may be verbal, spatial, or a mix. Discussing various representations can help students see the power of words, pictures, and symbols to communicate ideas. Figure 2.3 shows two examples of sixth-grade students' responses to this situation.

Student 1:

The building is red. It has ten cubes altogether. On one side there is 5 blocks. 4 of these blocks are piled up. 3 is on the bottom and 2 is on the Top on the rigth 2 blocks. The 3 blocks behind the middle 2 blocks are on each other and behind those 3 blocks there is one. Next to the block of 3 on the right side there is one right there and the cubes are tape together and it is placed on a little piece of paper.

Student 2:

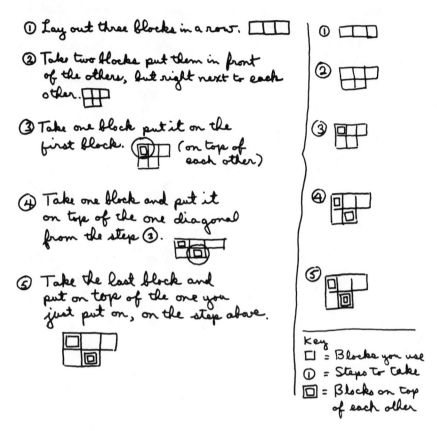

① Lay out three blocks in a row. ⊏⊓⊐

② Take two blocks put them in front of the others, but right next to each other. ⊞⊞

③ Take one block put it on the first block. (on top of each other)

④ Take one block and put it on top of the one diagonal from the step ③.

⑤ Take the last block and put on top of the one you just put on, on the step above.

Key
□ = Blocks you use
① = Steps to take
◫ = Blocks on top of each other

Fig. 2.3

## III. Seeing and Describing Patterns

Pattern blocks provide children with many opportunities to reason inductively and deductively. First, the children can use the square with the length of an edge equal to 1 unit to reason about the length of the edges of the other pieces. These activities (see fig. 2.4) use the triangle, square, and trapezoid. The children should have already determined that the triangle has edges of 1 unit; the trapezoid has slant edges of 1 unit, a base of 1 unit, and the other base of 2 units. Each problem has three big questions associated with the situation:

1.  What is the next figure in the sequence?

    "Describe a rule in words that would tell a friend how to build the figures in the pattern. Why do you think your rule will work?"

2. How many pieces will it take to build the next figure in the sequence? "Describe a rule that would let you find out how many pieces it would take to build a particular figure in the sequence. Why do you think your rule will work?"

3. What is the perimeter of the next figure in the sequence? "Describe a rule that would let you find out the perimeter of a particular figure in the sequence. Why do you think your rule will work?"

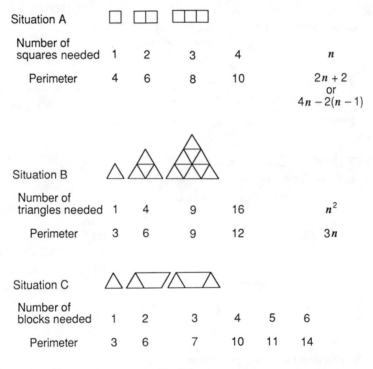

| Situation A | | | | | |
|---|---|---|---|---|---|
| Number of squares needed | 1 | 2 | 3 | 4 | $n$ |
| Perimeter | 4 | 6 | 8 | 10 | $2n + 2$ or $4n - 2(n - 1)$ |

| Situation B | | | | | |
|---|---|---|---|---|---|
| Number of triangles needed | 1 | 4 | 9 | 16 | $n^2$ |
| Perimeter | 3 | 6 | 9 | 12 | $3n$ |

| Situation C | | | | | | |
|---|---|---|---|---|---|---|
| Number of blocks needed | 1 | 2 | 3 | 4 | 5 | 6 |
| Perimeter | 3 | 6 | 7 | 10 | 11 | 14 |

Fig. 2.4

*Discussion.* Situation C can be looked at in different ways. Some students will see that the rule for perimeter could be described as "add 3, add 1, add 3, add 1." Others might separate the pattern into odd positions and even positions. The odd positions give 3, 7, 11, 15, . . ., etc., which is an "add 4" rule. The even positions give 6, 10, 14, 18, . . . , which is also an "add 4" rule. Others might generalize on odds and evens by observing that for position $N$ if $N$ is odd, then the perimeter is $2N + 1$; if $N$ is even, then the perimeter is $2N + 2$. The important thing is to have children make conjectures about a pattern and to try to convince others that their conjectures are valid. These problems can be responded to at many different levels. For some children, figuring out how the next figure will be made is a sufficient challenge. Other children can tackle all three types of questions.

Two final comments are important. First, this type of pattern work opens the door for surprises for the teacher as well as the students. Children often see a way of making sense of a pattern that is different from what the teacher has in mind. This creative aspect of making sense of mathematics can be a real confidence builder for children. Second, in problems of this sort reasoning and communication can be enhanced even further by letting the children create the patterns. For example:

> Create a pattern of your own to share with a friend. Write down a description of your pattern. Tell how the number of blocks needed and the perimeter change as the pattern continues.

## IV. Can You Read My Picture?

Graphs occupy a special place in mathematical communication and reasoning. Two-dimensional graphs show concise information about the relationship between two variables. Currently, students have few opportunities to reason from graphical information prepared by others or to think about how to portray information about change, as shown in this example (see fig. 2.5) by Malcolm Swan (1986).

*Discussion.* In this example the dynamic relationship between height and age has to be considered. As students read information from the graph and interpret this information in light of the queue of interesting people, they see how young-old and short-tall can vary across a set of people. Recognizing how a dot on the graph conveys these two characteristics of a person has

Agatha  Barbara  Cathy      Dennis    Ernie      Freda
(& baby Gavin)

Fig. 2.5. Each person shown in the queue above is represented by a point on the graph that follows. Copy the graph and label each point with the name of the person it represents.

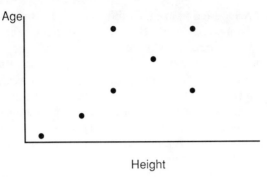

Fig. 2.5 (*cont.*)

direct application to understanding graphical representations of other variables in mathematics.

## V. Bending Straws

Here is an excellent problem for small groups. Ask each group to write a story telling how they solved the problem. Ask them to tell about anything that they observed as they worked on the problem.

> You have a straw that is 8 cm long. You can bend it in two places, but only at a centimeter mark. How many different triangles can you make?

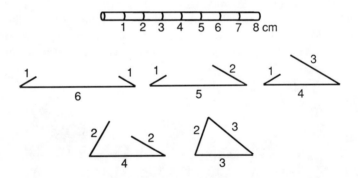

*Discussion.* The surprising result is that only one triangle can be made, and it is isosceles. But think of what children can learn about the structure of triangles from trying all the possibilities. They can discover that in triangles the sum of the length of two sides is less than or equal to the third. Extensions could include posing the same situation with a 9-cm straw and a 10-cm straw. The 10-cm straw is similar to the 8-cm straw in that only isosceles triangles can be formed. The 9-cm straw is interesting because one can make a scalene, an isosceles, and an equilateral triangle. (2, 3, 4; 1, 4, 4; and 3, 3, 3.)

## VI. How Does My Building Grow?

Children also need experiences with three-dimensional objects. The following problem can be explored as a pattern problem by building physical models from cubes (see fig. 2.6). It gives children an opportunity to reason about how measurement relationships change as objects grow. Children working in small groups can be asked to explore and to write about how they thought about the problem, what they tried, what their answers are, and why they think they are correct.

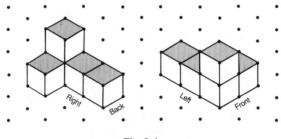

Fig. 2.6

Two views of a simple building are shown. If you construct a building like this one except that each dimension is two times as large, how many cubes would be needed to build the new building?

What would be the perimeter of the new base?

What is the new surface area?

Draw a picture of the new base.

Describe what you think would happen if you tripled each dimension.

*Discussion.* To answer the question "What is the new surface area?" students will have to decide whether to include the base of the building. If they think of the surface area as that part of the building that might be painted, they probably will not include the base. If they view the building as a block structure that can be moved freely in space, they may include the base. It may help younger children to think of the building as "growing up" in every direction (dimension). Children who have had no experience with blocks or growth ideas may need to experiment with "growing" a single cube before they tackle this problem.

Figure 2.7 shows the building with each dimension doubled—if it took 5 cubes to build the original (fig. 2.6), it will take eight times as many cubes to double the building (40 cubes) and twenty-seven times as many (135 cubes) to triple it. The surface area of the original is 22 square units. The surface area of the doubled building is four times the original (88 square units); for the tripled building the surface area would be nine times the original (198 square units).

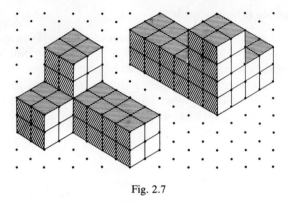

Fig. 2.7

## VII. That's Stretching It

This geometry game created by Romberg, Harvey, Moser, and Montgomery (1976) is appropriate for two or three players. The game is played on a five-nail geoboard. To start the game, make a parallelogram on the board as shown in figure 2.8. Children take turns rolling a pair of dice. The smaller

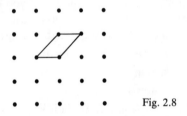

Fig. 2.8

number locates a position on the bottom row of the chart in figure 2.9; the larger number tells how far up the column to go to locate the attribute for that turn. The student must change the existing figure on the board to a new quadrilateral that has the attribute rolled. A change must be made even if the existing figure has the attribute rolled. The person with the most points wins.

Scoring:
Four points if you change only one corner.
Three points if you change two corners.
Two points if you change three corners.
One point if you change all four corners.

*Discussion.* The game provides opportunities for reasoning about geometric properties of figures and relationships among figures. Students have an opportunity to deepen their thinking through the discussions required to check each other's moves. The emphasis on trying to minimize the

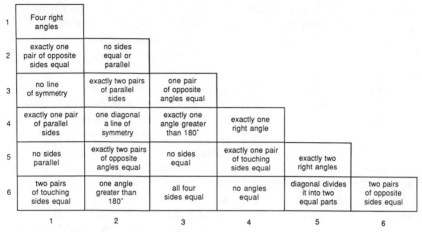

| | 1 | 2 | 3 | 4 | 5 | 6 |
|---|---|---|---|---|---|---|
| 1 | Four right angles | | | | | |
| 2 | exactly one pair of opposite sides equal | no sides equal or parallel | | | | |
| 3 | no line of symmetry | exactly two pairs of parallel sides | one pair of opposite angles equal | | | |
| 4 | exactly one pair of parallel sides | one diagonal a line of symmetry | exactly one angle greater than 180° | exactly one right angle | | |
| 5 | no sides parallel | exactly two pairs of opposite angles equal | no sides equal | exactly one pair of touching sides equal | exactly two right angles | |
| 6 | two pairs of touching sides equal | one angle greater than 180° | all four sides equal | no angles equal | diagonal divides it into two equal parts | two pairs of opposite sides equal |

Taken from Romberg, Harvey, Moser, and Montgomery (1976)

Fig. 2.9

number of corners changed encourages the students to consider many alternatives. The dynamic nature of the game—focusing on changing an existing figure—raises the question of relationships among figures in a way that simply forming a rectangle or a trapezoid on a geoboard cannot. How far from a particular trapezoid is a rectangle? What do they have in common? What needs to be changed? What is the minimum change that will work? This activity provides an excellent opportunity for reasoning and communicating ideas.

## CONCLUSION

Any mathematics lesson can incorporate opportunities to reason and to communicate ideas. Areas of mathematics that are now receiving increased attention—estimation, mental computation, geometry, measurement, statistics, probability—have the additional advantage of being the source of particularly appropriate and natural experiences that are accessible to all children for developing communication and reasoning skills in the process of making sense of the mathematics. Asking children to describe what they think is going on in a mathematical situation, why they think they are correct, what their answer means in the context of the original problem situation, or what they thought about that helped them solve the problem can turn a routine lesson into a "learning to think" lesson. It takes time to listen to children, but the rewards can be very great for both children and teachers. For example, in one classroom the teacher had been working very hard to improve the quantity and quality of thinking and communication. She gave

Sam a chance to answer a question on decimals. When he gave a number response, the teacher's head came up and she opened her mouth to ask a follow-up question. Before she could speak, Sam said, "I know, I know, Ms. Davis. You want me to tell you why and to draw a picture!" He then proceeded to do exactly that.

It is not easy to change students' perceptions and beliefs about mathematics. It is also not easy to change our own perceptions about what students can and cannot do in mathematics. If we want to help our students to value mathematics, to develop mathematical power, and to have the confidence to tackle new situations, we must pose interesting, challenging problem situations and give our students time to explore, to formulate problems, to develop strategies, to make conjectures, to reason about the validity of these conjectures, to discuss, to argue, to predict, and, of course, to raise more questions! If we listen carefully to our students, showing them that we value their thoughts, we are likely to learn that children are remarkably clever at making sense of mathematical situations.

### REFERENCES

Bright, George W., and John G. Harvey. "Learning and Fun with Geometry Games." *Arithmetic Teacher* 35 (April 1988): 22–26.

Burns, Marilyn. *A Collection of Math Lessons from Grades 3 through 6.* San Francisco: Math Solution Publications, 1987.

Hoyles, Celia. "What Is the Point of Group Discussion?" *Educational Studies in Mathematics* 16 (2) (1985): 205–14.

National Council of Teachers of Mathematics. *Curriculum and Evaluation Standards for School Mathematics.* Working draft. Reston, Va.: The Council, 1987.

Romberg, Thomas A. "A Common Curriculum for Mathematics." In *Individual Differences and the Common Curriculum,* edited by G. D. Fenstermacher and J. I. Goodlad, pp. 121–59. Chicago: Rand McNally & Co., 1976.

Schoenfeld, Alan H. "On Mathematics as Sense-making: An Informal Attack on the Unfortunate Divorce of Formal and Informal Mathematics." Paper presented at the Office of Educational Research and Improvement/Learning Research and Development Center Conference on Informal Reasoning and Education, University of Pittsburgh, March 1987.

Swan, Malcolm. *The Language of Graphs,* p. 13. Draft version. Nottingham, England: Shell Centre for Mathematics Education, University of Nottingham, 1986.

Welch, William. "Science Education in Urbanville: A Case Study." In *Case Studies in Science Education,* edited by R. Stake and J. Easley, p. 6. Urbana, Ill.: University of Illinois, 1978.

# 3

# Developing Understanding in Mathematics via Problem Solving

Thomas L. Schroeder
Frank K. Lester, Jr.

**E**ARLY in this decade the theme of school mathematics shifted from "back to the basics" to "problem solving." In fact, in recent years problem solving has been the most written-about and talked-about part of the mathematics curriculum and at the same time the least understood. Now that there has been nearly a decade of attempts to make problem solving "the focus of school mathematics" (NCTM 1980, p. 1), we need to assess the results of these efforts. This article addresses the role of problem solving in elementary school mathematics in the hope of adding some much-needed clarity to the discussion. Our main point is that the most important role for problem solving is to develop students' understanding of mathematics.

## APPROACHES TO PROBLEM-SOLVING INSTRUCTION

In the main, the discussions about problem solving and the efforts to develop curricula and materials for students and teachers have been worthwhile and helpful. Today the notion that problem solving should play a prominent role in the curriculum has widespread acceptance. During the past decade quite a large number of problem-solving resources have been developed for classroom use in the form of collections of problems, lists of strategies to be taught, suggestions for activities, and guidelines for evaluating problem-solving performance. Much of this material has been very useful in helping teachers make problem solving a focus of their instruction. However, it has not provided the sort of coherence and clear direction that is needed, primarily because to date little agreement has been reached on *how* this goal is to be achieved. Undoubtedly there are several reasons for this state of affairs, but the confusion probably stems from the vast differences among individuals' and groups' conceptions of what it means to make problem solving the focus of school mathematics. One of the best ways of coming to grips with these differences is to distinguish among three approaches to problem-solving instruction: (1) teaching *about* problem solving, (2) teaching *for* problem solving, and (3) teaching *via* problem solving. An explicit statement of this distinction appeared in a paper written more than a decade ago by Hatfield (1978), but we suspect that others may have espoused a similar point of view as well. Let us explain what each of these three approaches entails.

### Teaching about Problem Solving

The teacher who teaches *about* problem solving highlights Pólya's (1957) model of problem solving (or some minor variation of it). Briefly, this model describes a set of four interdependent phases in the process of solving mathematics problems: understanding the problem, devising a plan, carrying out the plan, and looking back. Students are explicitly taught the phases that, according to Pólya, expert problem solvers use when solving mathematics problems, and they are encouraged to become aware of their own progression through these phases when they themselves solve problems. Additionally, they are taught a number of "heuristics," or "strategies," from which they can choose or which they should use in devising and carrying out their problem-solving plans. Some of the strategies typically taught include looking for patterns, solving a simpler problem, and working backward. At its best, teaching about problem solving also includes experiences with actually solving problems, but it always involves a great deal of explicit discussion of, and teaching about, how problems are solved.

### Teaching for Problem Solving

In teaching *for* problem solving, the teacher concentrates on ways in which the mathematics being taught can be applied in the solution of both routine and nonroutine problems. Although the acquisition of mathematical knowledge is of primary importance, the essential purpose for learning mathematics is to be able to use it. Consequently, students are given many instances of the mathematical concepts and structures they are studying and many opportunities to apply that mathematics in solving problems. Further, the teacher who teaches *for* problem solving is very concerned about students' ability to transfer what they have learned from one problem context to others. A strong adherent of this approach might argue that the sole reason for learning mathematics is to be able to use the knowledge gained to solve problems.

## Teaching via Problem Solving

In teaching *via* problem solving, problems are valued not only as a purpose for learning mathematics but also as a primary means of doing so. The teaching of a mathematical topic begins with a problem situation that embodies key aspects of the topic, and mathematical techniques are developed as reasonable responses to reasonable problems. A goal of learning mathematics is to transform certain nonroutine problems into routine ones. The learning of mathematics in this way can be viewed as a movement from the concrete (a real-world problem that serves as an instance of the mathematical concept or technique) to the abstract (a symbolic representation of a class of problems and techniques for operating with these symbols).

An example from the Middle Grades Mathematics Project can serve to illustrate teaching via problem solving (Shroyer and Fitzgerald 1986). A fifth-grade teacher who has decided to introduce the concepts of area and perimeter gives each student a set of twenty-four one-inch-square tiles that are to be regarded as small tables. The students are challenged to determine the number of small tables (tiles) needed to make banquet tables of different sizes (area) and the number of people who can be seated at these banquet tables (perimeter). The students are told that one small table can seat four people, one on each side, and that the banquet tables made from the small tables are usually rectangular. The real-world situation (forming banquet tables and seating people around them) serves as a context in which students explore area and perimeter and the relationships between them. At first no formulas are used or developed; they will come in a later activity. Examples of the challenges presented by the teacher include the following (Shroyer and Fitzgerald 1986):

*Example A:* Use your tiles to make different arrangements that will seat twenty people.

*Example B:* Add squares to the following arrangement so that the perimeter is 18. What is the new area?

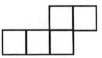

## Some Observations about the Three Approaches

Although in theory these three conceptions of teaching problem solving in mathematics can be isolated, in practice they overlap and occur in various combinations and sequences. Thus, it is probably counterproductive to argue in favor of one or more of these types of teaching or against the others.

Nevertheless, if curriculum developers, textbook writers, or classroom teachers intend to make problem solving the "focus of instruction," they need to be aware of the limitations inherent in exclusive adherence to either of the first two types of problem-solving instruction. One such limitation stems from the fact that problem solving is not a topic of mathematics, and it should not be regarded as such. If teaching *about* problem solving is the focus, the danger is that "problem solving" will be regarded as a strand to be added to the curriculum. Instead of problem solving serving as a context in which mathematics is learned and applied, it may become just another topic, taught in isolation from the content and relationships of mathematics.

A different shortcoming arises from teaching *for* problem solving. When this approach is interpreted narrowly, problem solving is viewed as an activity students engage in only *after* the introduction of a new concept or following work on a computational skill or algorithm. The purpose is to give students an opportunity to "apply" recently learned concepts and skills to the solution of real-world problems. Often these problems appear under a heading such as "Using Division to Solve Problems," and a solution of a sample story problem is given as a model for solving other, very similar problems. Often, solutions to these problems can be obtained simply by following the pattern established in the sample, and when students encounter problems that do not follow the sample, they often feel at a loss. It has been our experience (which is supported by several studies) that when taught in this way, students often simply pick out the numbers in each problem and apply the given operation(s) to them without regard for the problem's context; as often as not, they obtain the correct answers. In our view this practice is certainly not problem solving. Indeed, it does not even require mathematical thinking. Furthermore, a side effect is that students come to believe that all mathematics problems can be solved quickly and relatively effortlessly without any need to understand how the mathematics they are using relates to real situations. Unfortunately, this approach to problem-solving instruction has been quite common in textbooks.

Unlike the other two approaches, teaching *via* problem solving is a conception that has not been adopted either implicitly or explicitly by many teachers, textbook writers, and curriculum developers, but it is an approach to the teaching of mathematics that deserves to be considered, developed, tried, and evaluated. Indeed, teaching via problem solving is the approach that is most consistent with the recommendations of NCTM's Standards Commission that (1) mathematics concepts and skills be learned in the context of solving problems; (2) the development of higher-level thinking processes be fostered through problem-solving experiences; and (3) mathematics instruction take place in an inquiry-oriented, problem-solving atmosphere (NCTM 1987).

## TWO MODELS OF THE PROCESS OF SOLVING
## MATHEMATICS PROBLEMS

Problem solving has sometimes been conceptualized in a simplistic way by a model like that in figure 3.1. This model has two levels, or "worlds": the everyday world of things, problems, and applications of mathematics; and the idealized, abstract world of mathematical symbols, operations, and techniques. In this model the problem-solving process has three steps: Beginning with a problem posed in terms of the everyday physical reality, the problem solver first translates (arrow A) the problem into abstract mathematical terms, then operates (arrow B) on the mathematical representation to come to a mathematical solution of the problem, which is then translated back (arrow C) into the terms of the original problem.

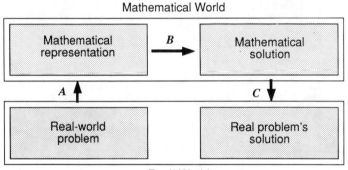

Fig. 3.1. A simplistic model of the process of solving mathematics problems

According to this model, mathematics can be, and often is, learned separately from its applications. In teaching *for* problem solving, instructors are very concerned to develop students' abilities to translate real-world problems into mathematical representations, and vice versa. But they tend to deal with problems and applications of mathematics only *after* those mathematical concepts and skills have been introduced, developed, and practiced. The difficulty with this model is that it applies to routine problems better than to nonroutine ones. Problems classified as "translation problems" (Charles and Lester 1982) are solved exactly as the model indicates, but for more challenging problems, like those categorized by Charles and Lester as "process problems," the problem solver has no single already-learned mathematical operation that will solve the problem. As well as translation and interpretation, these nonroutine problems also demand more complex processes, such as planning, selecting a strategy, identifying subgoals, conjecturing, and verifying that a solution has been found. For nonroutine problems, a different type of model is required.

Figure 3.2 shows a modification of the problem-solving model for translation problems that can be used to illustrate thinking processes when nonroutine problems are involved and when teaching *via* problem solving is adopted. This model also contains two levels that represent the everyday world of problems and the abstract world of mathematical symbols and operations. In this model, however, the mathematical processes in the upper level are "under construction" (i.e., being learned, as opposed to already learned), and its most important features are the relationships between the steps in the mathematical process (in the upper level) and the actions on particular elements in the problems (in the lower level).

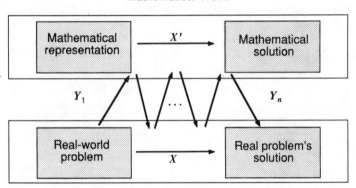

Fig. 3.2. A model of the process of solving process problems

In the figure, some of the Y arrows point upward to indicate that the problem solver is learning to make abstract written records of the actions that are understood in a concrete setting. These arrows pointing upward represent the processes of abstraction and generalization. Some of the arrows point downward to show that the problem solver is able to explain a mathematical process by referring to the real-world actions that the mathematical symbols represent. Arrows pointing downward might also suggest that a problem solver who had forgotten the details of a mathematical procedure would be able to reconstruct that process by imagining the corresponding concrete steps in the world in which the problem was posed. The collection of Y arrows illustrate the correspondence between the process of solving the problem in concrete terms (labeled X) and the parallel, abstract mathematical process (labeled X'). The Y arrows also show that the problem solver typically moves back and forth between the two worlds—the real and the mathematical—as the need arises. For a particular problem the problem solver might move directly along arrow $Y_1$ from the real world to the mathematical world and proceed directly along arrow X' to a mathematical generalization and hence to a solution of the original real-world problem. In such a situation the solution process can be modeled as shown in figure 3.1.

## PROBLEM SOLVING AND UNDERSTANDING IN MATHEMATICS

Central to our interest in teaching via problem solving is the belief that the primary reason for school mathematics instruction is to help students *understand* mathematical concepts, processes, and techniques. During the back-to-basics movement of the 1970s, and also with the more recent focus on problem solving, this fundamental tenet of good mathematics instruction has been given far too little attention. Moreover, some commentators have limited their discussion of understanding to the question of students' comprehension of the information presented in mathematical text, especially in the statements of verbal problems. In our view, students' understanding of mathematics involves much more than this.

A large number of mathematics educators have written about mathematical understanding by distinguishing between types or qualities of understanding. Brownell's work (e.g., 1935, 1945, 1947) on "meaningful arithmetic" in the 1930s and 1940s is especially relevant, but only during the past ten to fifteen years has any substantial activity taken place in this area. Of particular note are the works of Skemp (1976, 1979), Herscovics and Bergeron (1981, 1982), Davis (1984), and Hiebert (1984, 1986). A common thread running through these considerations of the nature of understanding in mathematics is the idea that to understand is essentially to relate. In particular, a person's understanding increases (1) as he or she is able to relate a given mathematical idea to a greater number or variety of contexts, or (2) as he or she relates a given problem to a greater number of the mathematical ideas implicit in it, or (3) as he or she constructs relationships among the various mathematical ideas embedded in a problem.

Indications that a student understands (or misunderstands, or does not understand) specific mathematical ideas often appear as the student solves a problem. Relationships of the kinds mentioned above are evident in students' attempts to solve the following problem (fig. 3.3), which is an adapta-

You have opened your piggy bank, and these are the coins you have. In how many ways can you give all your money to your four friends so that they will all have the same amount of money?

Fig. 3.3. A coin problem

tion of one suggested for students in grade 2 (Alberta Education 1983, p. 54). This problem was used by Croft (1987), a teacher who conducted individual interviews with several of her grade 1 students.

Croft noticed that different children had distinct levels of understanding that corresponded to the number of different mathematical concepts and processes they used in solving the problem. All the children began by sorting the coins by value and repeatedly using one-to-one correspondence; they placed the four dimes into four piles, then four of the nickels, then four more nickels, then the pennies. But some students got stuck when they reached the situation shown in figure 3.4. Although they were satisfied that the coins in each of the four piles matched, they did not know what to do with the nickel and three pennies that were left over. The children at the lowest level of understanding never got beyond this impasse, despite being encouraged to "try a different way" and to "share out all the coins." One child suggested that he could solve the problem if only he could take the nickel to the store and exchange it for five pennies. Other children used the making-change idea and recognized that by "undoing" part of the sharing, they could remove the three pennies from one pile and replace them with the "extra" nickel so that six pennies could then be put in the other three piles. This solution represents the next level of understanding. When the teacher asked, "Can you find another way? Could the piles have different coins in them but the same amount of money?" some children rearranged the coins but found no new solutions. However, the students at the highest level of understanding noticed that the value of the coins in each pile was twenty-five cents and used this fact to find several different ways of making change, such as those shown in figure 3.5.

These differences in students' performance indicate the variety of mathematical operations inherent in the problem, including sorting, finding a one-to-one correspondence, iterating, exchanging sets of equal value, and counting the value of a collection of coins and using the value (rather than the coins themselves) to find other collections of the same value. The pupils'

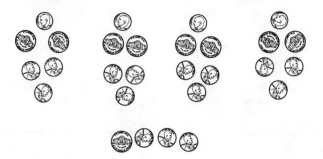

Fig. 3.4. An impasse on the way to solving the coin problem

Fig. 3.5. Some different ways to make twenty-five cents

ability to recognize and use these ideas gives a measure of their understanding. It is interesting to note that some children's understanding seemed to deepen and grow as they worked on the problem; their progress with the problem came in stages, by discovery, rather than all at once. This suggests that these students were learning *via* problem solving, even though the teacher's purpose was to assess their understanding rather than to teach them via problem solving.

## DEVELOPING UNDERSTANDING VIA PROBLEM SOLVING

We believe that instead of making *problem solving* the focus of mathematics instruction, teachers, textbook authors, curriculum developers, and evaluators should make *understanding* their focus and their goal. By doing so they will shift from the narrow view that mathematics is simply a tool for solving problems to the broader conception that mathematics is a way of thinking about and organizing one's experiences. As a consequence, problem solving will not be de-emphasized, but the role of problem solving in the curriculum will change from being an activity students engage in after they have acquired certain concepts and skills to being both a means for acquiring new mathematical knowledge and a process for applying what has been learned previously. Fundamental to the view that understanding should be a primary goal of instruction is the belief that children's learning of mathematics is richest when it is self-generated rather than when it is imposed by a teacher or textbook. A primary advantage of self-generated knowledge is that it is tied to what the learner already knows. Furthermore, when children construct new mathematical knowledge for themselves, they learn not only concepts, facts, skills, and so on, but also how to manage and regulate the application of this new knowledge. That is, they are in charge of this knowledge (and of their learning in general), thereby making it more useful to them in solving problems and in learning new concepts and skills. A benefit of having acquired mathematical knowledge in this way is that problem-solving efforts are less susceptible to error. We believe that teaching via problem solving and teaching for understanding are not only compatible but in fact mutually beneficial.

### Problem Solving Enhances Understanding

Beatriz D'Ambrosio has suggested the following challenge as an illustration of the fact that solving a problem can deepen a student's understanding of a topic of mathematics.

> On centimeter graph paper outline all the shapes that have an area of 14 square cm and a perimeter of 24 cm. For each shape you draw, at least one side of each square must share a side with another square. Here's an example:

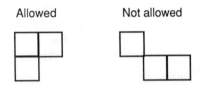

It is assumed, of course, that students given this problem would already have a basic understanding of the concepts of area and perimeter for rectangular shapes. The intention is not simply to allow the students an opportunity to apply their knowledge of these two concepts. Rather, it is to enhance their understanding of the relationships between area and perimeter. The solution to this problem requires that students make many decisions, among them how to keep track in a systematic way of the shapes that have been made so that all possibilities will be found and none will be duplicated. Such decisions and the associated skills needed to carry them out are an important part of learning how to solve problems successfully and efficiently. But learning what decisions to make and when to make them is not the only benefit of this task. In addition, as shapes are modified to fit the conditions of the problem, the learner is exposed to relationships between area and perimeter that, if noticed, can facilitate a richer understanding of both concepts. Thus, through investigation and exploration, students not only learn some useful problem-solving skills but also deepen their understanding of two important measurement concepts.

### Understanding Aids Problem Solving

Of course, success in solving a problem depends on the student's having a good understanding of the information in it. However, the value of understanding in successful problem solving goes far beyond this. In particular, when understanding is viewed in the way we have discussed, it aids problem solving in at least four distinct ways.

1. *Understanding increases the richness of the types of representations that the problem solver can construct.* During problem solving it is necessary for the problem solver to internalize the information in a problem. That is, the problem solver must develop a representation of the information. The more accurately the representation depicts the information and links pieces of information together, the more likely it is that the problem will be solved correctly.

2. *Understanding assists the problem solver in monitoring the selection and execution of procedures (e.g., strategies, algorithms).* Successful problem solving requires the ability to monitor the selection and subsequent execution of procedures, and the ability to evaluate the extent to which local actions (e.g., performing computations) conform to goals, and the ability to make various trade-off decisions (e.g., deciding that an estimate will give a "close enough" answer). The problem solver who understands the relationships among the conditions and variables in a problem and who can place the problem in a meaningful context is well equipped to anticipate the consequences of various decisions and actions and to evaluate the progress being made toward a solution.

3. *Understanding aids the problem solver in judging the reasonableness of results.* The ability to create a meaningful and appropriate internal representation of the information in a problem enhances the problem solver's ability to determine whether the answer makes sense.

4. *Understanding promotes the transfer of knowledge to related problems and its generalizability to other situations.* Brownell (1947), among others, has pointed out that a solution to a problem that is meaningful (i.e., well understood) transfers readily to problems that are similar in structure even if they are different in context. That is, since understanding involves the ability to apply a particular concept, skill, or procedure to unfamiliar situations, an individual who has a good understanding of certain mathematical ideas and techniques is likely to be able to apply that learning to contexts that might be very different from the contexts in which the mathematics was originally learned.

## CONCLUSION

We believe that there can be a mutually supportive relationship between emphasizing problem solving and emphasizing understanding in mathematics instruction. When teachers teach *via* problem solving, as well as *about* it and *for* it, they provide their students with a powerful and important means of developing their own understanding. As students' understanding of mathematics becomes deeper and richer, their ability to use mathematics to solve problems increases.

## REFERENCES

Alberta Education. *Let Problem Solving Be the Focus for 1980's*. Edmonton, Alberta: Author, 1983.

Brownell, William A. "Psychological Considerations in the Learning and Teaching of Arithmetic." In *The Teaching of Arithmetic*, Tenth Yearbook of the National Council of Teachers of Mathematics, pp. 1–31. New York: Bureau of Publications, Teachers College, Columbia University, 1935.

———. "When Is Arithmetic Meaningful?" *Journal of Educational Research* 38 (March 1945): 481–98.

———. "The Place of Meaning in the Teaching of Arithmetic." *Elementary School Journal* 47 (January 1947): 256–65.

Charles, Randall, and Frank Lester. *Teaching Problem Solving: What, Why, and How*. Palo Alto, Calif.: Dale Seymour Publications, 1982.

Croft, Monica. "A Problem-solving Interview." Unpublished paper, University of Calgary, 1987.

Davis, Robert B. *Learning Mathematics: The Cognitive Science Approach*. Norwood, N.J.: Ablex Publishing Corp., 1984.

Hatfield, Larry L. "Heuristical Emphases in the Instruction of Mathematical Problem Solving: Rationales and Research." In *Mathematical Problem Solving: Papers from a Research Workshop*, edited by Larry L. Hatfield and David A. Bradbard, pp. 21–42. Columbus, Ohio: ERIC/SMEAC, 1978.

Herscovics, Nicolas, and Jacques C. Bergeron. "Psychological Questions regarding a New Model of Understanding Elementary School Mathematics." In *Proceedings of the Third Annual Meeting of the North American Chapter of the International Group for the Psychology of Mathematics Education*, edited by Thomas R. Post and Mary P. Roberts, pp. 69–76. ERIC Document Reproduction Service No. ED 223-449, 1981.

———. "A Constructivist Model of Understanding." In *Proceedings of the Fourth Annual Meeting of the North American Chapter of the International Group for the Psychology of Mathematics Education*, edited by Sigrid Wagner, pp. 28–35. ERIC Document Reproduction Service No. ED 226-957, 1982.

Hiebert, James. "Children's Mathematical Learning: The Struggle to Link Form and Understanding." *Elementary School Journal* 5 (May 1984): 497–513.

———. *Conceptual and Procedural Knowledge: The Case of Mathematics*. Hillsdale, N.J.: Lawrence Erlbaum Associates, 1986.

National Council of Teachers of Mathematics. *An Agenda for Action: Recommendations for School Mathematics of the 1980s*. Reston, Va.: The Council, 1980.

———. *Curriculum and Evaluation Standards for School Mathematics*. Working draft. Reston, Va.: The Council, 1987.

Pólya, George. *How to Solve It*. 2d ed. Princeton, N.J.: Princeton University Press, 1957.

Shroyer, Janet, and William Fitzgerald. *Mouse and Elephant: Measuring Growth*. Middle Grades Mathematics Project. Menlo Park, Calif.: Addison-Wesley Publishing Co., 1986.

Skemp, Richard R. "Relational Understanding and Instrumental Understanding." *Mathematics Teaching* 77 (December 1976): 1–7. (Reprinted in *Arithmetic Teacher* 26 [November 1978]: 9–15.)

———. *Intelligence, Learning and Action*. New York: John Wiley & Sons, 1979.

# 4

# The Role of Computation in the Changing Mathematics Curriculum

## Terrence G. Coburn

**I**T IS widely recognized that written computation dominates the instructional program in elementary school mathematics. Paper-and-pencil computation is also prominent in the public's perception of what it means to be mathematically proficient. Yet written computation is in reduced demand both at home and on the job. In fact, mathematics education leaders, national reports, and some state and local school curriculum guidelines are calling for curriculum reform with limits on paper-and-pencil computation because the electronic calculator is making much written computation obsolete. Reform will not come smoothly, however. The public will be skeptical about any proposals for de-emphasizing computation. Those having vested interests in current standardized testing, current textbooks, and the traditional curriculum will also be resistant to such change.

The role of computation in the emerging curriculum will require wide-ranging examination and discussion. To stimulate this discussion, the following major points are made:

1. The definition of computation must be broadened.
2. The importance of computation in the curriculum must be clarified and reaffirmed and limitations set for written computational skills.
3. We must become more effective at teaching computation.

### BROADEN THE DEFINITION OF COMPUTATION

Much has already been written about reforms in the teaching of computation. Reform documents consistently support the position of elevating the importance of problem solving and reducing the level of written computation. In addition, thoughtful and compelling arguments have been made for a broadened definition of computation that will include three modes of

43

performing computation and two purposes for computing (see fig. 4.1). Six categories of computation result from combining the three modes with the two intended outcomes. Category A-1 currently receives the overwhelming share of time and emphasis.

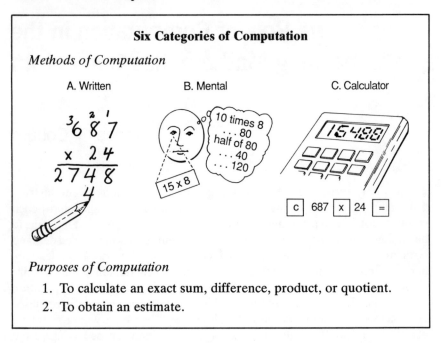

**Six Categories of Computation**

*Methods of Computation*

A. Written          B. Mental          C. Calculator

10 times 8
... 80
half of 80
... 40
... 120

15 × 8

c 687 x 24 =

*Purposes of Computation*

1. To calculate an exact sum, difference, product, or quotient.
2. To obtain an estimate.

Fig. 4.1

We envision a curriculum in which students would also be taught to select an appropriate computational procedure depending on the problem situation. Their computational repertoire would range from mental-oral procedures for obtaining exact answers to estimation with the assistance of a calculator.

### Written Computation

Some paper-and-pencil algorithms will continue to be useful, especially with fractions. As a rather precarious analogy, electronic word processors are certainly more powerful, but the average person will still find it useful to be able to produce a handwritten note. Similarly, calculators and computers will not completely eliminate the need for doing some paper-and-pencil computing. For example, people may still wish to verify a restaurant bill.

### Calculators

Won't the calculator become a crutch? Dependence on a device like a calculator is inevitable to some degree. We become by nature dependent on things we use regularly; this in and of itself is not bad. The fact that many children are overly dependent on written computation is often overlooked. A child who multiplies 300 by 122 using the traditional paper-and-pencil algorithm is dependent on written computation. The child who receives good instruction should decide to do this type of computation mentally, or at least take a written shortcut to the conventional algorithm (i.e., not use three partial products).

The term *crutch* implies a dependency without understanding. The real issue is not dependency but understanding. We need to examine this issue carefully because it is a common belief that if children use calculators, they will not understand what they are doing. It is as if understanding always enters the brain on a pathway from a pencil through the fingers. The understanding of a computational procedure must be seen as only one of at least three different aspects of computation: concepts, calculation procedures, and applications. Square roots and long division illustrate this point. Calculating a square root is only one dimension of understanding square root. Although the written algorithm is obsolete, we still teach the major understandings related to the concepts and applications of square root. The situation with square root is prophetic of what may be happening to long division. Like the square root algorithm, the long division algorithm may be becoming obsolete. When we say that a child needs to understand division, we mean more than just how to perform the algorithm. Working through the complex steps of the digit-by-digit algorithm does not contribute to the understanding of any of the important ideas and applications of division.

One of the primary understandings in computation involves knowing which arithmetic operation to perform: the child still needs to decide which buttons to push (see fig. 4.2). The child should also be taught to evaluate whether the computed answer is reasonable. This process requires more thinking than that which is needed for the rote manipulation of a paper-and-pencil algorithm.

## Mental Computation and Computational Estimation

Why teach mental computation or computational estimation? We teach them because they are practical skills and because they help a child concentrate on meanings and grasp relationships. Some have observed that the average adult makes more use of mental computation and estimation on a daily basis than written computation (Hope 1986, p. 46). All students need to acquire skills that will enable them to be accurate and speedy with simple number questions. We don't want to run for a calculator (or look for paper and pencil) to find the product of $20 \times 30$. Current efforts toward teaching computational estimation, teaching for understanding, and teaching for

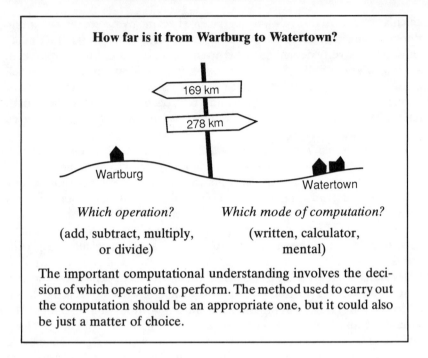

**How far is it from Wartburg to Watertown?**

*Which operation?*
(add, subtract, multiply, or divide)

*Which mode of computation?*
(written, calculator, mental)

The important computational understanding involves the decision of which operation to perform. The method used to carry out the computation should be an appropriate one, but it could also be just a matter of choice.

Fig. 4.2

higher-order thinking will benefit from a renewed emphasis on mental computation.

## THE IMPORTANCE OF COMPUTATION

Computation is an important part of the K–8 mathematics curriculum, but it is not the most important part. Both the National Council of Supervisors of Mathematics and the National Council of Teachers of Mathematics have recommended that computation be recognized as just one part of a mathematics program. And within computation itself, skill in using written procedures is being subordinated to the development of concepts and applications.

Essentially, two major reasons are usually given for including the teaching of computation within the mathematics curriculum. The first is that computation is a useful skill both in everyday life and in various occupations. Society needs people who can compute and who are knowledgeable about computation. Of course, society has to accept the fact that computation includes the use of calculators.

The second reason is that computational skills assist the learner in learning other topics, such as measurement, statistics, and problem solving. It is important to note that the purpose of learning computational skills is not to perform them per se but to use them in solving problems, in making applications, and in exploring new knowledge in mathematics and other courses of study. As Trafton and Suydam (1975) have stated as one of their tenets on teaching computation, "The study of computation should promote broad, long-range goals of learning" (p. 531).

The thrust of the current curriculum reform, then, is not to reduce the importance of computation but rather to broaden the definition of computation and to elevate the importance of problem solving. The amount of time given to teaching written computation can be reduced, and the time saved can be given to increased emphasis in concept development, problem solving, mental computation, and estimation.

## WHAT COMPUTATION SHOULD BE TAUGHT?

The suggestions for specific changes that follow have been developed and shaped by reading the professional literature, talking to colleagues, and participating in countless state and local curriculum revision meetings. In this land of local automony, we can hope only to gradually influence test-item writers and textbook editors, who in turn influence (and are influenced by) local and state curriculum committees. It is perhaps a mistake to focus too intently on grade-level outcomes. There should be an open forum for the continual examination of what should be taught. In the meantime, however, we need some notions of what to strive for in order to allocate our resources better to the job of equipping each child with the computational understandings and skills needed in a high-quality mathematics curriculum.

Change in the content of the computation portion of the curriculum involves three actions: dropping antiquated skills, adding new content, and readjusting the pace of development for certain skills. We shall first consider the areas of computation that are important for all children (see fig. 4.3). Next we shall consider those traditional skills that could be dropped (see fig. 4.4). Finally, we discuss some reasonable outcomes for each of the major areas of computation. Readjusting the instructional pace will be discussed in the next section.

### Mental Computation

Mental computation has been neglected in school mathematics for some time. Very little hard data (that we are aware of) are available to guide us in setting performance outcomes for mental computation. One guide to use would be a parallel development with written computation and computational estimation. We should also consider how mental computation can help learning in related areas. For example, mental addition with two-digit num-

---

**Six Areas of Computation That Are Important for All Children**

1. Conceptualization of the four operations with whole numbers and fractions

2. Immediate recall of the basic facts for the four operations with one-digit numbers

3. Written computation using standard algorithms to obtain exact answers

   *a*) Whole numbers—addition and subtraction with three-digit numbers and multiplication with two-digit numbers

   *b*) Selected fractions (commonly used denominators)—standard algorithms for addition, subtraction, and multiplication; do not exclude division, but emphasize the concept, not the algorithm

   *c*) Renaming with equivalent fractions and mixed numbers

   *d*) Decimals—addition, subtraction, and multiplication (The level of complexity should parallel that used with whole numbers; the division operation can be handled with calculators.)

   *e*) Solving proportions

4. Mental computation for exact answers (more emphasis on conceptualization than on computational speed)

   *a*) Whole numbers—four operations with appropriate numbers (e.g., compatible number situations and shortcuts with special numbers: 10, 15, 25, 50, 100, 500, 1000, etc.)

   *b*) Selected fractions—four operations

   *c*) Selected decimals and multiples of powers of 10

   *d*) Selected percents

5. Computational estimation and approximation (Include the four operations with rational numbers and percent. Written procedures and calculator use are also envisioned here. Estimation is not solely an oral-mental process.)

6. Calculator use with appropriate rational numbers and percent (limited use with fraction notation)

The competencies above should be learned in the context of real-life applications.

---

Fig. 4.3

bers is helpful in the memorization of the multiplication facts. In trying to recall the product for $6 \times 7$, the child may recall that $5 \times 7$ is 35 and that $35 + 7$ is 42. If the child cannot add 35 and 7 without paper and pencil, then this strategy of building on a known fact is not very helpful.

## Estimation

As with mental computation, grade-level outcomes for computational estimation are speculative. National test results suggests that students do not perform very well in this area. This poor performance is more likely due to a lack of instruction than to any intrinsic difficulty. As with mental computa-

---

### Paper-and-Pencil Skills to Be Deleted

*Examples*

1. Written computation to find sums and differences with whole numbers larger than 999 and products with numbers larger than 99

$$853$$
$$\times\ 476$$

$$3874$$
$$6921$$
$$+\ 5438$$

2. The standard algorithm for long division with two-digit or three-digit divisors (There may be some reason to teach short division with one-digit divisors—this skill is really a combination of mental computations with written assistance.)

$$62\overline{)27\ 159}$$

3. Written computation with decimal fractions to find products or quotients (other than simple cases that parallel related whole number skills)

$$64.7$$
$$\times\ 8.82$$

$$4.7\overline{)1.772}$$

4. Written computation involving uses of percent

$$82.9\%\ \times\ 924$$

---

Fig. 4.4

tion, the grade-level outcomes for estimation can be established parallel to the traditional sequence with written computation. We recommend, however, that simple cases of estimation with a particular operation precede the related written computational procedure for obtaining exact answers. In this way students may acquire more of a number sense prior to the use of formal written computation.

### HOW CAN WE TEACH COMPUTATION MORE EFFECTIVELY?

In 1956, William Brownell stated that "it is assumed that both meaning and computational competence are proper ends of instruction in arithmetic" (1987, p. 18). Will children learn to compute better given the new definition of computation with its reduced levels of written computation? It is tempting to speculate that they will, but we think that the revised content will not be any easier to learn. Teachers will still strive to teach effectively using manipulatives, taking appropriate time to develop the concepts, and making efficient use of drill.

Teaching for understanding is still a major ingredient in a high-quality program of instruction. With the implementation of this broadened view of computation, teachers will have a new opportunity to take an appropriate amount of time to help all children acquire a better understanding of quantitative ideas and the meanings of arithmetic operations. The mathematics education literature has long advocated the use of manipulatives and conceptual models to help children develop better understandings of computational procedures. However, many classroom teachers feel pressed to develop written computational skills quickly and do not take the time to concentrate on concepts. Now is the time to make a change.

### Will Children Need to Have Immediate Recall of the Basic Facts?

The memorization of the 390 basic arithmetic facts will remain a priority. Once an operation is understood, instruction can begin to help the child attain immediate recall of the one-digit-by-one-digit facts for that operation. The use of "thinking strategies" may be more effective than mere rote memorization at helping children memorize facts (Rathmell 1978). The speedy recall of the basic facts is the foundation of mental computation, estimation, and written computation.

The conceptualization stage of instruction can encompass the basic facts portion of the instructional program. There is little need to proceed quickly to a written algorithm until the related concepts, meanings, and basic facts are in place to support the rationalization of an algorithm. A comfortable pace for mastering the facts would be five new facts a week. This pace would allow for the addition and subtraction facts to be mastered in grades 1–3 and for the multiplication and division facts to be mastered by the end of grade 4. This pace would also allow the instructional program to be as comprehensive as possible over these early years without getting bogged down in a heavy program of drill.

### Move Some Traditional Whole Number Milestones

The pace of development may be relaxed somewhat for teaching some of the written computational algorithms, and the traditional grade-level outcomes can be adjusted up to a later grade level. For example, renaming in addition and subtraction with two- and three-digit numbers can be established as a grades 3–4 skill instead of a grades 2–3 skill. Also, there is no reason to require that all fourth graders master multiplication with a two-digit multiplier. This can become a grades 4–5 skill.

Readjusted levels of written computation will not necessarily make computation easier to teach. They should, however, allow for better balance in the time allocated for teaching skills, concepts, and applications. Modern programs of instruction will concentrate their efforts in the areas of conceptualization and problem solving. One of the key principles for teaching computation given by Trafton and Suydam (1975) summarizes this issue: "Computation needs to be continually related to the concepts of the operations and both concepts and skills should be developed in the context of real-world applications" (p. 532).

## Readjust the Teaching of Written Computation with Fractions

More time needs to be spent carefully developing the initial fraction concepts and the connections between the concepts and algorithmic procedures. It is not true that fractions are obsolete and that computation with fractions should be dropped from the curriculum (Payne 1980; Usiskin 1979). It is true, however, that many students do not attain computational skills with fractions, because of inadequate understanding of basic fraction concepts and a premature emphasis on computation rules.

Some calculators can handle fraction notation. Nonetheless, it seems wise to continue teaching written procedures for computing with fractions. There may be some relationship between learning to manipulate fraction symbols and learning related symbol manipulations in algebra. Coxford (1985) raised a cogent point when he observed that we do not completely understand the psychological relationships between manipulative skill and concept learning. It is possible that skills involving least common denominators, renaming fractions in lower terms, and so on, may be best learned in the environment of written computation and not at the push of a button. How can this be true for fractions and not true for whole numbers? A partial response is that the whole number algorithms are place value driven whereas the algorithms used with fractions are more directly related to ratio and measurement concepts.

The purpose for readjusting formal instruction in computation is to allow for a stronger development of fraction concepts and the meanings of the operations. This reorganization means spending more time with conceptual models and manipulatives before stressing the rules for manipulating the symbols.

Written computation should be taught for all four operations. With division the stress should be on conceptualization, and easy fractions should be used (such as $2/3 \div 1/6$). Estimation and mental computation should be equally mixed with written computation. Instruction should emphasize understanding and applying the computational procedures.

It does not seem to affect achievement if decimal computation precedes or follows computation with fractions. Fraction concepts (such as the idea of a part of a unit region) should precede the extension of the decimal numeration system to the right of the ones place. Obviously decimal fractions are just that—fractions expressed in a different notation scheme. Since computation with decimals is easier to do than computation with fractions, it makes sense to undertake decimal computation first. However, there is an important caveat here: the ease in computation makes it easy to hide poor understanding of decimals. The meaningful development of decimal computation is just as important as whole number computation with fractions and whole numbers.

### How Can We Teach Percent More Effectively?

One of the main contributors to low levels of achievement with percent is the lack of understanding most students have about the relationships among ratios (expressed as fractions), decimals, and percent. Textbooks have not given adequate space to the meaningful development of this interrelationship.

Another reason for our lack of success in teaching percents is that we do not take enough "out of book" teaching time to help students develop some fundamental sense of quantity involving parts of a whole. We need to use estimation activities that help students visualize the amount involved with concrete representations of 1%, 10%, 25%, 50%, and 100%.

As with fractions, more time is needed to develop adequately the conceptualization and "number sense" of percents than is currently used in most textbooks and many classrooms. A calculator can help a student develop some estimation ability with percent by giving immediate reinforcement to repeated calculations. For example, the student can rapidly compute 25% of different amounts and check each display to see whether the part is about one-fourth of the whole.

Written computation should be de-emphasized in favor of the calculator. The major thrust of instruction should be in the direction of meaning and application. Students should be taught to use the calculator while interpreting the different ways in which percent questions are asked in everyday life.

### Will There Be Less Drill?

One of the major criticisms of the way computation has been taught is the overreliance on drill as the main instructional strategy. Although drill remains an important activity in teaching computation, we must use more efficient approaches. A new trend toward more frequent, briefer periods of practice seems to offer promise for effective drill. As always, drill must follow adequate understanding. The "daily mixed practice sessions" contain a systematically determined mixture of previously taught skills. Mixing several skills in the same session forces the children to make decisions about the computational procedures. These short practice sessions distributed over a school year seem to help promote mastery beyond the initial instruction period as well as to help maintain acquired skills.

It is not possible to teach mental computation and estimation without a variety of drill sessions. Thus, in spite of a reduction in the amount of written computation, drill activities will continue to be an important tool in the teacher's arsenal. The main point, however, is that the drill must be brief, regular, systematic, and built on adequate understanding.

### SUMMARY

The role of computation in the mathematics curriculum will be much the same as it has always been: to furnish the individual with useful skills and to facilitate further learning in both mathematics and related disciplines. The broadened definition of computation will better serve all groups of children. The talented student will be challenged more appropriately by computation in problem solving. The slow learner and the learning disabled student will be less frustrated by complicated written algorithms. The prospect of more students spending more time learning mathematics is exciting.

The suggested changes in the content of the computation strand of the elementary school mathematics curriculum are summarized in figure 4.5. The proposed changes will come slowly, but they will come because there is a broad base of support. The change process must involve teachers of all subjects at all levels, textbook and test publishers, and the public.

The public will be skeptical of any attempt to reduce the amount of written computation taught in our schools. They have recent memories of the "new math" and the decline in test scores. Many parents want their children to bring home pages of computational drill from school. They are comforted to see their children "doing math" the way they did when they were in school. Consequently, we need to use all avenues to help them understand our objectives for computation. The National Council of Teachers of Mathematics has prepared several excellent brochures directed at parents. This parent communication/education program needs to be emphasized further. Other avenues of educating the public also need to be explored.

Current standardized tests focus heavily on written computational skills and symbol manipulation and pay less attention to problem solving and higher-order thinking skills. Calculator usage on these tests has not yet been established. Results on standardized tests heavily influence curriculum decision makers in local school districts. Change in this area of school policy is a "chicken or the egg" issue: many schools will not change their curriculum until the tests change. Recent signs indicate that the test makers are indeed willing to change.

Recent editions of popular textbook series have included calculator materials and lessons in mental computation. They are beginning to teach more about computational estimation than merely the strategy of computing with rounded numbers. Textbook editors, however, are loath to delete any skill that has been in the curriculum. They may continue to feature anachronistic algorithms alongside modern technology. State guidelines may be instrumental in influencing textbook writers to adopt the proposed reforms in teaching computation.

Many classroom teachers in grades 3–8 are accustomed to spending the majority of mathematics time in describing how adults perform written computations and then assigning large amounts of written practice. These teachers will not find change easy to accommodate. Funding for staff development must be increased across the nation.

### Proposed Changes in the Computation Curriculum—a Summary

| | Written Computation | Mental Computation and Estimation | Calculators |
|---|---|---|---|
| Whole Numbers | • Eliminate the long division algorithm.<br>• Significantly reduce the amount of multidigit written computation.<br>• Readjust some traditional grade-level outcomes. | • Increase emphasis in order to—support concept development; provide a practical skill; enhance problem solving; and develop quantitative thinking. | • Ensure routine use by all children at all grades.<br>• Develop concepts.<br>• Reinforce skills.<br>• Enhance problem solving.<br>• Promote higher-order thinking. |
| Fractions | • Delay rules for symbol manipulation to allow adequate time for conceptual development.<br>• Reduce complexity.<br>• Focus on developing generalizations required for success in algebra. | • Increase emphasis for same reasons as given above. | • Use with selected topics (e.g., change fractions to decimals). |
| Decimals and Percent | • Reduce complexity.<br>• Develop written computational procedures in parallel with related whole number algorithms. | • Increase emphasis for same reasons as given above for whole numbers. | • Use regularly both to help develop concepts and to make realistic applications. |

Fig. 4.5

Teachers need staff development programs that help them develop a broader, more global view of computation (see fig. 4.6). In this global view, conceptual models and the meanings of operations are foundational. All computation should relate to conceptualization and problem solving, and these important aspects are located at the "poles." The methods of doing computation are shown at the "equator." Mental computation, written computation, and the use of a calculator are each equally important, and

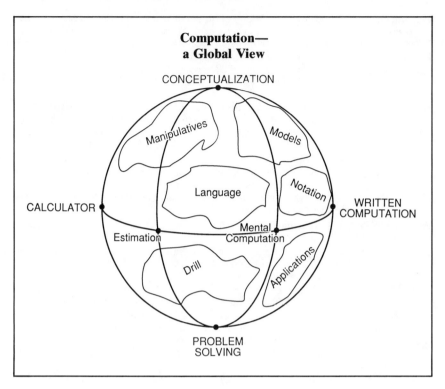

Fig. 4.6

children need to make appropriate choices. Manipulatives are used to deepen meaning and to connect language and symbols. Daily mixed practice and regular reviews help to further learning and maintain competence.

If teachers adopt this global view of computation, then we may begin to teach computation more effectively as well as find room in the curriculum to teach problem solving, measurement, geometry, statistics, and probability. We may then begin to see more students attain a broader and deeper understanding of mathematics than has previously been accomplished. The time may be at hand when it is deemed more important to understand mathematics and to attack problems with confidence than to be adept at performing written computation.

### BIBLIOGRAPHY

Brownell, William A. "Meaning and Skill—Maintaining the Balance." *Arithmetic Teacher* 34 (April 1987): 18–25. Originally published in 1956.

Conference Board of the Mathematical Sciences. *The Mathematical Sciences Curriculum K–12: What Is Still Fundamental and What Is Not?* Washington, D.C.: The Board, 1983.

Coxford, Arthur. "School Algebra: What Is Still Fundamental and What Is Not." In *The Secondary School Mathematics Curriculum,* 1985 Yearbook of the National Council of Teachers of Mathematics, pp. 53–64. Reston, Va.: The Council, 1985.

Hamrick, Katherine B., and William D. McKillip. "How Computational Skills Contribute to the Meaningful Learning of Arithmetic." In *Developing Computational Skills,* 1978 Yearbook of the National Council of Teachers of Mathematics, pp. 1–12. Reston, Va.: The Council, 1978.

Hope, John A. "Mental Calculation: Anachronism or Basic Skill?" In *Estimation and Mental Computation,* 1986 Yearbook of the National Council of Teachers of Mathematics, pp. 45–54. Reston, Va.: The Council, 1986.

Leinwand, Steven. "Curricular Improvement versus Standardized Testing." *Arithmetic Teacher* 33 (April 1986): 3.

Lindquist, Mary Montgomery. "The Elementary School Mathematics Curriculum Issues for Today!" *Elementary School Journal* 84 (May 1984): 595–608.

National Council of Teachers of Mathematics. *Estimation and Mental Computation.* 1986 Yearbook. Reston, Va.: The Council, 1986.

Payne, Joseph N. "Sense and Nonsense about Fractions and Decimals." *Arithmetic Teacher* 27 (January 1980): 4–7.

Rathmell, Edward C. "Using Thinking Strategies to Teach the Basic Facts." In *Developing Computational Skills,* 1978 Yearbook of the National Council of Teachers of Mathematics, pp. 13–38. Reston, Va.: The Council, 1978.

Rowan, Thomas E. "The Role of Computation." In *Selected Issues in Mathematics Education,* edited by Mary Montgomery Lindquist, pp. 46–53. Chicago: National Society for the Study of Education; Reston, Va.: National Council of Teachers of Mathematics, 1980.

Trafton, Paul R. "Assessing the Mathematics Curriculum Today." In *Selected Issues in Mathematics Education,* edited by Mary Montgomery Lindquist, pp. 9–26. Chicago: National Society for the Study of Education; Reston, Va.: National Council of Teachers of Mathematics, 1980.

——— . "Computation—It's Time for a Change." *Arithmetic Teacher* 34 (November 1986): 2.

Trafton, Paul R., and Marilyn N. Suydam. "Computational Skills: A Point of View." *Arithmetic Teacher* 22 (November 1975): 529–37.

Usiskin, Zalman P. "The Future of Fractions." *Arithmetic Teacher* 26 (January 1979): 18–20.

# FIFTH GRADERS
# INVESTIGATE GEOMETRY

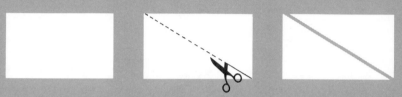

Cut the rectangle along the diagonal. Put the two triangles together by joining congruent sides. What shapes do you get? Describe your shape.

Joey Arms

sides are parallell
to the opposite
side
its quadrilateral
it doesn't have
any right angles
it has 4 corners
2 angles are
more than 90 degrees
and 2 are less
then 90 degrees
2 sides are
horazontal and
2 are diagonal

Anna Hamelton

This figure is called a
quadrilateral. It has four sides.
The top two sides are equal and
the bottom two sides are equal.
When you look at it this way
it looks like a kite if you turn
the paper upside down then look at the
figure it looks like a square pyramid. Best
of all it has two right angles.

Alan
Maiga 9/5
Math

This shape is a triangle, it has three sides. Two of the sides are the same length. This shape is closed. This shape has no right angles. All three angles are acute.

Kate and
9/5/88
Math

This shape is a triangle. If you cut this figure on a symetry line it would have two triangles. This shape has no right angles. Angle #1 is obtuse and angles #2 and 3 are acute angles. This shape also has no parralell lines.

Rou[...]neider

It has two acute angles and two obtuse. It is a quad[...], opposite sides are equal and parrellel, it is called a parrellelogram, it is flat, it is also a closed figure, it is black. Also about the obtuse and acute- the opposites are equal

**Questions to think about:**

1. Why can you get only five additional shapes?
2. Compare the perimeters. See if you can do this without measuring.
3. Compare the areas.

*Submitted by Alison Claus*

# 5

# Assessing and Building Thinking Strategies: Necessary Bases for Instruction

Harriett C. Bebout
Thomas P. Carpenter

I T WAS early September and Leigh Bailey was getting to know her first-grade class of twenty-seven children. She was especially interested in finding out about their mathematical thinking because she had attended a summer workshop in which she had learned about some recent research on children's thinking and problem solving in mathematics. (For reviews of this research see Carpenter [1985]; Carpenter, Carey, and Kouba [forthcoming]; Carpenter and Moser [1983]; or Riley, Greeno, and Heller [1983].) Leigh Bailey had taught first grade for five years so she was aware that most children enter first grade with some experience in using numbers and some basic knowledge of number concepts. During the summer workshop she learned that many children can solve a variety of simple word problems before they receive formal instruction in addition and subtraction in school. She also became familiar with the various modeling and counting strategies that children use to solve the different types of problems.

So that she could better plan her instruction to build on the children's informal mathematical knowledge, Leigh Bailey wanted to find out their mathematical understandings and strategies. She arranged to have a ten- to fifteen-minute interview with each child. The arrangements required some planning, but the interviews often could be scheduled during individual or small-group activity periods, special classes, or the autumn health screening.

Leigh Bailey's intention in these interviews was to assess children's problem-solving strategies by using different types of addition and subtraction word problems. She knew that during the first grade, children's solution strategies become progressively less concrete and increasingly more abstract. (Table 5.1 gives examples of this progression.) When children first come to school, most have invented strategies that directly model the actions or relationships described in problems; these early strategies are the simple joining and separating strategies that compose the most elementary strategy level. The elementary direct modeling strategies are followed by the more sophisticated direct modeling strategies of adding on and matching and by the more efficient counting strategies. The strategies at these first three levels provide essential physical modeling and counting backgrounds for the later strategies that involve meaningful recall of symbolic number facts. Knowledge of number facts is constructed by children over an extended learning period on the essential foundation provided by these earlier strategies.

The following section presents Leigh Bailey's interviews with four children at various strategy levels and describes her thoughts about their performances on the different types of problems.

### KATHY

*L.B.:*   Hi, Kathy. I'm going to tell you some stories. Each story has numbers in it and asks a question. You figure out the answers to the stories and show me how you did it with these little blocks. [Gives Kathy a cup of about twenty small blocks.]

*Kathy:*   Okay [nods].

*L.B.:*   Here's the first story:
   Sam had five stickers. His mother gave him some more stickers. Then Sam had eight stickers. How many stickers did his mother give him?

*Kathy:*   I think I can do this [nods]. He has ... five—one, two, three, four, five [counts out five blocks], and his mom gave him more ... and he's going to end up with ... eight. [Kathy then sets out more blocks as she counts on to eight.] Six, seven, eight. [Looks at the new group and quietly counts them.] One, two, three ... three. His mom must have given him three more stickers. [Looks questioningly at Leigh Bailey.]

*L.B.:*   That makes sense. Good, Kathy.

Leigh Bailey discovered that Kathy understood and could directly model

TABLE 5.1
Levels and Common Strategies for Addition and Subtraction Problem Types

| Critical Problem Types | Strategies |
|---|---|
| **Elementary Direct Modeling Level** | |
| *Result Unknown* | *Joining* |
| Polly had 3 cookies. Her brother gave her 4 more cookies. How many cookies did Polly have then? | Join together sets of 3 and 5 blocks and count the total. |
| Joe had 10 toy cars. He gave 4 of them to his friend Ruth. How many cars did Joe have then? | *Separating From* Make a set of 10 blocks, remove 4, and count the remaining blocks. |
| **Direct Modeling Level** | |
| *Change Unknown* | *Adding On* |
| Sam had 5 stickers. His mother gave him some more stickers. Then Sam had 8 stickers. How many stickers did his mother give him? | Make a set of 5 blocks, add blocks until there are 8 altogether, and count the blocks added. |
| *Comparison* | *Matching* |
| Some children are catching lightning bugs. Suzanne catches 4 and John catches 9. How many more does Suzanne need to catch to have as many as John? | Make two sets of 9 and 4 blocks, match the sets, and count the unmatched btocks. |
| *Start Unknown* | *Trial and Error* |
| Some children were in the park. Six children went home. Then 8 children were in the park. How many children were there at the start? | Make a trial set and separate 6. Count the items left, compare to 8, readjust initial set, and begin again. |
| **Counting/Transforming Level** | |
| Some children were in the park. Six children went home. Then 8 children were in the park. How many children were there at the start? | *Counting On* 8 . . . 9, 10, 11, 12, 13, 14 |
| **Number Facts Level** | |
| Some children were in the park. Six children went home. Then 8 children were in the park. How many children were there at the start? | *Recall and Derived Facts* 6 plus 8 is 14, or take 1 from the 8 and give it to the 6; 7 plus 7 is 14. |

the action in the problem. She knows from her experience with young children that first graders often need to use objects or fingers to represent the quantities in a problem.

Leigh Bailey then chose a slightly more difficult problem that involved comparing two groups of numbers.

*L.B.:*   Let's do another story:

Some children are catching lightning bugs. Suzanne catches four and John catches nine. How many more does Suzanne need to catch to have as many as John?

*Kathy:* Well, John caught more.

*L.B.:* Okay. How many more?

*Kathy:* I don't know [looks puzzled]. Can you tell me the story again?

*L.B.:* Sure. [Rereads the story.] Use the little blocks to show me what happens in the story.

*Kathy:* All right. Here are Suzanne's . . . one, two, three, four [counts out four] and here are John's . . . one, two, three, four, five, six, seven, eight, nine [counts out nine and then stares at the two groups, thinking.] John has nine . . . one, two, three, four, five, six, seven, eight, nine [moves the group of nine into a row], and the girl has four. [Matches up the second group of four with the row of nine.] Oh [looks at the blocks that are not matched and counts them] one, two, three, four, five . . . five! He has five more. See?

*L.B.:* I do see. Great, Kathy, you did a good job. I could see how you figured out that story.

Leigh Bailey learned a couple of important things about Kathy's mathematical thinking. She realized that Kathy understood and could solve different types of word problems. More specifically, she learned that Kathy could understand and directly model the action or relationships described in problems. Kathy was easily able to imagine what happened in each problem and to copy this action with physical items.

## LEWIS

With another child, Lewis, Leigh Bailey began with the same story about Sam and the stickers.

Lewis listens and looks at Leigh Bailey a long time. Then he counts out a group of five blocks, pauses, recounts the five blocks, and adds three more blocks as he counts to eight. Unlike Kathy, Lewis does not keep the three blocks separate from the original five, so he cannot figure out how many blocks he added to the original set. He looks at the eight blocks for a while and then recounts them.

*L.B.:* Can you tell me how many stickers Sam's mother gave him?

*Lewis:* Eight?

*L.B.:* Listen to the story again, Lewis, and then you tell me the story in your own words. [Rereads the problem.]

*Lewis:* Well, Sam has five stickers and he gets some more from this mother and then he has eight. So how many did he get from his mother?

*L.B.:* Yes, that's the story. Now use these blocks to show me the story.

*Lewis:* I don't think I can.

*L.B.:* Let's do it together. Let's pretend these blocks are Sam's stickers, and let's set out the stickers he has. [Lewis counts out five blocks.] Now what happened?

*Lewis:* His mother is going to give him some stickers.

*L.B.:*    Okay, let's give him another one, and keep it a little bit away from the others. [Lewis sets out another block.] How many does Sam have now?

*Lewis:*   One, two, three, four, five, six . . . six.

*L.B.:*    And give him another. [Lewis sets out another block.] How many now?

*Lewis:*   One, two, three, four, five, six, seven . . . seven. Wait! [Puts out a third block and counts both groups again.] One, two, three, four, five, six, seven, eight . . . eight! That's it. [Counts second group.] One, two, three . . . three. His mother gave him three more, I think.

*L.B.:*    That makes sense, Lewis. Good.

Leigh Bailey realized that this problem was too hard for Lewis, even though he did work it out with her help. She decided to give him two easier problems that required a simpler form of modeling. She read the following problem:

> Polly had three cookies. Her brother gave her five more cookies. How many cookies does Polly have now?

*L.B.:*    Show me with the blocks, Lewis, how you would figure out that story.

*Lewis:*   It's easy. Here are Polly's cookies, one, two, three, and here are the cookies from her brother, one, two, three, four, five. So now she has, one, two, three, four, five, six, seven, eight . . . eight [counts both groups].

*L.B.:*    Great, Lewis. Now try one more story. Here it is:

> Joe had ten toy cars. He gave four of them to his friend Ruth. How many toy cars did Joe have then?

*Lewis:*   Let's see. He had . . . ten toy cars? [Leigh Bailey nods.] And he gave away four?

*L.B.:*    That's the story.

*Lewis:*   So . . . let me see. He had ten cars . . . one, two, three, four, five, six, seven, eight, nine, ten [counts out ten blocks]. And then he gave away four . . . one, two, three, four [separates four from the group of ten]. So then, here [counts the remaining blocks] one, two, three, four, five, six . . . six! I think he had six left.

*L.B.:*    That makes sense. Good, Lewis.

From Lewis's performances on these last two problems, Leigh Bailey saw that he could tell the difference between addition and subtraction situations. He used a joining action for the addition problem and a separating action for the subtraction problem. Lewis was able to solve the two most basic types of problems—ones that had an unknown quantity as the result of an action— by taking one step at a time. For example, in the last problem he made one set of ten blocks, separated four blocks, and then counted the blocks that were left.

Lewis was not able to understand the more complex problem about Sam and the stickers, a problem in which the unknown is in the middle, in the change part of the problem. For this problem, he had to plan ahead. He needed to recognize that the set of five blocks that he made initially was part of the set of eight blocks that he would make next, and that the set of five blocks had to be kept separate so he could count the blocks that he added on.

## CARLOS

When Carlos came to see Leigh Bailey, she told him the story about Sam and the stickers.

*Carlos:* [Nods several times and responds quickly.] Three!

*L.B.:* That was quick. Can you tell me how you know it's three?

*Carlos:* I counted.

*L.B.:* How did you count?

*Carlos:* I went, Five . . . six, seven, eight.

*L.B.:* But how did you know the answer was three?

*Carlos:* 'Cause I counted three more times after the five.

*L.B.:* How did you know you had counted three more?

*Carlos:* 'Cause I put out a finger for each time I counted.

*L.B.:* I see. Good! Let's try another problem:

Polly had four cookies. Her brother gave her eight more cookies. How many cookies does Polly have now?

*Carlos:* [almost immediately] Twelve.

*L.B.:* Good. How did you get that so fast?

*Carlos:* I counted on my fingers again.

*L.B.:* Can you tell me what numbers you said when you counted?

*Carlos:* Eight . . . nine, ten, eleven, twelve.

Next Leigh Bailey gave Carlos the following problem:

Some children were in the park. Six children went home. Then eight children were in the park. How many children were in the park at the start?

*Carlos:* Fourteen.

*L.B.:* How did you get that?

*Carlos:* I counted, Eight . . . nine, ten, eleven, twelve, thirteen, fourteen.

Carlos's performance had several interesting aspects. He did not physically model the action in the problems with blocks or his fingers. Rather, he realized he did not have to make two sets, and he counted on from one of the numbers in the problem. Furthermore, he did not simply start with the first number stated in the problem and count on from it. In the last two problems he counted on from the larger number, a strategy that is more efficient than simply counting on from the first number given. Carlos was much more flexible in his responses than Kathy or Lewis. He did not have to model the action directly. This fact was seen most clearly in his response to the last problem. The unknown was at the start of the action sequence, which was a take-away situation. The problem was similar to the problem about Joe, Ruth, and the toy cars except that the unknown was at the beginning, rather than as a result of the action. Carlos was able to think of the problem as an addition problem rather than as a take-away situation. Neither Kathy nor Lewis could solve this problem—they could solve problems only by modeling them directly, and they did not know where to begin with this problem.

## ANGELA

Angela was the next child that Leigh Bailey interviewed. Again, she began with the story about Sam and the stickers. Angela's responses to this problem were different from those of Kathy, Lewis, and Carlos.

*Angela* [quickly]: Three.

*L.B.:* How did you know that so quickly, Angela?

*Angela:* Well, I know five and three are eight, so I knew I had to put three with the five to get eight.

Leigh Bailey saw that Angela knew some of the basic facts and used this knowledge to solve the problem quickly. She knew that many children are successful at solving straightforward problems that contain small numbers, but with problems that are more complex and have larger numbers, children often need some intermediate step between the problem statement and its solution. So, for Angela's next problems, Leigh Bailey used numbers that were based on facts with sums from 11 to 20. She wanted to see what number facts Angela knew and how she solved problems when she did not know the appropriate number facts. Leigh Bailey changed the numbers and some of the words as she read the same type of problem:

> Mary Anne had nine books. Her father gave her some more books. Then Mary Anne had fourteen books. How many books did her father give her?

*Angela* [after a slight hesitation]: Five.

*L.B.:* How do you know the answer is five?

*Angela:* Well, I know that ten and four more is fourteen, so you need five more to go from nine to fourteen.

*L.B.:* That's very good thinking, Angela. Let's do one more story. Here's one about some children playing in a park.

*Angela:* Good. I like to do that.

*L.B.:* Some children were in the park. Six children went home. Then eight children were in the park. How many children were in the park at the start?

*Angela:* Let me be sure . . . six children go home and then. . . ?

*L.B.:*    This is a long story. I better tell it again. [Repeats the problem.]

*Angela:*  Let's see . . . six and six is twelve . . . and two more is fourteen, so six and eight is fourteen. There were fourteen children in the park.

*L.B.:*    Angela, you are a really good thinker! That was great!

By asking additional questions about different number facts, Leigh Bailey discovered that Angela knew number facts for sums less than 10 and she knew some facts greater than 10, particularly doubles (7 + 7, 8 + 8, etc.). Angela used these facts to generate other facts that she did not know. Like Carlos, Angela also was able to solve the more difficult "start unknown" problem.

Leigh Bailey's experiences from listening to and observing children gave her an awareness both of the natural insights into mathematical situations that children have when they come to school and of the way children learn by building new knowledge onto their previous experiences. The information from the workshop on children's mathematical thinking provided her with an overview of the different types of addition and subtraction problems and the common strategies that children invent for solving each type (see table 5.1). Because children develop these strategies in a fairly predictable order, she knew which problem types were the easiest and which were increasingly more difficult. During the interview she usually began with a problem of average difficulty, similar to the one about Sam and the stickers, that many children directly model with an adding-on strategy. Then, depending on the child's success and choice of strategy, she decided either to drop back to the easier problems that children solve with simple joining or separating strategies or to progress to the more difficult problems that require more advanced strategies. Her knowledge about the progression of strategies and the position of the child in this progression allowed her to choose problems at an appropriate level of difficulty.

Leigh Bailey is a fictitious teacher used in this article to represent the growing number of teachers who have become aware of children's natural insights and of the way they learn by building onto past experience. Many of these teachers have tried to teach mathematics with traditional programs that emphasize memorization of basic facts and procedural practice on computations. They have questioned the effectiveness of their instruction because, although a few children memorize their facts well, others never achieve the expected level of rote responses even with a great deal of practice. These teachers have also become aware of assessments in later grades indicating not only that children are performing at a low level in mathematics but also that many children view mathematics as a formal and superficial school subject unrelated to their previous experience and knowledge. Ultimately, early emphasis on computations and procedures might be impeding rather than enhancing many children's learning of mathematics.

However, many teachers with experience in listening to and observing children have also noticed that some who do not know their facts are able to solve realistic addition and subtraction situations by using their fingers or counters to help them. Their awareness of children's insights and natural strategies has been substantiated by similar reports from other teachers and by articles on children's thinking in the *Arithmetic Teacher*. Although basic fact and procedural knowledge are important aspects of mathematics, many of these teachers have realized that to reach that goal effectively, they must help children build onto their previous understandings by capitalizing on their natural development of strategies. Some of these teachers have made significant changes in both the focus of their mathematics programs and the processes of their classrooms to help children continue to build mathematical understandings and thinking strategies.

## CURRICULUM CONNECTIONS TO THE REAL WORLD

A program based on realistic addition and subtraction word problems provides a meaningful basis for mathematics instruction because of its potential for connecting the informal experiences of children to the formal mathematics of the classroom. Many basic concepts in elementary school mathematics can be readily related to children's experiences by using realistic word problems. The major emphasis of instruction can be to help children become aware of this connection and to build on their own intuitions. To help children make this connection, the teacher can compose word problems with realistic settings or the children can be encouraged to describe situations or personal activities that involve numbers. With word problems children might be helped to understand mathematics as a language or system of symbols that can be used to describe their experiences.

The use of realistic word problems can help children continue to build the mathematical thinking strategies that they had invented before coming to school. Most children spontaneously develop rich and meaningful strategies for solving number situations by representing them with their fingers or other available concrete items. By using realistic word problems as the basis for instruction, these informally developed mathematical insights can be legitimized and children's mathematical thinking can become the primary goal of the curriculum and classroom instructional processes.

## CLASSROOM PROCESSES TO BUILD THINKING STRATEGIES

The processes and procedures of classrooms provide the settings that are essential for helping children build mathematical thinking strategies. There is a strong tradition of mathematics classrooms in which students work as individuals on symbolic tasks and compete to produce correct and quick rote answers or procedures. These conventional classroom models have to be replaced by classrooms with cooperative atmospheres that encourage children to discuss, share, demonstrate, and, ultimately, better develop their mathematical thinking through real-world addition and subtraction situations.

Such cooperative learning atmospheres can be established in both public and private classroom settings. In public settings with whole-class instruction, word problems can be used as the basis for children's discussions and sharing of thinking strategies. Children can demonstrate solution strategies by using concrete items on the overhead, by drawing pictorial representations on the chalkboard, by holding up their fingers, or by explaining their number-fact strategies. In private setttings, children in pairs or small groups can be encouraged to collaborate in solving word problems. Children can discuss and share their solution strategies; they can compose addition and subtraction stories and trade these with other groups. The assessment of children's growth in strategy use can be carried out by calling on a few children every day to explain their strategies in public settings and by listening in on the small groups in private settings.

Different parts of the daily mathematics lesson can accommodate the various levels of problems. For instance, during whole-class instruction, elementary-level problems can be used for the review part of the lesson and more challenging problems for the development part of the lesson. For practice with small groups or individuals, problems can be selected that students can readily solve at their current level or at the next higher level of difficulty. A knowledge about which problems are easier and which are more difficult and where individual children are in their strategies for solving problems enables the teacher to select the appropriate types of problems for different parts of the lesson.

## CONCLUSION

Teachers' experiences with children, their awareness of the mathematical understandings that children have when they come to school, and their knowledge about the research on children's development of addition and subtraction concepts can affect their approaches to teaching mathematics. Although the opening scenario in this article was based on Leigh Bailey and her first-grade students, many experienced teachers at higher grade levels have redesigned their mathematics programs and classroom processes to build on children's previous knowledge and experiences, with realistic addition and subtraction word problem situations as the medium for instruction. By capitalizing on, and coinciding with, children's informal mathematics, they believe that their programs provide a stronger basis for children's future knowledge in formal mathematics. Furthermore, they believe their approaches will help children not only succeed in mathematics but also understand mathematics as a school subject related to their experiences and to their previous knowledge. These teachers are tapping into children's informal knowledge and previous experiences to continue the rich and meaningful mathematical processes that children developed before coming to instruction. These teachers are also assessing and then helping children to build their thinking strategies as necessary bases for their classroom mathematics instruction.

## REFERENCES

Carpenter, Thomas P. "Learning to Add and Subtract: An Exercise in Problem Solving." In *Teaching and Learning Mathematical Problem Solving: Multiple Research Perspectives,* edited by Edward A. Silver, pp. 17–40. Hillsdale, N.J.: Lawrence Erlbaum Associates, 1985.

Carpenter, Thomas P., Deborah A. Carey, and Vicky Kouba. "Developing Understanding of Basic Operations." In *Mathematics in Early Childhood,* edited by Joseph Payne. Reston, Va.: National Council of Teachers of Mathematics, forthcoming.

Carpenter, Thomas P., and James M. Moser. "The Acquisition of Addition and Subtraction Concepts." In *The Acquisition of Mathematical Concepts and Principles,* edited by Richard Lesh and Marsha Landau, pp. 7–44. New York: Academic Press, 1983.

Riley, Mary S., James G. Greeno, and Joan I. Heller. "Development of Children's Problem-solving Ability in Arithmetic." In *The Development of Mathematical Thinking,* edited by Herbert P. Ginsburg, pp. 153–96. New York: Academic Press, 1983.

# 6

# Thinking Strategies: Teaching Arithmetic through Problem Solving

Paul Cobb
Graceann Merkel

THE evidence is clear, and supported by research findings (Steinberg 1985; Thornton 1978), that thinking strategies can help children learn the basic arithmetic facts. By *thinking strategies* we mean the child's use of a known sum or difference to find an unknown sum or difference. Consider, for example, the following thinking strategy used by Tyrone, a second grader (Cobb 1983, p. 187):

*Teacher:* What's 21 plus 23?

*Tyrone:* [Pauses] 44.

*Teacher:* How did you do that?

*Tyrone:* 'Cause I know 23 plus 23 is 46, and you have to take away two, and that would be 44.

*Teacher:* And why did you have to take away two?

*Tyrone:* Because it's 22 plus 22.

*Teacher:* But I asked you 21 plus 23.

*Tyrone:* Because put one over there, and then it would be 22.

Tyrone's last comment implies that if 1 is taken from the 23 of 21 + 23 and put with the 21, then the result is 22 + 22, which has the same sum. He

The project discussed in this article is supported by the National Science Foundation under grant no. MDR-8470400. All opinions expressed are solely those of the authors.

found 22 + 22, and thus 21 + 23, by relating it to the known sum 23 + 23 = 46. His solution illustrates that thinking strategies need not be limited to the basic facts. It also shows that they can be viewed as ways of thinking about, and constructing relationships between, numbers, rather than merely as methods for producing correct answers. In turn this view suggests some compelling reasons for making thinking strategies a central focus of mathematics teaching.

## GOALS OF THINKING-STRATEGY INSTRUCTION

When thinking strategies are viewed as thought processes, children's improved learning of the basic facts can be seen as the result of a more profound development—the construction and organization of relationships among numbers (Baroody 1985; Brownell 1935). In other words, children's construction of increasingly powerful thinking strategies goes hand in hand with their development of increasingly sophisticated conceptual understandings. Instruction that encourages children's construction of thinking strategies simultaneously nurtures the development of key arithmetical concepts, particularly more mature concepts of addition and subtraction. Such concepts, of course, constitute a basis for further learning. At the same time, the emphasis on creating or inventing relationships encourages children to view mathematics as an activity that makes sense. The following are some additional reasons for teaching thinking strategies:

1. To help children develop increasingly powerful concepts of addition and subtraction (Steffe 1979; Cobb 1983)
2. To serve as a basis for subsequent learning (Carpenter 1980), particularly children's invention of algorithms for adding and subtracting two-digit numbers (Cobb 1983; Labinowicz 1985)
3. To help children view mathematics as an activity that is supposed to make sense rather than one that involves memorized rules (Skemp 1976; Cobb 1983)

## THE PROBLEM-CENTERED APPROACH

The problem-centered approach attempts to achieve the objectives above by developing a setting in which children can invent and discuss their own strategies. In the second-grade curriculum that we are implementing for the entire school year in a public school classroom with twenty pupils, all mathematical concepts and skills, including arithmetic computation, are taught in small-group problem-solving sessions that are followed by whole-class discussions of pupils' solutions. Two video cameras are used to record every mathematics lesson to help us clarify the pupils' thinking and learning processes. From our analysis of these recordings and of individual interviews conducted with all the pupils, it is clear that the problem-centered approach has generally been successful. Without prompting, all but one of the pupils used a variety of strategies to solve a range of problems. Further, by January, over half the pupils had built on their strategies to invent efficient algorithms for adding two-digit numbers. A key feature of the instructional activities is that they can be solved in a variety of ways that make sense to pupils at different conceptual levels. The most advanced pupils have expanded on their powerful concepts as they invented sophisticated strategies. Initially, the less conceptually advanced pupils counted on their fingers or used manipulative materials. Thus, the problem of individual differences is addressed by encouraging the children to use methods that make sense to them. Of course, we hope that all the pupils will eventually develop powerful strategies, and all but one had invented several strategies before the winter holidays. However, the less conceptually advanced pupils initially gave meaning to problems by counting (Steffe et al. 1983). Because they were not explicitly taught to use more advanced methods, they were able to make progress by building on what was meaningful to them. At the same time, they developed an interest in, and curiosity about, mathematics. Further, they were extremely persistent and tried to think things through for themselves (Cobb, Yackel, and Wood, forthcoming). In January, for example, the pupils attempted to solve a single problem in three one-hour lessons. The problem asked them to put the numbers 1 through 12 in twelve boxes arranged to form the sides of a four-by-four square, so that numbers along each side added to 26. We had intended to introduce a new activity, but the pupils insisted that they wanted to continue working on "their problem."

## Children Inventing Thinking Strategies

Many of the activities we have used most successfully do not involve elaborate materials or complicated instructions. These activities created many more learning opportunities than the more complex activities we tried earlier. The activities were not designed to lead pupils to "see" specific relationships, because "we [and children] see what we understand rather than understand what we see" (Labinowicz 1985, p. 7). Instead, their function was to give the children opportunities to think about what they were doing as they solved arithmetic problems. We shall briefly describe four of the activities and give examples of the children's solutions.

*Double ten-frame activity.* This introductory whole-class activity was adapted from recommendations made by Wirtz (1977) and Labinowicz (1985). The teacher used an overhead projector, plastic chips, and a transparency of two ten-frames (see fig. 6.1). The teacher placed chips in the two frames to make patterns and then turned on the projector for, at most, two seconds to show the class the patterns. This procedure was repeated if the pupils indicated that they needed a second look. Finally, the projector was turned on during discussion and the teacher asked, "How many did you see?" "How did you see them?" This activity led to many stimulating discussions. On one occasion, for example, the teacher made the patterns shown in figure 6.2.

Fig. 6.1          Fig. 6.2

*Andy:*     15, there's one more on each side. [He relates these patterns to the previous task, which had patterns of 8 and 5, but "saw" 9 and 6.]

*Teacher:* Did anyone see it a different way?

*Juan:*     It's 14, there's 6 blanks.

*Teacher:* How did you figure that out?

*Juan:*     Twenty take away six is 14.

*Teacher:* Oh, you know there were 20 squares all together and you saw three of them were empty here and three were empty on the other one?

*Juan:*     Yeah.

*Teacher:* O.K., Jack.

*Jack:*     I saw six and six first, and that makes 12, but they both have one more, so it has to be 14.

*Lisa:*     I agree, it's 14.

*Teacher:* How did you get 14?

*Lisa:*     I counted them up on my fingers.

*Teacher:* Yes, Tricia.

*Tricia:*     [Leaves her desk and goes to the screen.] It's the same thing as the one we just did. It was 8 and 6 and you take one from the 8 and put it with the 6, and that makes 7 and 7. [The teacher had made patterns for 8 and 6 earlier in the session.]

The pupils' solutions indicate that they think at a variety of different levels when they solve these tasks. Juan, one of the most advanced students, understood the task in terms of subtraction. In contrast, Lisa recognized two patterns of seven and had to count to find the sum. Both engaged in productive thinking that made sense to them. The practice of having children explain their solutions also allows them to realize that problems can be solved in more than one way and improve their ability to verbalize their thinking.

This ten-frame activity has, of course, many variations, for example:

a) Chips can be added to, or removed from, one or both frames, rather than make patterns from scratch each time.

b) Chips can be transferred from one frame to the other.

c) After the children are familiar with the activity, they can be encouraged to write number sentences for what *they* saw.

Two previous versions of this activity were unsuccessful. In the first, each group of students was given two ten-frames and chips and asked to find sums to, say, 15 or to make patterns for each other. In the second version, the teacher made patterns while the overhead projector was turned on. In both instances, the pupils found these activities uninteresting, as evidenced by frequent off-task behavior. The third version was far more challenging, which is why it was successful. The pupils became immediately involved because they had problems to solve. We have found that restlessness often indicates that a given activity may not give pupils the opportunity to think.

*Balance activity* (developed with Grayson Wheatley). Children solve these problems by finding numbers that "balance the scale." (The use of the balance format also gives them the opportunity to develop a more sophisticated understanding of arithmetical equality and suggests a real-world situation in which to think about numbers.) The activity begins with a discussion of the idea of balancing the scale. A few problems are solved as a class before the children work in groups of two or three. A whole-class discussion follows in which the pupils explain and justify their solutions. The four problems on each activity sheet are usually sequenced so that the children can use a previous solution. However, they are not required to do so; they frequently make alternative relationships that did not occur to us when we developed the activity sheets.

As can be seen from the sample activity sheet (see fig. 6.3), most of our problems go beyond the basic facts. They do so for two reasons: First, problems with "small numbers" do not challenge most of the students—they either know the fact or can solve it easily by counting. Manipulatives, such as multilinks as well as hundred boards, are available for less able pupils whenever they feel the need. Second, because thinking strategies are, as the term implies, ways of thinking, they are applicable to numbers of any magnitude. For example, the fourth grader who finds, say, $7002 - 25$ by relating the problem to $7000 - 25 = 6975$ is using a thinking strategy.

We have observed numerous interesting exchanges both when the chil-

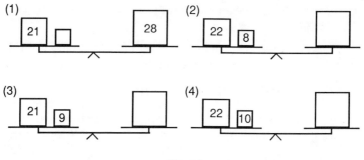

Fig. 6.3

dren work in groups and during class discussions. The following protocols are excerpted from a dialogue between two children, Andy and Eric. Andy was initially one of the more advanced students, whereas Eric was about average. (The number sentences at the left refer to the four balance tasks.)

21 + __ = 28    *Andy:*    What's that one? 28, 21.

                *Eric:*    That's easy.

                *Together:* Seven more.

                *Andy:*    If it was 20, you would just add 8 more [relates 21 + __ = 28 to 20 + 8 = 28].

Here, Andy verbalizes his insight that 21 + __ = 28 can be related to 20 + 8 = 28 because Eric is his audience.

22 + 8 = __    *Eric:*    22 and 8. Hey, that's nine . . . 29, yeah ["sees" only the increase in the second addend].

              *Andy:*    30 . . . O.K., 21 . . . no, it's 29.

              *Eric:*    Yes, it is.

              *Andy:*    [Points to first and then second problems.] 21 . . . 22 . . . yeah, it's 30 [relates 22 + 8 = __ to 21 + 7 = 28].

              *Eric:*    [Writes 30.]

In this example, the two boys quickly resolve the conflict between their answers. Andy realizes that he is obliged to justify his answer, and Eric accepts his explanation.

21 + 9 = __    *Eric:*    21 and a 9. . . . Hey, that's easy, same as this [points to the second problem] except two higher. So. . . .

              *Andy:*    It's 32.

              *Eric:*    32 [both believe that each addend increases by one].

> *Andy:* Wait, no, it isn't.
>
> *Eric:* Yes, it is.
>
> *Andy:* Let me see, 21 add 7 [looks at the first problem], 21 add 8 would make. . . .

Andy is trying to relate $21 + 9$ to $21 + 7 = 28$. Eric insists the second problem, $22 + 8 = 30$, is "going to help us out better." Here, they are consciously considering which of two alternative strategies to use. Now Andy explains why he thinks the first problem, $21 + 7 = 28$, is of more help.

> *Andy:* 'Cause it has a 21 [points to the 21s in the first and third problems]. This is two more than that [points to the 7 and the 9 in the first and third problems]. 21 and 8.
>
> *Eric:* [Interrupts.] That would be two more than 28, so that's 30 [relates $21 + 9$ to $21 + 7 = 28$].

They have arrived at an answer by relating the first and third problems. However, this is not sufficient for Andy. He does not believe that their answers to the second and third problems can both be correct. At first he thinks 31 should be the answer to the second problem—he only "sees" that the first addend of this problem is one higher than 21. But he counts to check and finds, "No, it's thirty." The two pupils have answers for all three problems, yet they cannot relate each problem to the other two. Eric argues that the answer to the third problem should be 32 because he believes that each addend has increased by one from the second problem. Finally, Andy has an insight:

> *Andy:* They're the same thing [the second and third problems].
>
> *Eric:* No, no.
>
> *Andy:* See, see, one lower [points to 9 and 8 in the second and third problems]. It's the same thing.
>
> *Eric:* [Interrupts.] One lower than that one [points to 9 and 8 in the second and third problems]. 30 [relates $21 + 9$ to $22 + 8 = 30$].

They then solve the final balance problem, $22 + 10 =$ ___, without difficulty.

$22 + 10 =$ ___

> *Eric:* 22 plus 10.
>
> *Andy:* 22 plus a 10, what was that? [Points to the third problem.]
>
> *Eric:* Hey, two more than this . . . 32.
>
> *Andy:* 32.

Using thinking strategies has become a natural process for these two second graders. They expect their answers to make sense, and things that do not fit together are regarded as problems to be solved. For them, mathematics is about understanding, not just producing a page of correct answers.

A second example is the interchange between Billy and Karen as they complete the same balance-activity sheet. Billy is one of our weakest students, whereas Karen was initially slightly above average. They both solve the first two balance problems by counting on.

21 + __ = 28    *Karen:*    O.K., 28 take away 21.

                 *Billy:*    28 take away 21, hmmm.

                 *Karen:*    I'm thinking about 8 [i.e., an estimate].

                 *Billy:*    21 . . . 22, 23, 24, 25, 26, 27, 28 [puts up seven fingers as he counts]—7.

                 *Karen:*    [Counts on to check Billy's answer]  7.

22 + 8 = __    *Billy:*    22 take away 8.

                 *Together:* 22 . . . 23, 24, 25, 26, 27, 28, 29, 30.

                 *Karen:*    30.

                 *Billy:*    28 . . . I counted 8 more. 22 . . . 23, 24, 25, 26, 27, 28, 29, 30.

21 + 9 = __    *Billy:*    31 [attempts to relate second and third problems but only "sees" that the second addend increases].

                 *Karen:*    [Points to first and third problems.] 21, 22, 23 [finds that first addend increases by 2].

                 *Billy:*    It should be 31.

                 *Karen:*    That one's 30. Same as that one [points to the first problem], 'cause you add 2 more to 28 and you get 30. Seven and nine, look [puts up 7 fingers] and you add 2 more [puts up 2 fingers] and you get 9. We add 2 more to 28 and we get 30.

                 *Billy:*    That should be 30.

Billy, the less conceptually advanced of the two students, is the first to attempt to use a thinking strategy, which leads Karen to relate the first and third problems. Conversely, Karen gives Billy some support as he attempts to solve problems (the teacher cannot be everywhere!). Her frequent explanations also give her an opportunity to think about what she is doing. At the same time, Billy tries to solve problems in ways that make sense to him. For example, he feels free to count whenever he needs to. Karen also explains to

Billy how she solved the last of the four problems.

22 + 10 = ___    *Karen:*  That one should be 32 because counting by twos
                      . . . 2, 4, 6, 8, 10 and you get up to . . . [Karen
                      initially solved the problem by noting that as 2
                      and 8 more would complete a decade, 2 and 10
                      more will be 2 more in the next decade] . . . and
                      that's the same thing as the one [points to the
                      fourth and second problems] except that one is
                      two more.

                *Billy:*  Oh [writes 32].

Karen seemed to realize that Billy would not be able to understand how she
initially solved the problem. She then explained an alternative solution
method—relating the second and fourth problems—that might make sense
to him. As this example illustrates, the problem-centered approach also
gives children the opportunity to improve their social and communication
skills.

*Number sentences.* We have also produced sequences of number sentences
to encourage the children to invent their own strategies, for example:

$$10 + 10 = \underline{\quad} \qquad 22 - 8 = \underline{\quad}$$
$$9 + 11 = \underline{\quad} \qquad 20 - \underline{\quad} = 15$$
$$12 + \underline{\quad} = 20 \qquad 20 - \underline{\quad} = 13$$
$$8 + \underline{\quad} = 21 \qquad 18 - \underline{\quad} = 11$$
$$21 - 8 = \underline{\quad} \qquad 11 + 8 = \underline{\quad}$$

The following excerpt from a whole-class discussion of the pupils' solutions
captures their creativity and inventiveness:

*Teacher:*  O.K., 9 plus 11.

*Andy:*     10 plus 10 is 20, take away one would be 19, and add one more,
            it will still be 20.

*Teacher:*  How did you get 10 plus 10?

*Andy:*     'Cause 9 is one lower than 10 and 11 is one higher, so it must be
            the same thing.

*Teacher:*  He took one away from the 11, which made a 10 over here.
            Karen?

*Karen:*    Um . . . 9 plus 9.

*Teacher:*  What about 9 plus 9?

*Karen:*    9 and 9 is 18, plus 2.

*Teacher:*  So all together what does that make?

*Karen:*    20.

*Teacher:*   Who has a different way you could do this?

*Scott:*      Seven and 7 is 14, 8 and 8 is 16, 9 and 9 would equal 18, so 9 plus 11 must equal 20.

*Teacher:*   So you know your doubles. This is our last one.

*Susie:*      11 and 11 is 22. Then take 11 and switch it to a 10, 10 plus 11 is 21, and um . . . 9 plus 11 is 20.

In a simple variation of this activity conducted with the whole class, the teacher writes an incomplete sentence on the chalkboard and encourages the children to solve it in as many ways as possible. Other activities that have proved successful include card games, four-in-a-row, and story problems sequenced to facilitate the children's construction of numerical relationships.

## Thinking Strategies as a Basis for Further Learning

The teaching of thinking strategies should be an end in itself, not just a means to an end, such as the learning of the basic facts. As children invent strategies that make sense to them, they develop increasingly powerful arithmetical concepts that they can build on in subsequent learning. This process was particularly apparent when our students invented their own algorithms for adding two-digit numbers. To illustrate such invention, we will present excerpts from interviews conducted in January with pupils who were about average in ability. This occasion was the first on which the pupils had been asked to solve purely symbolic tasks with such large numbers. Further, it was also the first time that they had been exposed to the column format since the end of first grade. For the pupils, these apparently routine tasks were genuine mathematical problems. The children consistently used the same methods to solve problems presented in either format. All solutions presented are for

$$39 + 53 = \underline{\quad} \quad \text{or} \quad \begin{array}{r} 39 \\ +53 \\ \hline \end{array}$$

*a.* Anna's algorithm involves the compensation strategy. As she explained, "50 plus 30 is 80, then 9 plus one more would be 90, plus 2 more would be 92." She took one from the three to complete an additional ten and then added the remaining two ones.

*b.* Joel's solution was this: "You have 53, ten more is 63, plus ten more is 73, plus ten more is 83, plus nine . . . 92."

*c.* The following exchange with Mark gives a clue to the origin of the type of iterative algorithm that Joel used:

*Interviewer:*   What is 39 plus 10?

*Mark:*          49.

*Interviewer:*   Can that help you [to solve 39 + 53]?

*Mark:*    Yeah, because 39 plus 10 is 49, and so you used up ten one time [puts up one finger], then you use up 10 again and that would make 59 [puts up a second finger], then 69, then 79, then 89 [sequentially puts up three more fingers] and that makes 50, then you put . . . so you add 39 and all these tens together and that makes . . . 39 . . . 49, 59, 69, 79, 89 [touches each extended finger]—89, then you add this in and that makes . . . 92.

Mark succeeded in solving the problem once he related 39 + 53 to 39 + 10 = 49. His algorithm is an extremely sophisticated thinking strategy that involves units of both ten and one.

*d.* Jenny's algorithm is a curtailed, or shortened, version of Mark's iterative algorithm: "See, 39 and 50 more is 89, then add 3 makes 92." She implicitly related 39 + 53 to 39 + 50 = 89.

*e.* Eric's algorithm is the closest to the standard algorithm. "30 plus 50 is 80, and 9 plus 3 is 12, put all those together and I come up with 92." This algorithm is also a sophisticated strategy that involves units of ten and one. Eric related 39 + 53 to 30 + 50 = 80.

In general, any efficient, meaningful algorithm is a thinking strategy that involves units of different values (e.g., units of one, ten, and one hundred). This idea also applies to the meaningful use of standard algorithms. The children's two-digit addition algorithms are efficient ways of finding the sum 39 + 53 = ___. Because they "see" a relationship between this problem and a sum that they know or can find easily (e.g., 30 + 50 = 80 or 39 + 50 = 89), they do not have to count on from 53 by ones. Instruction that views these strategies as ways of thinking contributes to children's meaningful learning of computational algorithms.

## CONCLUSION

We have proposed three reasons for teaching thinking strategies that extend beyond memorization and the recall of the basic facts: conceptual development in arithmetic, beliefs about mathematics, and further learning. We believe that thinking strategies should be an essential feature of mathematics instruction in the early grades. Thinking-strategy instruction is compatible with recent recommendations that emphasize the importance of mental computation. The examples of children's thinking strategies and computational algorithms that we have presented are, in fact, mental-computation strategies. Thus, mental computation is an integral part of the instruction rather than a separate topic. The same can be said of estimation. Initially, we were surprised that the pupils spontaneously made estimates when they solved certain problems and evaluated each other's answers. As the year progressed, it became apparent that the instructional activities that we intended to facilitate the development of estimation strategies were unnecessary.

Although our discussion has focused on thinking strategies, we have also attempted to outline a general approach to teaching arithmetic. It involves small-group work followed by whole-class discussions of pupils' solutions, together with shorter, teacher-led activities, such as the ten-frame activity. It is possible to extend this approach to such advanced arithmetic topics as multiplication and division and even to such subjects as telling time, which are typically taught as social conventions (Cobb, Wood, and Yackel forthcoming). A basic premise of the approach is that children must be given more responsibility for their own learning if we expect them to learn meaningfully. They are the best judges of what is a problem, of what makes sense, and of what is helpful. In our opinion, elementary school mathematics instruction should capitalize on this resource and respect children's judgments.

### REFERENCES

Baroody, Arthur J. "Mastery of Basic Number Combinations: Internalization of Relationships or Facts?" *Journal for Research in Mathematics Education* 16 (March 1985): 83–98.

Brownell, William A. "Psychological Considerations in the Learning and Teaching of Arithmetic." In *The Teaching of Arithmetic*, Tenth Yearbook of the National Council of Teachers of Mathematics, pp. 1–31. New York: Bureau of Publications, Teachers College, Columbia University, 1935.

Carpenter, Thomas P. "Heuristic Strategies Used to Solve Addition and Subtraction Problems." In *Proceedings of the Fourth International Conference for the Psychology of Mathematics Education*, edited by Robert Karplus, pp. 317–21. Berkeley, Calif.: University of California, 1980.

Cobb, Paul. "Children's Strategies for Finding Sums and Differences." Ph.D. diss., University of Georgia, 1983.

Cobb, Paul, Terry Wood, and Erna Yackel. "A Constructivist Approach to Second-Grade Mathematics." In *Constructivism in Mathematics Education*, edited by Ernst von Glasersfeld. Dordrecht, Netherlands: D. Reidel, forthcoming.

Cobb, Paul, Erna Yackel, and Terry Wood. "Young Children's Emotional Acts While Doing Mathematical Problem Solving." In *Affect and Mathematical Problem Solving: A New Perspective*, edited by Douglas B. McLeod and Verna M. Adams. New York: Springer-Verlag, forthcoming.

Labinowicz, Ed. *Learning from Children*. Menlo Park, Calif.: Addison-Wesley Publishing Co., 1985.

Skemp, Richard R. "Relational Understanding and Instrumental Understanding." *Mathematics Teaching* 77 (December 1976): 1–7. (Reprinted in the *Arithmetic Teacher* 26 [November 1978]: 9–15.)

Steffe, Leslie P. "A Reply to 'Formal Thinking Strategies: A Prerequisite for Learning Basic Facts?'" *Journal for Research in Mathematics Education* 10 (November 1979): 370–74.

Steffe, Leslie P., Ernst von Glasersfeld, John Richards, and Paul Cobb. *Children's Counting Types: Philosophy, Theory, and Applications*. New York: Praeger Publishers, 1983.

Steinberg, Ruth M. "Instruction on Derived Fact Strategies in Addition and Subtraction." *Journal for Research in Mathematics Education* 16 (November 1985): 337–55.

Thornton, Carol A. "Emphasizing Thinking Strategies in Basic Fact Instruction." *Journal for Research in Mathematics Education* 9 (May 1978): 214–27.

Wirtz, Robert. *Making Friends with Numbers*. Monterey, Calif.: Curriculum Development Associates, 1977.

# CHILDREN WRITE ABOUT PROBLEM SOLVING

A road crew is building a 9-km road along the side of a mountain. Each day they complete 3 km, but each night rock slides destroy 1 km of the road. At this rate, on what day will the road be completed?

my name is John Rihn Gade 4 Top math group

Dear Wesley @ Que class thought really deep into the problem and it was very hard to do it it took about 1 hour And here is my thinking

they get 2 4½ km a day

| days | km | Rocks destroyed |
| --- | --- | --- |
| 1 | 2 | |
| 2 | 4 | |
| 3 | 6 | |
| 4 | 8 | |
| 5 | X 9 | |

10 - 1 = 9
= 9½

*Submitted by Randall Charles*

How do you share three cookies among four people?

Names  Dusty          Hannah
       David          Katie

Share **3** cookies equally among 4 people Paste each person's share in a box.

| Dusty | Hannah |
| --- | --- |
| David | Katie |

How much did each person get? Every won gets a half and a gorter

*Submitted by Marilyn Burns*

Bianca      Jackson
Lisa    math 6th  10-19-87
David         3
Chris

mrs. Weynand was
having a party. She
went to the store
to buy some cookies.
She bought a box of
cookies that contained
125 cookies. She has 20
guests. How many cookies
can each guest get.

Group 3                    Jackson
Math 6(2)                  Oct 16, 1987

$$\text{answer: } 6\tfrac{1}{4} \quad 20\overline{)125}\ ^{6R5}$$

Each person could have
6 and ¼ cookies. And each
person could get 6 cookies
with 5 left over.

Your remainder should
be reported by a fraction
because you can divide
cookies into fractions

by Carissa, Seth, Stephanie and
Joseph

Vanessa Phillips

① The reason a triangle can't have two square courness is beacuse every triangle hase etleast one slanted side the ones that have one slante side only have one square corner.

And the ones that have two slanted sids have ziro squar corners.

slanted side ← → slanted side

And the ones that have three slanted sids dont exist becaus triangles only kan have two slanted sids other wise they wouldent be triangles.

Vanessa Phillips

④ The reason there can't be an equilateral that is also a right is.... pretend you took a equilateral triangle and tryed to fit a squar in it how would you do it?

You can't no mader how you try you just can't. So you can't have an equilateri triangle that is also a right.

⑤ I'll prove that a triangle can't be an Isosceles and a scalen all at one time. If you took an Isosceles triangle and eraced on sid and mad it oneven from all the other sid it would be a plane old scalen and if you changed it it would be an Isoscle and no mader how meany times you da this you will never get it.

Isosceles ↙

△ scalen↙

△

# 7

# Language Experiences:
# A Base for Problem Solving

### Rosemary Reuille Irons
### Calvin J. Irons

**G**OOD problem solvers possess a broad understanding of the concepts involved in a problem. They are not only able to identify quickly what concepts are involved *without* relying on "clue" words or particular phrases but also able to identify a particular concept in situations that use varied vocabulary and language structures. For teachers, this means that children need to experience a broad range of language to help them develop the fullest understanding possible.

In problem-solving situations children need to be able to form a clear picture of the information provided. They need to be able to sort out the information and then relate it to their knowledge of mathematical concepts. The language used in the problem helps them create a picture. Language also helps to build the understanding that children possess of mathematical concepts. To be most effective, children should have an understanding of mathematical concepts that involves more than the notation that is used to record them.

Young children begin school with a reasonable knowledge of strategies that are helpful in problem-solving situations (Romberg and Carpenter

1986). Children's knowledge and excitement about mathematics grow if situations are provided to encourage discussion about their learning. This allows children to extend their own strategies and build new ones. It is important to plan learning experiences that will foster exploration and investigation. These activities will promote the use of language that can be gradually extended to more sophisticated ideas that might be associated with the important mathematical concepts.

Planning learning experiences that will encourage the development of language in mathematics can occur in four stages. Within each stage are three phases (modeling, creating, and sharing). Figure 7.1 summarizes the stages and phases from the language a child naturally uses to the most sophisticated use of language within mathematics.

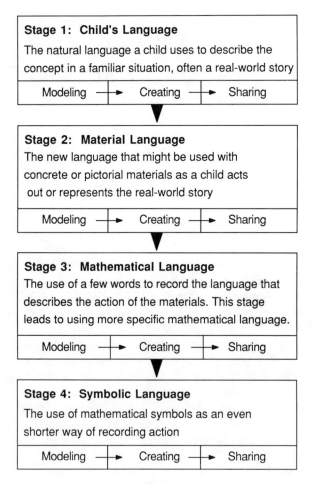

Fig. 7.1

The activities within each stage should occur over a period of time. A wide variety of experiences should be available for children to develop each mathematical concept. These experiences should represent the many kinds of problems that can be solved using an operation. The three phases included within each stage involve the children in three different and important aspects of learning.

## THE PHASES

### Phase 1: Modeling

In this phase, the children are involved in some learning experience that has been planned by the teacher. The purpose of the activity is to model an aspect of the concept being developed. It may be real-world activity, an activity to show something new using concrete materials, an experience with mathematical language, or an activity using mathematical notation. In this phase, the teacher is the initiator and models an activity that is appropriate for the language stage. The important aspect is that the children participate through describing in their own words what they have observed.

### Phase 2: Creating

After the children have participated in the modeling activities, they contribute further to the activity by creating something new. This allows them to clarify and extend their ideas. This creating can occur by constructing concrete, pictorial, or written records of the activity.

### Phase 3: Sharing

In phase 3, children take turns sharing their own work with others. This phase encourages an exchange of ideas. The sharing can occur through showing, describing, or reading their records. In this phase new ideas can be contributed by all the children as each creation is shared.

Since most children are eager to share their ideas, they will strive to create something new. As a result, the teacher might be able to use the sharing phase in one stage to lead into the next stage in the language model.

## THE LANGUAGE STAGES

Developing an understanding of mathematical concepts requires ample time for discussion in each of the four stages. Within each stage, activities should be planned for children to describe and discuss real-world situations. This discussion allows them to develop, clarify, refine, and extend their own ideas about the concept. The ideas described below should be used chiefly in the modeling phases.

## Stage 1: Child's Language

In the first stage, children use their own natural language to talk about real-world situations related to a mathematical operation. The situations may be in the form of stories or pictures. The stories should suggest direct action that the children can talk about, rephrase, and put into their own words. Pictures should encourage children to be creative when they make up their own stories and use their own language. The actions of baking, eating, picking, planting, and sharing, along with many other real-world activities, will suggest words the children can use. Children need to spend more time talking about real-world situations to allow a greater variety of language to be used and to encourage them to create their own stories to extend their language. This discussion needs to occur prior to the introduction of the operation.

The following activities will promote maximum involvement of the children and encourage use of their own language:

• *Use interesting pictures.* Discuss aspects of number and action ideas. For example, show a picture of several children playing at a playground or park. For the purposes of teaching addition, talk about the number of children on the swings and the number of children on the slide. At another time use the same pictures to show subtraction ideas: Talk about the number of children at the playground or park and then the number of children starting to walk home from the playground. Encourage children to use their own words to describe what is happening in the picture. You may need to focus their attention on a particular part of the picture, but let the main ideas and words used come from the children.

• *Use stories.* Stories in a "big book" format are particularly appealing to children (see photos 1–8). These stories can be looked at and then discussed with a whole group. At first, ignore the words; have the children tell what they think is happening on each page and share their ideas with the whole group. Let them add their own words. This is a good way for those children who have a limited vocabulary to make a contribution as well as to learn new vocabulary from the suggestions of other children. Select or create stories that focus on a particular concept, but encourage the children to use their own language to talk about the story or individual episodes in the story. This example was originally created for a discussion about multiplication using the well-known character, Peter Piper.

• *Act out the story ideas.* Encourage children to describe and dramatize the story ideas. In the "Peter Piper" story, the children may want to play the roles of the different characters: Peter, the buyer at the market, a pepper packer, a potato peeler, and so on. Each child can then tell what she or he would do in the story.

• *Use magnetic-board materials.* This activity makes a good transition

Photo 1. Cover of our "big book"

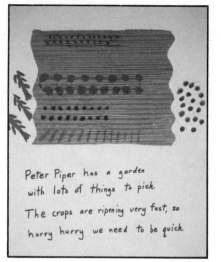

Peter Piper has a garden with lots of things to pick. The crops are ripening very fast, so hurry hurry we need to be quick.

Photo 2. Page 1

Peter Piper pulled potatoes and put three on each plate. When Peter cooks the potatoes he is sure they will taste great.

Photo 3. Page 2

Peter Piper picked peaches. and put six in each pail. Now Peter can go to market and put the peaches up for sale.

Photo 4. Page 3

from a fixed, completed story in a book to a more open-ended situation. Acting out the stories with magnetic boards is also a good way to show the action involved. Some concepts have a before-and-after aspect; children often need to "see" this aspect to help them describe what has happened.

Peter Piper piled pumpkins
carefully into two piles.
All the pumpkins in neat stacks
makes Peter burst out in smiles.

Photo 5. Page 4

Peter Piper packed pickles
into tall and skinny pots.
Peter plans to sell the pickles
and knows he will make lots.

Photo 6. Page 5

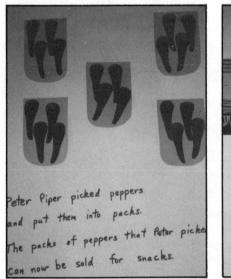

Peter Piper picked peppers
and put them into packs.
The packs of peppers that Peter picked
can now be sold for snacks.

Photo 7. Page 6

Peter Piper's work is done.
His crops are the best.
He has picked, pulled, piled and packed
and is now ready for a rest.

Photo 8. Page 7

    • *Ask children to create their own stories.* This activity will motivate children to describe—using a real-world context—what they understand about the concept. Initial ideas may be given through a picture or story or by acting out the activities. Then have the children use their own words to write a story. Encourage them to use any words they want and their own spellings; this allows them to focus on the concepts rather than the mechanical details. Misspellings can be corrected later. Figure 7.2, for example, shows a story a first-grade child wrote about subtraction after discussing a similar story as a whole group. Using familiar language ensures that children's understanding will match their maturity level.

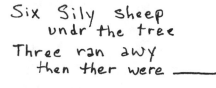

Six Sily sheep
undr the tree
Three ran awy
then ther were ____

Fig. 7.2

## Stage 2: Material Language

This stage introduces the use of physical objects in acting out a situation or part of a story. Material language is used with the activities in the first stage soon after children start to ask questions that they want to answer. This stage is incorporated in the current development of the concepts of operations. However, it needs to be treated as a separate stage and not become combined with the writing of mathematical symbols. New language (e.g., "take away" or "cover up" for subtraction) can be incorporated as the materials are manipulated, thus giving an opportunity to extend the language that the child used in the first stage.

The use of action pictures with materials at this stage helps to broaden the language used to describe the action. The use of hands-on concrete materials will suggest some words; pictures may suggest others. For example, concrete materials alone used with subtraction tend to suggest the use of the words *take away*. If pictures are used, these words cannot easily describe the action involved and the child does not learn to associate the concept of subtraction with just two words.

Pictures, in this stage, may refer to objects (e.g., counters, blocks, or just dots). The child can then describe what to do, for instance, with the simple picture in figure 7.3 to act out a story.

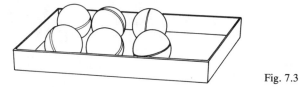

Fig. 7.3

- Tell what happens if 2 balls roll down the hill.
- Tell what happens if the box holds 10 balls.
- Tell what happens if a friend has 4 balls.

The following activities would be appropriate:

- Have children make in class objects that are suggested in stories and then act out the story. For example, the children might make fish from flat rocks. The fish could be stored in clear plastic bags with lines drawn on them to look like fishnets (fig. 7.4). Use the "bags" idea in different ways to discuss all the operations.

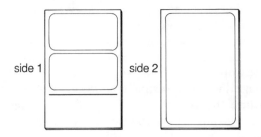

Fig. 7.4

- Use heavy cardstock to draw the designs in figure 7.5. It will help organize the materials that the children use for addition. Place objects on the cards to help children act out addition and subtraction (figs. 7.6 and 7.7). This will begin to show them the relationship between these two operations.

side 1    side 2

Fig. 7.5

**For addition**

Three cherry pies are on the top shelf. Four apple pies are on the next shelf. How many pies can the baker sell?

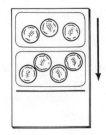

Fig. 7.6

**For subtraction**

Eight cars are in the parking lot. Two cars drive away. How many cars are still in the parking lot?

Fig. 7.7

Explain the many possible ways of describing a situation when concrete materials are used. In the parking lot example, ask the children to tell what happened in different ways in their own words. Some of the confusing aspects of relying on "clue" words (e.g., the idea of "left") will arise. Ask the children to tell how they would act out the same story if they had only a *picture* of eight cars and they could not "drive" two away. This will help generate new language (e.g., *cover up, hide, cross out*) that suggests subtraction. It will also help to establish the idea that subtraction is finding a missing part.

• Use cards like those in figure 7.8 to help discuss missing-addend subtraction stories. This pictorial model encourages verbalizing in a way that represents the idea better than using counters. It broadens the language used and also shows that the whole is known and the answer is a missing part. In this example the missing part is covered up.

The trailer holds six cars. There are already two cars on the trailer. How many more cars can fit on the trailer?

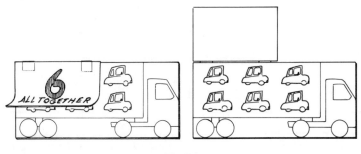

Fig. 7.8

• Show comparison examples using materials that help to show the overall idea of "finding an amount left over" for this type of subtraction. Slide a piece of paper across columns of materials to cover up matching amounts. The missing part is the part that is left uncovered. (See fig. 7.9.)

Alternatively, make a set of pattern cards. Use two cards from the set to

Fig. 7.9. How many more stamps with flowers?

represent a story. Have children use one card to cover up the matching number on the other (fig. 7.10). This will show the missing part.

Fig. 7.10

- Draw designs like those in figure 7.11 on heavy cardboard to help organize the materials used to discuss multiplication and division. Turn the card one way for multiplication and another way for division. This helps to establish which aspect of the (many equal parts) idea is multiplication and which is division.

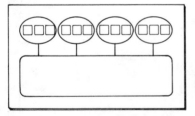

How many pies did the baker make? (There are 4 equal parts. What is in the whole?)

How many pies for each of the 4 customers? (There are 4 equal parts. What is in each part?)

Fig. 7.11

- Use arrays like the ones in figure 7.12 to show certain aspects of multiplication and division. Using a pictorial model will reinforce the relationship between the two operations. One card can be used for both concepts.

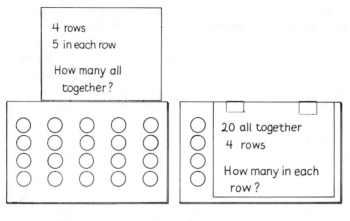

Fig. 7.12

• Relate any of the activities used in this stage to the previous stage. Ask the children to tell or write stories that might go with the materials and then share their stories with the other children. Have them check that the story matches the original activity.

### Stage 3: Mathematical Language

This stage has not usually been a part of the development of mathematical concepts. As children begin to use words to describe action, it is helpful to record these words on cards and use them to create stories, draw a picture, or act out with materials (see fig. 7.13). Using the cards these ways can help

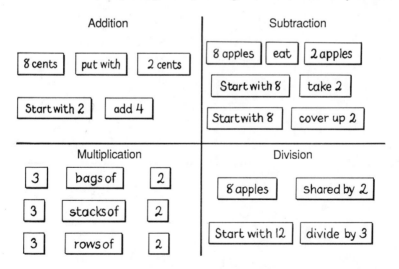

Fig. 7.13

reinforce the language already established and continue the development of new language. Some examples of how the cards might be used are shown in figure 7.13.

The particular cards that are produced will depend on the suggestions made by the children and the teacher. The children should suggest the words to be written on the cards. The mathematical language stage allows activities to extend the development of language without introducing symbols. The use of words also links mathematics with language arts and encourages children to use mathematics in writing activities. It is also a good way to show that mathematics can be read horizontally (fig. 7.14) or vertically (fig. 7.15).

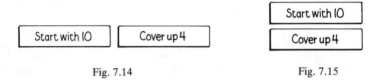

Fig. 7.14                             Fig. 7.15

The following activities will encourage the use of written language for the operation instead of the mathematical symbol:

• Use cards with counters described in the material language stage (fig. 7.16). The cards can be used in the horizontal or vertical form (see fig. 7.17).

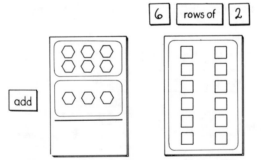

Fig. 7.16

Fig. 7.17

• Design a language box to provide good storage for the language cards. Milk or drink cartons cut to size and covered with contact paper are an inexpensive way to form the language box (see fig. 7.18).

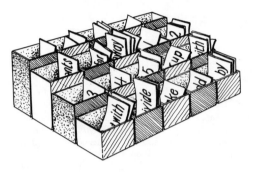

Fig. 7.18

The columns of cartons are for each operation: addition, subtraction, multiplication, division, and equality. The language cards can be used on a magnetic board if magnetic strip tape is placed on the back of each card. Magnetizing the cards makes a workable class set of materials. If the language box is available during the children's free time, they can make their own story sentences with cards selected from the box and act them out with materials or show a picture.

### Stage 4: Symbol Language

This stage introduces the mathematical symbol for each concept. At first it can be recorded on a card:

As children's confidence grows, they may begin to write the expressions. The following activities will be helpful in promoting the use of symbols:

• Ask the children to select cards with the appropriate symbols that match a story or a particular episode within a story. The children can arrange the cards to describe the story: for example, $3 \times 6$ for three buckets with six peaches in each.

• The children can select cards that go with activities with concrete materials or language used to describe pictures.

• Use the symbol cards as "starting points" for the children to make up stories. Have them select the cards and make up a story to match. This might be done as a creative-writing lesson or contest.

The previous activities encourage children to be the creators of their mathematical knowledge. When they create their own knowledge, they gradually build a picture of concepts and ideas that will be useful in problem-solving situations. Through the language experiences in the stages described here, the child has a better base from which to interpret and make decisions in new problem situations.

## REFERENCES

Irons, Calvin, and Rosemary Reuille-Irons. "A Language Model for Developing the Concepts of Operations for Mathematics in the Early Years of School." In *Proceedings of the Fourth Southeast Asian Conference on Mathematics Education,* edited by Sit-tui Ong, pp. 137-42. Singapore: Institute of Education, 1987.

Reuille-Irons, Rosemary. "Integrating Language and Mathematics to Teach the Concepts of the Operations." In *Mathematics Curriculum, Teaching and Learning,* edited by Peter Sullivan, pp. 263-68. Melbourne, Australia: Twenty-second Annual Conference of the Mathematical Association of Victoria, Monash University, 1985.

Romberg, Thomas, and Thomas Carpenter. "Research on Teaching and Learning Mathematics: Two Disciplines of Scientific Inquiry." In *Handbook of Research on Teaching,* 3d ed., edited by M. Wittrock, pp. 850-73. New York: Macmillan Publishing Co., 1986.

# 8

# Using "Part-Whole" Language to Help Children Represent and Solve Word Problems

Edward C. Rathmell
DeAnn M. Huinker

S OLVING word problems is an important component of the elementary
school mathematics curriculum. Word problems offer a context in which
a rich variety of meanings for the basic arithmetic operations can be developed. Children should have a broad conceptual framework of understandings for each of the operations so that they can apply them meaningfully in a variety of situations. Word problems serve as a setting for the
experiences that lead to these broader understandings.

Unfortunately, children often acquire a narrow conceptual view of an
operation. When new operations are introduced from a single perspective,
children may maintain that single idea for extended periods. They may
believe that addition is joining, that subtraction is take away, that multiplication is repeated addition, or that division is repeated subtraction. Each
operation has a structure that encompasses other interpretations. For example, the concept of subtraction should eventually also include missing-
addend and comparison situations. Narrow conceptual views may be important contributing factors in children's failure to solve some word problems.

Children need extended informal experiences with word problems in a
variety of contexts. Textbook lessons often devote only minimal attention to
the concept of an operation and quickly move on to practice of the basic
facts. Unfortunately, premature practice with procedures places an undue
emphasis on getting answers rather than on understanding how an operation
is related to various real-life situations. This approach can give students a
limited concept of an operation.

Children need to establish meaningful connections between problems and

99

arithmetic operations. Students with incomplete understandings often have difficulty selecting an appropriate operation to solve a word problem. They are forced to rely on cues that are often superficial because they are not yet able to understand how the structure of the problem matches an operation.

It is not uncommon for students to use strategies that are immature (Sowder 1986). These strategies help students with single-step problems in special contexts and give them an initial understanding of the operations. However, they do not result in the kind of understanding that they need to analyze a variety of problems successfully, especially those with extra information or multiple-step problems. The following are some examples of these immature strategies:

• *Action sequences.* Initially, action sequences allow pupils to act out or use models to represent problems. The structure they abstract from those actions can later be applied to static situations.

• *Key words.* Key words or phrases are often derived from descriptions and discussions of the actions in problems. This language often helps pupils complete the word problems on a worksheet or textbook page because all the questions are nearly identical. However, when the format or language of problems varies, key words are of little help.

• *Size of the answer.* The expected size of an answer can also help children with some problems. For whole-number operations, they can use addition or multiplication (or subtraction or division) to obtain an answer that is greater (or less) than the numbers in the problem; such a procedure, however, does not differentiate between addition and multiplication or between subtraction and division.

• *Compatible numbers.* Problems with compatible numbers can lead students to base their choice of an operation on the numbers without regard to the structure of the problem. For example, a problem that involves the numbers 42 and 7 may be "solved" by dividing, but a different operation might be appropriate. No logical connection exists between the numbers in a problem and a choice of an appropriate operation. Since many problems in textbooks have compatible numbers, pupils sometimes are misled to believe that they only need to look at the numbers.

These immature strategies do not offer pupils a way to decide which operations are appropriate for different types of problems (Carpenter, Moser, and Romberg 1982; Hendrickson 1986; Thompson and Hendrickson 1986). Both teachers and children need a simple way of analyzing problems.

Generally, children need to solve problems in one of two broad categories—part-whole or comparison. In part-whole problems, one set of objects is considered in two or more parts. In comparison problems, two sets are compared to one another. With these two categories, instruction can focus on the internal structure of the problems, which in turn enables the teacher to give students an opportunity to develop understandings of the operations that generalize to a variety of problem situations.

## INSTRUCTIONAL SUGGESTIONS

The following examples illustrate how children might think to solve a variety of word problems and how teachers might facilitate their thinking. Instruction should include concrete representations of the problems and development of language that enhances understanding of the operations.

To represent the problems concretely, children can be encouraged to solve problems by manipulating counters and using intuitive counting strategies. If necessary, teachers can ask guiding questions to help children build an accurate representation. Then, modeling these representations on the overhead projector can facilitate discussion.

The language used in the examples that follow illustrates how a teacher can call attention to the part-whole concept. Acquiring the part-whole concept is an important intellectual achievement. Because it is an abstract idea, complete understanding requires many experiences with the concept over an extended period. Continued use of part-whole language in discussing concrete representations will focus attention on the relationships.

The examples are situations that children will encounter during their introduction to each type of problem. Only discrete situations in which children can use their counting skills are illustrated. As they gain competence and confidence in representing problems, similar problems in different contexts can be given. For example, children can extend these ideas to continuous situations that can be represented by number lines or regions.

### Addition and Subtraction: Part-Whole

The pupils' initial work with addition and subtraction is done in part-whole situations. Two parts are combined to form a whole set (addition), or a whole set is separated into two parts (subtraction). The language in the examples attempts to make explicit the part-whole relations among the sets. (*Note:* In all the examples, asterisks denote key questions for all students. Questions without asterisks can be used for additional guidance if needed by some students.)

*Example 1:* Rick has some pencils. Three of them are red. The other 5 are green. How many pencils does Rick have?

**Representation**                                   **Questions**

*Thinking about the structure (without numbers)*

|  |
|---|

What does Rick have? (Pencils)

What do you know about the pencils? (Some are red and some are green.)

*Representing the situation*

| ooo |
|---|

How many pencils are red? (3)

How can you show the 3 red pencils? (Put 3 counters in the set.)

| ooo        ooooo |
|---|

How many pencils are green? (5)

How can you show the 5 green pencils? (Put 5 more counters in the set.)

*Solving the problem*

| oooooooo |
|---|

*What will the solution to the problem tell you? (The number of pencils Rick has)

*Are the 3 red pencils part or all of the pencils? (Part)

*Are the 5 green pencils part or all of the pencils? (Part)

*When you know both parts, how do you find the whole? (Add)

*How many pencils does Rick have? (8)

---

*Example 2:* Lisa had 3 apples. Her mother gave her some more. Now she has 8 apples. How many apples did her mother give her?

**Representation**                                   **Questions**

*Thinking about the structure (without numbers)*

|  |
|---|

What does Lisa have? (Apples)

Lisa had some apples. Then what did her mother do? (Gave her some more.)

*Representing the situation*

| ooo |
|---|

How many apples did Lisa have to start? (3)

How can you show the 3 apples? (Put 3 counters in the set.)

| ooo        ooooo |
|---|

Lisa's mother gave her some more apples. How many did Lisa have then? (8)

How can you show what her mother did? (Put more counters in the set until it contains 8.)

*Solving the problem*

| ooo        ooooo |
|---|

*What will the solution to the problem tell you? (The number of apples that Lisa's mother gave her)

*How many counters did you put with the 3 to make 8? (5)

*How many apples did Lisa's mother give her? (5)

As children become more sophisticated in solving problems of this type, they will recognize that Lisa's 8 apples are the whole set and the 3 she started with are part of that whole. Subtraction can be used to find the other part. To promote such thinking, the teacher can follow the questions above with a discussion and illustration of the parts and the whole, for example:

> The 3 apples that Lisa started with are part of the apples. The 8 apples are the whole set. We need to find the other part, the part that her mother gave her. When you know the whole and one part, you can subtract to find the other part. Eight minus 3 is 5, so her mother gave her 5 apples.

## Addition and Subtraction: Comparison

After part-whole problems, children can be introduced to comparison problems. In such problems, three amounts need to be considered: the number of the small set, the number of the large set, and the difference between them. The difference between the sets is the number of extras in the large set after the small set has been matched to part of it. The work area should include space for pupils to represent both sets and match the small set to part of the large set.

After children become familiar with comparison problems, they need opportunities to discriminate part-whole from comparison situations. They will be able to decide which work area is appropriate, the area for one set or the area for two sets.

The language in these examples attempts to make explicit a one-to-one match between the smaller set and part of the larger set. Instead of asking "how many more (fewer) than" for comparative subtraction, the problems are cast in a context where a one-to-one match is natural. The questions that then can be asked are, "How many counters are extras?" or "How many [of one set] don't match [the other set]?"

---

*Example 3:* Jeff has some pencils. He has 4 more than Sarah. Sarah has 2 pencils. How many pencils does Jeff have?

**Representation**                    **Questions**

*Thinking about the structure (without numbers)*

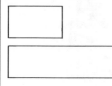

What do Jeff and Sarah have? (Pencils)

Do you know how many pencils Sarah has? (Yes)

Are the two sets of pencils being joined or compared? (Compared)

Part of Jeff's pencils match Sarah's. Does he have some more? (Yes)

*Representing the situation*

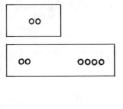

Who has the smaller set of pencils? (Sarah)

How can you show Sarah's pencils? (Put 2 counters in the smaller set)

Part of Jeff's pencils match Sarah's. How can you show this part? (Put counters in the larger set until they match the counters in the smaller set.)

How many extra pencils does Jeff have? (4)

How can you show this extra part? (Put 4 extra counters in the larger set.)

*Solving the problem*

*What will the solution to the problem tell you? (How many pencils Jeff has)

*Are the 2 of Jeff's pencils that match Sarah's pencils part of his pencils or all of them? (Part)

*Are the 4 extra pencils part or all of Jeff's pencils? (Part)

*When you know both parts of Jeff's pencils, how do you find the whole? (Add)

*How many pencils does Jeff have? (6)

*Example 4:* There are 7 children but only 3 chairs. How many children do not get to sit on a chair?

| Representation | Questions |
|---|---|

*Thinking about the structure (without numbers)*

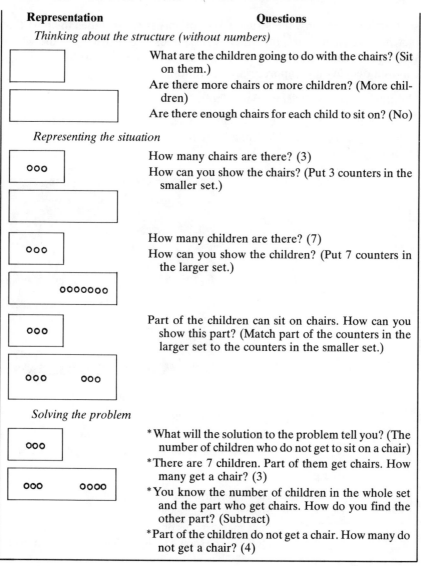

What are the children going to do with the chairs? (Sit on them.)

Are there more chairs or more children? (More children)

Are there enough chairs for each child to sit on? (No)

*Representing the situation*

How many chairs are there? (3)

How can you show the chairs? (Put 3 counters in the smaller set.)

How many children are there? (7)

How can you show the children? (Put 7 counters in the larger set.)

Part of the children can sit on chairs. How can you show this part? (Match part of the counters in the larger set to the counters in the smaller set.)

*Solving the problem*

*What will the solution to the problem tell you? (The number of children who do not get to sit on a chair)

*There are 7 children. Part of them get chairs. How many get a chair? (3)

*You know the number of children in the whole set and the part who get chairs. How do you find the other part? (Subtract)

*Part of the children do not get a chair. How many do not get a chair? (4)

To help children begin to understand the typical language found in word problems in textbooks, teachers can restate the solution to the problem in those terms:

Yes, that's right. Four children do not get a chair. There are 4 more children than chairs. (There are 4 fewer chairs than children.)

Children who have learned to analyze problems using the part-whole concept are also able to analyze comparison problems. For addition and subtraction problems, the structure of the larger set includes the part that matches the smaller set, the other part composed of extras, and the whole set. A part-whole analysis of the larger set can serve as a structure to help children decide on an appropriate operation.

## Multiplication and Division: Part-Whole

The initial work with multiplication and division involves equal parts composing a whole. The language attempts to make explicit the relations among equal parts and the whole.

---

*Example 5:* Four children went fishing. Each of them caught 3 fish. How many fish did the children catch?

**Representation**             **Questions**

*Thinking about the structure (without numbers)*

What are the children doing? (Fishing)

Did they each catch the same number of fish? (Yes)

*Representing the situation*

ooo  ooo  ooo  ooo

How many fish did each child catch? (3)

How many children went fishing? (4)

How many groups of 3 fish were caught? (4)

How can you show 4 groups of 3 fish? (Put 4 groups of 3 counters in the set.)

*Solving the problem*

ooo  ooo  ooo  ooo

*What will the solution to the problem tell you? (How many fish the children caught)

*How many fish are in each group? (3)

*How many children caught 3 fish? (4)

*When you know the number of equal parts and the number in each part, how can you find the whole? (Multiply)

*How many fish did the children catch? (12)

*Example 6:*  Misha has 12 pineapples to pack in boxes. He packs 3 in each box. How many boxes does he use?

**Representation**                                    **Questions**

*Thinking about the structure (without numbers)*

What is Misha doing with the pineapples? (Packing them into boxes)

Does he put the same number in each box? (Yes)

*Representing the situation*

How many pineapples did Misha have to pack? (12)

How can you show the 12 pineapples? (Put 12 counters in the set.)

How many pineapples does Misha put in each box? (3)

How should the pineapples be grouped? (In groups of 3)

How can you show the pineapples in groups of 3? (Make groups of 3 with the counters.)

*Solving the problem*

* What will the solution to the problem tell you? (The number of boxes needed to pack the pineapples)

* Is 12 all or just part of the pineapples that have to be packed? (All of them, or the whole set)

* How many pineapples are in each box? (3) Each of the equal parts has 3 pineapples.

* When you know the whole and the number in each part, how can you find the number of parts? (Divide)

* How many boxes does Misha need? (4)

## Multiplication and Division: Comparison

After part-whole problems, children can be introduced to comparison problems. As with addition and subtraction comparison problems, three amounts need to be considered: the number in the small set, the number in the large set, and the number of times the small set can be matched to equal parts of the large set.

*Example 7:*  Jill and Paul each have some cookies. Paul has 2 cookies. Jill has 4 times as many cookies as Paul. How many cookies does Jill have?

**Representation**                                    **Questions**

*Thinking about the structure (without numbers)*

What do Jill and Paul have? (Cookies)

Do you know how many cookies Paul has? (Yes)

Who has more cookies? (Jill)

Are the two sets of cookies being joined or compared? (Compared)

Can Paul's cookies be matched several times to equal parts of Jill's cookies? (Yes)

*Representing the situation*

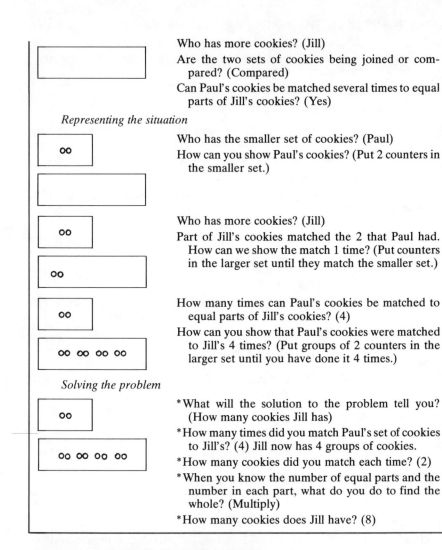

Who has the smaller set of cookies? (Paul)

How can you show Paul's cookies? (Put 2 counters in the smaller set.)

Who has more cookies? (Jill)

Part of Jill's cookies matched the 2 that Paul had. How can we show the match 1 time? (Put counters in the larger set until they match the smaller set.)

How many times can Paul's cookies be matched to equal parts of Jill's cookies? (4)

How can you show that Paul's cookies were matched to Jill's 4 times? (Put groups of 2 counters in the larger set until you have done it 4 times.)

*Solving the problem*

*What will the solution to the problem tell you? (How many cookies Jill has)

*How many times did you match Paul's set of cookies to Jill's? (4) Jill now has 4 groups of cookies.

*How many cookies did you match each time? (2)

*When you know the number of equal parts and the number in each part, what do you do to find the whole? (Multiply)

*How many cookies does Jill have? (8)

*Example 8:* Jason and Angie have some stickers. Jason has 12 stickers. He has 3 times as many as Angie. How many stickers does Angie have?

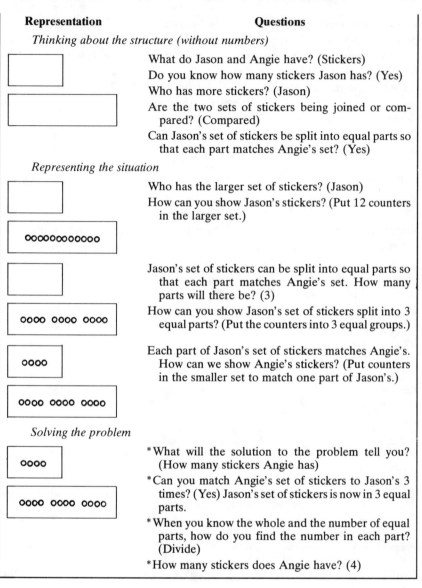

| **Representation** | **Questions** |
| --- | --- |

*Thinking about the structure (without numbers)*

What do Jason and Angie have? (Stickers)
Do you know how many stickers Jason has? (Yes)
Who has more stickers? (Jason)
Are the two sets of stickers being joined or compared? (Compared)
Can Jason's set of stickers be split into equal parts so that each part matches Angie's set? (Yes)

*Representing the situation*

Who has the larger set of stickers? (Jason)
How can you show Jason's stickers? (Put 12 counters in the larger set.)

Jason's set of stickers can be split into equal parts so that each part matches Angie's set. How many parts will there be? (3)
How can you show Jason's set of stickers split into 3 equal parts? (Put the counters into 3 equal groups.)

Each part of Jason's set of stickers matches Angie's. How can we show Angie's stickers? (Put counters in the smaller set to match one part of Jason's.)

*Solving the problem*

*What will the solution to the problem tell you? (How many stickers Angie has)
*Can you match Angie's set of stickers to Jason's 3 times? (Yes) Jason's set of stickers is now in 3 equal parts.
*When you know the whole and the number of equal parts, how do you find the number in each part? (Divide)
*How many stickers does Angie have? (4)

## CONCLUSION

The instructional procedure described in this article was used with third graders for about fifteen minutes a day over nineteen consecutive days. Comparisons of pretest and posttest results indicate that this approach was very effective in helping pupils (1) answer word problems correctly and (2) write appropriate number sentences for the problems. The pretests and posttests contained a wide variety of problems requiring all four operations. A similar instructional procedure focusing on part-whole relationships was used successfully with younger students.

The instructional method described here is an effective way to help children construct broad meanings for the basic operations. Language is developed that encourages students to reflect on the relationships between their representation of a problem and the arithmetic operations. Recognizing these relationships eventually enables them to make thoughtful decisions about applying the operations to real-world settings.

Discussing the relationships between a whole and its parts can establish a language that allows teachers and children to communicate effectively. Children can explain their thinking and their reasons for choosing an operation, and teachers can evaluate children's understanding of the mathematical structure of word problems and the process used to analyze them.

Children who have experienced this part-whole instructional program over an extended period develop confidence in their ability to reason with numbers and have little difficulty recognizing the mathematical structures of a wide variety of single-step problems. They also have the conceptual understanding necessary to successfully analyze more complex word problems.

## BIBLIOGRAPHY

Carpenter, Thomas P., James Hiebert, and James M. Moser. "Problem Structure and First-Grade Children's Initial Solution Processes for Simple Addition and Subtraction Problems." *Journal for Research in Mathematics Education* 12 (January 1981): 27–39.

Carpenter, Thomas P., James M. Moser, and Thomas Romberg, eds. *Addition and Subtraction: A Cognitive Perspective.* Hillsdale, N.J.: Lawrence Erlbaum Associates, 1982.

De Corte, Eric, L. Verschaffel, and L. De Win. "Influences of Rewording Verbal Problems on Children's Problem Representations and Solutions." *Journal of Educational Psychology* 77 (1985): 460–70.

Hendrickson, A. Dean. "Verbal Multiplication and Division Problems: Some Difficulties and Some Solutions." *Arithmetic Teacher* 33 (April 1986): 26–33.

Hudson, Tom. "Correspondences and Numerical Differences between Disjoint Sets." *Child Development* 54 (February 1983): 84–90.

Huinker, DeAnn. "Multiplication and Division Word Problems: Improving Students' Understanding." *Arithmetic Teacher,* in press.

Mahlios, Jan. "Word Problems: Do I Add or Subtract?" *Arithmetic Teacher* 36 (November 1988): 48–52.

Rathmell, Edward C. "Helping Children Learn to Solve Story Problems." In *The Fifth Mathematics Methods Conference Papers,* edited by Alan Sollman, William Speer, and John Meyer. Bowling Green, Ohio: Bowling Green State University, 1986.

Sowder, Larry. "Strategies Children Use in Solving Problems." Paper presented at the Tenth International Conference on the Psychology of Mathematics Education, July 1986.

Thompson, Charles S., and A. Dean Hendrickson. "Verbal Addition and Subtraction Problems: Some Difficulties and Some Solutions." *Arithmetic Teacher* 33 (March 1986): 21–25.

# 9

# Making Sense of Numbers

## Larry P. Leutzinger
## Myrna Bertheau

**A** PRIMARY objective of the elementary school mathematics curriculum is to instill in students a basic understanding of the number system. It is not enough to teach students just to manipulate symbols—calculators and computers do that, and much more effectively. To develop an internal sense of number, children need guidance within a classroom environment that encourages reasoning and creativity. They need to learn that mathematics is not simply pushing a pencil around on paper, calculating answers to problems and exercises. It is a wondrous study of concepts, relationships, and patterns that are timeless and possess an orderly beauty all their own. All too often students' mathematical knowledge is superficial and leads to misconceptions about numbers. Results like the following are the norm in many classrooms:

- Seventeen out of twenty students in a fourth-grade class responded that 1/2 is the largest fraction less than 1.
- Sixty-five percent of a class of sixth-grade students selected 0.39 as a decimal that is larger than 0.6.
- A third-grade student adamantly argued that 20 is closer to 90 than to 5.
- Several students were playing a calculator "target" game. The problem was 24 + _____ = (the answer was to be between 60 and 65). After an initial choice of 10 gave a sum of 34, their second guess was 11.

The responses above indicate inadequate understanding of basic number concepts. In addition, they also indicate a lack of "number sense," that is, sound, thoughtful judgment about the approximate quantity represented by a number. Number sense permits students to make decisions concerning the relationships between numbers and enables them to give valid reasons for their decisions.

One goal of a mathematics program should be to help students develop the awareness that numbers have consistency and sense. The abilities to use objects to demonstrate an understanding of numbers, to compute, and to solve problems do not, by themselves, insure that students possess number sense.

Number sense is recognized as an important part of a forward-looking mathematics program. NCTM recommends that the development of number sense be included as a criterion for judging the quality of the mathematics curriculum. As the working draft of the *Curriculum and Evaluation Standards for School Mathematics* states, "Children who have acquired a good number sense have well understood number meanings, have developed many relationships among numbers, recognize the relative magnitudes of numbers, and the relative effect of operating on numbers" (NCTM, 1987, p. 30).

Presently, little emphasis is given to number sense in the mathematics curriculum. A strong commitment needs to be made to instruction that emphasizes the development of number sense and the thinking skills required to nurture it. This instruction should be ongoing and integrated with the teaching of concepts and skills. In fact, an emphasis on number sense can increase the understanding of basic concepts by strengthening the link between physical models and symbols. It is the responsibility of the elementary school teacher to imbue students with a feel for how numbers are related to each other and how they "behave" when added, subtracted, multiplied, and divided. Hiebert (1984, p. 510) states, "If students can be assisted in developing rich meanings for the symbols and in recognizing that solutions to written problems should make sense, their struggle to link form and understanding, to learn mathematics in a meaningful way would be greatly enhanced."

Number sense is developed by a careful and deliberate move from a "hands on" involvement of the students with manipulatives to a "minds on" involvement, where physical contact, so important for the development of understanding, is used to create mental imagery, so important for the development of thinking skills. Activities that aid students in making this transition include flashing familiar concrete models for one second (or less) on an overhead projector. The students are then asked to explain what they saw in terms of the model. These "flash math" activities require extensive use of oral language both by the students in describing what they saw and by the teacher in restating or questioning the responses. The activities should be used only after the students have had many experiences with manipulating objects. The following are some ways to use flash math to help students better understand the concepts of numeration, multiplication, fractions, and decimals.

## FLASH MATH ACTIVITIES

*Teacher does*

Using "ten blocks," place 4 tens and 6 ones on the overhead projector (see fig. 9.1). Cover the display with a piece of paper. Show the tens and ones to the students for less than one second. Call on one of the students.

Accept any answer, provided the student can describe it in terms of the model. (Some teachers call any answer that relates to the model and uses the proper language a "smart" answer. A student whose answer matches the tens and ones on the overhead is "smart" and "lucky.")

Ask other students for their answers. Repeat the procedures.

Before uncovering the tens and ones, give the students a clue related to them.

*Teacher says*

On this overhead are some tens and ones. I'm going to show them to you for less than one second. Tell me how many you see.

How many did you see, Karl? ("54.") How many tens did you see? ("5.") How many ones did you see? ("4.") Then you were smart to say "54." Fifty-four is 5 tens and 4 ones. Who agrees with Karl? Marcie, what did you see? ("Four tens and 5 ones.") How many would that be in all? ("45.") Right, 4 tens and 5 ones is 45. Then you were smart to say 4 tens and 5 ones. Who agrees with Marcie?

There are 4 tens on the overhead. You can change your guess if you like.

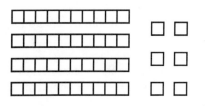

Fig. 9.1

This activity encourages students to think about the model they have been studying. They are called on to use the required oral language and can even be asked to write the symbols. Their answers are accepted if the students can describe what they saw in terms of the model. One example can elicit many different responses. When students are asked to manipulate models or identify pictures of models, they frequently rely on simple counting techniques and fail to internalize the concept. The development of number sense requires a mental fluency that begins with a solid mental model that students can use to determine quickly and accurately the characteristics of the numbers as they perceive them. Since "flash math" activities do not allow counting, it is more likely that they will encourage the students to form mental pictures of the models. These pictures are of great benefit for developing mental thinking skills, strengthening concept development, and promoting number sense.

The previous activity can be expanded to develop mental computation skills, as illustrated by the following examples:

1. Flash a set of tens and ones on the overhead projector and then ask the students to indicate a number that is more or less than the given number. Ask questions such as, What number would be 2 tens more than this number? Three ones less? Forty more than? Twice as large? Half as much? Twenty-one less than? What are two numbers you could add (or subtract) to get this number? What would be the next odd number?

2. After the pupils have made several responses, give hints and let them change their guesses. Such hints might include the following: "The number of tens is 2 more than the number of ones." "There are 6 ones." "There are an even number of tens." "The answer should be in the forties." "The sum of the digits in the number is even." Initially, give only one hint. Later, you can give two or more hints. This activity evolves naturally into one where clues are given without the models being present. After each new clue, the students should write down three or four numbers that satisfy the conditions. Students' responses are assessed after each clue. The primary goal is to develop further the concept under study.

3. Flashing pairs of numbers on the overhead improves students' comparison and estimation skills as well as develops their sense of the size of numbers. If 4 tens and 7 ones are placed near the top of the overhead and 6 tens and 3 ones are placed near the bottom and both sets "flashed," the students can be asked to tell which set contained the larger number and then to explain their thinking. This activity focuses the students' attention on the fact that in two-digit numbers the number of tens is more important in determining numerical value than the number of ones.

Obviously, these activities can be expanded to three-digit numbers using pictures of hundreds, tens, and ones. These "flash math" activities should be used only after the students have had many concrete, hands-on experiences with the models.

Any model used to develop concepts can be flashed. Below are some commonly used models and some accompanying activities.

## Multiplication

Flash math can also help students internalize multiplication. Students should know their multiplication facts fairly well before these activities are attempted.

Using rows of squares like those in figure 9.2, flash 4 rows with 5 in each row. Ask the students one of the following questions, depending on their previous experience: (1) "How many rows did you see, and how many were in each row?" (2) "What multiplication combination did you see?" (4 × 5—but any multiplication combination is acceptable if the student can explain it correctly in terms of the rows and the number in each row.) (3) "How many were there in all?" (20—again accept any reasonable answer that the student can properly explain.)

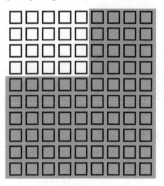

Fig. 9.2

Arrays can be expanded by using dimes as the individual units. Then an additional question can be asked—"What is the total value of all the coins you saw?" For 4 rows of dimes with 7 dimes in each row, the students could respond, "I saw 4 rows with 7 in each row, which is 4 × 7, or 28, which would be $2.80."

## Fractions

Fraction bars, pie shapes, set models, and number-line models should all be used in activities to develop number sense for fractions. The first model should be the area model. After students are familiar with the fraction-bar or pie-shape model, flash for one second on the overhead an example of the model with unit-division marks shown on it. Focus especially on fractions with a value near 0, near 1, and slightly larger or smaller than 1/2. If students can learn the characteristics of these fractions, the benchmarks created are very valuable for later work with fractions.

After the students have stated or written a fraction for the diagram, give them a hint—the number of shaded units or the total number of units. Allow them to make another estimate of the fraction on the basis of this additional information. If the students wrote 5/6 for the fraction and the additional information they received was that the total number of equal parts was 10, the students might change their answers to 8/10 or 9/10, depending on their visual image of the model.

Later, models should be presented without unit markings. These models can be flashed for a longer time but not long enough to allow students to copy the model and mark the unit divisions for themselves. This activity helps develop a sense of the size of the fraction without counting.

The following are some examples of models that can be used for fraction activities:

"What fraction of this bar is shaded?" [Flash it and ask for answers.] "Three parts were shaded. You can make another guess."

"What fraction of this bar is shaded?" [Flash it and ask for answers.] "I am thinking of a fraction equivalent to this one that has 40 parts. What fraction am I thinking of?" [4/40, 5/40, 6/40, 7/40, 8/40, 9/40, or 10/40 are acceptable answers.]

"What fraction of this circle is shaded?" [Flash it and ask for answers.] "There are 8 parts in all. You can make another guess."

"What fraction of this circle is shaded?" [Flash it and ask for answers.] "I am thinking of an equivalent fraction that has a 12 in the numerator. What fraction am I thinking of?" [12/14 or 12/15]

Activities using set and number-line models for fractions can also be used.

"What fraction of these squares have dots in them?"

"To what fraction is the arrow pointing?"

### Decimals

Although any of the models used for developing decimal concepts can be flashed, the examples given are for a 10 × 10 grid (see figs. 9.3 and 9.4). The students are asked to identify the number of columns completely filled in

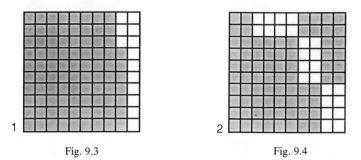

Fig. 9.3 Fig. 9.4

(tenths) and the number of extra squares (hundredths). For the first example, the students might respond "8 columns and 7 extras" or "8 tenths 7 hundredths." The teacher can then ask how many small squares in all are filled in (87). Students can write their answers in several ways. For any model, many different answers are usually given. Each time a different answer is given, the link between the model and oral language is reinforced.

Later, grids shaded in other ways should be presented (fig. 9.4). With these examples, students can develop a sense of the relative size of decimals and can practice mental computation with decimals. For instance, when presented with figure 9.4, one student stated that 3 groups of 8 squares were not shaded, so $100 - 24$, or 76, squares were shaded, which was 0.76. Another student said that about three-fourths of the big square was shaded, so the value was 0.75. When many answers are allowed, the students can share their responses and their thinking.

These grids can also be used to develop the concepts of percents and common fractions. Flash math activities, although a natural extension of the students' work with concrete materials, add a new dimension to their thought processes. They can no longer simply count to find the answer; they must form strong visual images and internalize the concept being studied. With this internalization come the foundations on which number sense is based.

## RELATIONSHIP ACTIVITIES

Although number sense is founded on strong mental imagery, students must also learn how numbers are related to one another. It is important for students not only to realize that 23 479 contains 23 thousands and that the "4" stands for 4 hundreds but also to understand that 23 479 is slightly less than 25 000 and about twice as much as 12 000 and that if 20 000 is added to 23 479, the sum is around 43 000. In fact, to perform mental calculations and estimation, these latter skills are much more important. With the advent of the calculator, more emphasis should be placed on the relative size of numbers, that is, as compared to other numbers or to certain "benchmarks" (e.g., 0, 1/2, 1, multiples of 10). The following activities allow students to compare and contrast numbers, first in a concrete way and then in a representational way.

Present three "trains" of interlocking cubes as in figure 9.5. Inform the students of the value associated with the longest and shortest trains, and ask them to determine the value associated with the middle train.

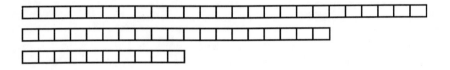

Fig. 9.5

*Teacher says*

"This train [points to the shortest one] contains 10 cubes. This train [the longest one] contains 25 cubes. Watch while I quickly place another train between the other 2—it will only be there for 2 seconds. Try to figure out how many cubes are in that train."

"Hank, how many did you think were in the middle train?"

"Why did you say 20?"

"What do you think, Kevin?"

*Student says*

"20"

"It was closer to 25 than it was to 10, but more than 2 or 3 away from 25."

"I said 20 because it looked like twice as much as the short one."

Students should be encouraged to explain their thinking for each answer given. Exact answers are not required, and in fact, the actual answer need not be given (although the students will want to know). The language of "smart" and "lucky" can be used again in these activities.

The size of the numbers should be appropriate for the grade level of the students; but rather than putting together mammoth trains that reach out the door and down the hall, use the same trains to *represent* the value of numbers. In the following activity, for instance, the shortest train can represent, say, 3570 and the longest one 8160. Refer again to figure 9.5.

| *Teacher says* | *Student says* |
|---|---|
| "Leah, what number is represented by the middle train?" | "Maybe about 7000." |
| "Why do you say that?" | "That's about twice as big as the small one." |
| "So you think that this one [points to the middle one] is twice as big as this one" [the short one]. The teacher slides the end of the shortest train to where its front was. | "It's not quite twice as long. Can I change my guess to 6500?" |
| "Sure. What is your guess, Gene?" | "I think it's 5200, because it's about half again as long as the short one. One-half of 3500 is about 1700, and 3500 plus 1700 is 5200." |
| "What do you think, Sara?" | "I'm close to that, but I thought it was halfway between the big and little one and maybe closer to the little one. Halfway is about 6000, so I guessed 5500." |

Students often give lucid answers like these to accompany their guesses. By listening to classmates' responses, other students can gain insights that help develop number sense. The teacher can encourage these types of answers by asking direct questions related to closeness, twice or half as much, or how much more or less one train appears to be than either of the others.

The same types of questions can be asked about fraction models.

If the larger rod represents 2 1/2, what does the smaller one represent?

The preceding activities develop number sense and make it more likely that students will be able to apply their skills properly in other situations. The activities that follow also encourage students to make a judgment on the basis of comparing known and unknown quantities.

What is the approximate height of the larger mountain?

14 593

About how much larger is New York than Chicago?

——————— Chicago

————————————— New York City   8 534 715

Approximately what is the length of the window?

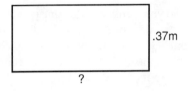

.37m

?

Additional activities stressing the relationships between numbers can use the number line as the model. For these activities skills such as doubling, halving, estimating, adding on, and subtracting should be stressed. Students can do these activities individually or with a group. The teacher should circulate, asking students how they determined where each number should be placed.

Where should the following numbers be placed on this number line? 80, 120, 100, 10

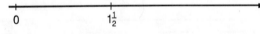

Indicate where these numbers belong: 1 000 000, 100 000, 700 000, 143 679.

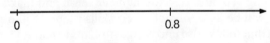

Where should the following numbers be placed on this number line? 2/3, 1 1/3, 1/6, 3

Indicate where these numbers belong: 0.4, 0.73, 1.2, 0.05

## SYMBOLIC ACTIVITIES

The first section of this article was devoted to developing mental imagery and hence improving number sense through the direct use of manipulatives, and the second section emphasized the relationship between numbers in a representational way; some time also should be spent on how number sense can be developed at the symbolic level. Here again the emphasis is on oral language, the link that connects two worlds—here, symbols and mental concepts. Students are asked to explain their thinking as it applies to the symbols that represent numbers. Before that can occur, they need strong concepts based on work with concrete objects, and the relationships between related numbers must be firmly in place. It is only then that students can fluently give meaning to the symbols involved.

| *Teacher says* | *Student says* |
|---|---|
| "Is the fraction 6/7 closer to 0 or to 1?" | "It is closer to 1. It's real close to 1!" |
| "How do you know that?" | "Well, 7/7 is the same as 1 and 6/7 is only 1/7 from that." |
| "But just look at the numbers 6 and 7. How could you tell just by looking at those that 6/7 is real close to 1?" | (After a pause) "Six is close to 7 and it is less than it. So 6/7 must be close to 1 and less. Is that what you mean?" |
| "Yes, that is right. Can you say a general rule that will tell you if a fraction is close to 1 and less than it?" | "If the top number is close to the bottom number, then the fraction is close to 1." |
| "So would 13/12 be close to 1?" | "Yes, very close. It's bigger than 1 by 1/13." |
| "How did you know that it was bigger? | "Because 13 is bigger than 12—the top number is bigger." |

A similar series of questions can deal with decimals:

| | |
|---|---|
| "Sharon, how do you know that 0.4 is larger than 0.29?" | "4 tenths is the same as 40 hundredths and 40 hundredths is larger than 29 hundredths." |
| "Very good! Could you tell that just by looking at the numbers 0.4 and 0.29?" | "Sure; the tenths part of 4 tenths is bigger than the tenths part of 29 hundredths, so 4 tenths is larger." |
| "But the tenths part of 5.9 is larger than the tenths part of 9.3, but 9.3 is larger than 5.9. Why doesn't your rule work on those?" | "To see if one number is bigger you always look at the value of the biggest digit—I mean, the digit farthest to the left. Whichever number has that digit the biggest is the biggest number." |
| "What if the leftmost digits are the same in two numbers?" | "Then you go to the next digit. Just keep doing this until one of the same digits is bigger." |

Computational exercises can be similarly questioned:

"Estimate the sum of 2345 and 5589, Mandy."

"It's about 7000. Because 2000 something and 5000 something is about 7000 something."

"Do you agree, Justin?"

"Yeah, sort of. It's 7000 something but 300 and 500 make 800, so it's 7800—almost 8000."

"Dave?"

"5589 is about 6000 and 6000 and 2000 is 8000."

After the students have worked with models and representations, they should be able to express a sense of number based on their understanding of what the symbols mean. And a well-rounded mathematics education allows the student to move freely from the concrete to the symbolic and back again, at all times maintaining a feeling for the numbers involved. Adequate instructional time should be devoted to the teaching of thinking skills. This article provides an instructional framework within which the development of number sense can occur in the regular mathematics curriculum. Higher-level thinking and problem-solving skills can be developed with the activities suggested here, and concept development can be enhanced and internalized. It takes time, commitment, and willingness to take a risk, but the results are worth it. Not only will students develop a real sense of number, but they will also become aware that mathematics is more than a system of symbols and more than just calculations on paper. It is a logical and consistent study of relationships and patterns, which possesses a beauty and a grace all its own.

## BIBLIOGRAPHY

Bright, George W. "Using Manipulatives—One Point of View." *Arithmetic Teacher* 33 (February 1986): 4.

Coxford, Arthur F., and Lawrence W. Ellerbruch. "Fractional Numbers." In *Mathematics Learning in Early Childhood,* Thirty-seventh Yearbook of the National Council of Teachers of Mathematics, edited by Joseph N. Payne, pp. 191–203. Reston, Va.: NCTM, 1975.

Hiebert, James. "Children's Mathematics Learning: The Struggle to Link Form and Understanding." *Elementary School Journal* 84 (May 1984): 497–513.

Leutzinger, Larry P., Edward C. Rathmell, and Tonya D. Urbatsch. "Developing Estimation Skills in the Primary Grades." In *Estimation and Mental Computation,* 1986 Yearbook of the National Council of Teachers of Mathematics, edited by Harold L. Schoen, pp. 82–92. Reston, Va.: NCTM, 1986.

National Council of Teachers of Mathematics. *Curriculum and Evaluation Standards for School Mathematics.* Working Draft. Reston, Va.: NCTM, 1987.

Payne, Joseph N., and Edward C. Rathmell. "Number and Numeration." In *Mathematics Learning in Early Childhood,* Thirty-seventh Yearbook of the National Council of Teachers of Mathematics, edited by Joseph N. Payne, pp. 125–60. Reston, Va.: NCTM, 1975.

Rathmell, Edward C. "Teaching Mathematics Concepts." In *A Guide to Curriculum Development in Mathematics,* p. 13. Des Moines: Iowa Department of Education, 1986.

Van de Walle, John A. "Focus on the Connections between Concepts and Symbolism." *Focus on Learning Problems in Mathematics* 5 (1983): 5–13.

# 10

# Teaching for Understanding: A Focus on Multiplication

## Marilyn Burns

NEW instructional emphases are needed to meet the goals of current mathematics programs. All too frequently, educators are preoccupied with teaching paper-and-pencil computational skills. Too often, skills are taught in isolation from their underlying concepts and from their usefulness in real-world situations. This preoccupation is reflected in school districts' statements of learning objectives and reinforced by the questions on the tests students take.

There is strong evidence that instruction driven by the goal of mastering algorithmic procedures has not been effective. Large amounts of instructional time are required to develop proficiency with computational skills. Still, students lack the understanding necessary to apply their learning in problem-solving situations.

From an instructional focus on algorithmic proficiency, students acquire a narrow and misleading view about what it means to be able to compute. They see paper-and-pencil computation as the "real" goal of learning arithmetic. They fail to learn that there are other equally important and viable ways to compute, including figuring mentally, making estimates, and using calculators. They are not aware that knowing when to apply an operation is as important as being able to compute an answer.

Surveys of adult uses of arithmetic indicate that mental computation and calculators are more commonly used in situations that require computation than paper-and-pencil computation. Also, there are many situations in which estimates suffice or are even more appropriate than exact answers. Current objectives for computation need to be broadened: helping students learn to estimate, compute mentally, and use a calculator, as well as to select appropriate approaches for problem situations, should become integral to instruction.

Teachers and educators need to reconsider the allocation of instructional time. Limited instructional time and the needs of today's society make the current time-consuming development of computational proficiency untenable. Devoting large amounts of time to learning and practicing paper-and-pencil skills made sense when these skills were essential for many jobs, such as accounting and bookkeeping, and calculators were not readily available. This is, however, no longer the situation. Of much greater importance today is the ability to reason with numbers, to judge the reasonableness of results, and to make effective decisions based on numerical information. Instruction now must emphasize developing the ability to reason numerically and to use numerical data to solve problems.

Shifting the emphasis from teaching for computational proficiency to teaching for the understanding of fundamental concepts has profound implications. Students will no longer see understanding and applying mathematical concepts as by-products or afterthoughts of developing computational skills. Educators will see thinking, reasoning, and solving problems rather than demonstrating algorithmic proficiency as the most important goals of instruction.

Thus, it is time to examine carefully the full scope of instructional goals for arithmetic. Educators should reevaluate the underlying rationale for traditional objectives and then make instructional decisions that emphasize the broader objective of developing mathematical understanding.

In order to understand the new directions needed for today's programs, it is helpful to consider specific examples. Multiplication serves well as a vehicle for investigating the implications of a strong commitment to teaching for understanding while limiting the role of computation. The multiplication ideas, however, apply equally well to addition, subtraction, division, and other traditional topics of the elementary school mathematics curriculum and can shed light on a broader view of instruction.

## A FOCUS ON TEACHING MULTIPLICATION

The multiplication of whole numbers is a topic basic to the mathematics curriculum in most of the elementary grades. The development of understanding, insight, and competence is essential to children's learning about multiplication.

### Rethinking Multiplication Objectives

The left column of table 10.1 presents some of the standard objectives for instruction in multiplication. Unfortunately, in classroom practice, not all these objectives receive adequate attention. Typically two of the objectives, knowing basic facts and developing computational facility, receive the largest portion of instructional time and emphasis. Paper-and-pencil proficiency is generally the most important goal.

TABLE 10.1
Standard Objectives for Instruction in Multiplication and Their Rationales

| *We want children to—* | *so that they—* |
| --- | --- |
| • know the basic multiplication facts | can compute and estimate with facility. |
| • perform simple computations mentally, such as with multiples of 10 | can compute confidently and accurately in appropriate situations. |
| • develop computational facility | can select and use an appropriate method of computing in problem situations, including estimating, using a calculator, computing mentally, and computing with paper and pencil. |
| • understand the logic of the multiplication algorithm | become flexible in their mathematical thinking and can adapt and re-create rules for computation. |
| • solve problems involving multiplication | can use multiplication appropriately in problem situations. |
| • estimate products | can decide if results are reasonable in problem situations. |
| • understand the relationship of multiplication to addition and division | see mathematics as a unified subject. |
| • learn properties of numbers—factors and multiples, evens and odds, composites and primes, commutativity and associativity, properties of 0 and 1, and the distributive property. | develop an understanding of, and appreciation for, patterns and order in mathematics. |

Not only are most of these objectives ignored, but the purposes for them are also ignored. The right column gives the rationale for each of the objectives. The statements in this column can make clear to teachers and students the reasons for studying multiplication and shape the kind of instruction students receive.

In order for understanding, insight, and competence to receive primary focus in instruction, perhaps the objectives for multiplication should be stated with the "so that" statements first (see table 10.2). In this way, mathematical understanding gets emphasized rather than algorithmic skills.

## Structuring Classroom Instruction

The primary goal of instruction should be students' understanding of fundamental mathematics concepts rather than their acquisition of rules and procedures for computing. Teaching for mathematical understanding emphasizes relationships rather than sequential skills. Skill development should be viewed as a way of demonstrating and furthering conceptual understanding instead of as the goal of instruction.

Rather than focusing on one specific objective, instructional experiences should be designed so that children interact with several goals simultaneously. Children do not develop mathematical understanding through a bit-by-bit approach in which concepts are broken into pieces and presented to them in manageable "bites." Such an approach reinforces the notion that

TABLE 10.2
Refocused Objectives for Multiplication

| We want children to— | so we have them— |
|---|---|
| • compute and estimate with facility | learn basic multiplication facts. |
| • compute confidently and accurately in appropriate situations | perform simple computations mentally, such as with multiples of 10. |
| • select and use an appropriate method of computing in problem situations, including estimating, using a calculator, computing mentally, and computing with paper and pencil | develop computational facility. |
| • become flexible in their mathematical thinking and adapt and re-create rules for computation | understand the logic of the multiplication algorithm. |
| • use multiplication appropriately in problem situations | solve problems involving multiplication. |
| • decide if results are reasonable in problem situations | estimate products. |
| • see mathematics as a unified subject | learn the relationship of multiplication to addition and division. |
| • develop an understanding of, and appreciation for, patterns and order in mathematics | study properties of numbers—factors and multiples, evens and odds, composites and primes, commutativity and associativity, properties of 0 and 1, and the distributive property. |

mathematics is a collection of unrelated ideas, rules, and skills. Instead, children learn by being surrounded by concepts in a variety of ways and encouraged to make sense out of their experiences, see connections in their ideas, and look for relationships among mathematical concepts.

Suggestions for multiplication instruction throughout the elementary grades are provided in the following sections. They do not constitute a complete instructional sequence but offer ideas that model the kinds of experiences that help children develop understanding.

These instructional ideas include certain common elements. All are designed to—

1. present all concepts in several different contexts;
2. involve children in problem-solving situations;
3. interweave several strands of the mathematics curriculum;
4. have children work cooperatively in small groups;
5. use concrete materials when appropriate;
6. incorporate the ongoing investigation of patterns.

## Introducing Multiplication in Contexts

Since multiplication involves thinking about groups of objects, primary-grade students benefit from exploring natural groupings that occur in the world around them. The following activities can occur over several days or weeks.

The class first brainstorms things that come in twos, such as eyes, ears, hands, thumbs, bicycle wheels, slices of bread in a sandwich, scoops on double-dip ice-cream cones, wings on a fly, children needed to play checkers. Their ideas are listed on a chart or chalkboard and titled "These Come in Twos."

Children will often suggest things that do not occur in groupings—for example, doors or buttons. These suggestions need to be discussed and the concept of groups explained again. Also, children may suggest things that appear in groupings other than twos, such as tricycle wheels, fingers on a hand, spider legs. These objects can be used to start other lists.

After the children's responses indicate that they understand, they continue brainstorming in small groups and creating lists with as many things as they can think of that come in twos, threes, fours, and so on. Their findings are later compiled on class lists for the different numbers and used to generate problems. For example, the problem "How many eyes are there on six children?" can be posed. Six children come to the front of the room, and the others count their eyes. They count by ones and by twos. It is important for the teacher to present the mathematical notation for multiplication so that children begin to connect the situation to the symbolism: each child has 2 eyes, so with 6 children there are 12 eyes all together, or $6 \times 2 = 12$.

Over several weeks, other problems can be posed, such as "How many fingers do ten children have all together?" "How many soft drinks are in three six-packs?" "How many wheels are there on four tricycles?" Objects or drawings can be used when the problems do not involve children; the symbolism should always be connected to problem situations.

### Relating Multiplication to Functions

The class lists can also be used to investigate patterns that are functions. Such investigations can be initiated by posing a problem such as the following:

> If we count all the ears in this room, how many ears do you think we'll have all together?

Children's guesses will vary. One systematic way to solve this problem is to develop a chart. After one child comes to the front of the room and the other children verify that he or she has two ears, the teacher records this number pair on a chart. Then another child comes up; the class verifies that there are now four ears up and this is recorded, and so on:

| People | Ears |
|--------|------|
| 1 | 2 |
| 2 | 4 |
| 3 | 6 |
| 4 | 8 |
| 5 | 10 |

The numbers in the "Ears" column are used to reinforce counting by twos, and the number pairs are related to the multiplication symbolism:

> With 5 people, there are 10 ears; that's 5 people with 2 ears each; we write that as $5 \times 2 = 10$.

> How can the chart tell you how many ears there are for 8 people? What about for 3 people? How would I write a math sentence to show how many ears there are in all?

> What does $10 \times 2 = 20$ tell about people and ears?

> What if there were 100 people? How many ears would there be?

This exploration can be repeated over time using other entries from the lists.

## Writing Multiplication Stories

Writing stories for multiplication sentences also helps children relate multiplication to real-world situations. Each story should end with a question that can be answered by the multiplication sentence.

It is important that teachers model what children are expected to do. First present a multiplication sentence, such as $7 \times 3 = 21$, and tell a story that ends with a question and fits the multiplication sentence, as in the following example:

> Billy was sent home from school because he was sick. His dad took him to the doctor, who told him he would have to go to bed and rest until he was well. The doctor prescribed some pills for Billy to take to help him get well. She told Billy he would have to take 3 pills a day for one week. How many pills would Billy have to take?

Then each child writes a different story for that multiplication sentence. They then read their stories to each other in small groups. After a child reads a story, the other children verify that it ended with a question and that the question could be answered by the multiplication sentence.

The students can write stories for other multiplication sentences, using a sentence they select or one drawn from an envelope. The stories can be used in several ways. Students can have other children in their small group give the multiplication sentence that goes with the story. The stories can be used as activity cards at a learning center. They can also be displayed on a bulletin board for students to read.

At a later time, children can write stories that contain extraneous information as well. Too often, children use all the data presented in a problem, even if it is not appropriate. Having children create their own stories and discuss them with their peers helps them focus on the meanings in situations rather than on getting an answer. Again, a sample story should be modeled for the children.

> Sara agreed to do chores for her dad as a Father's Day present. Her dad gave her a list of what he would like done. The list included the following tasks: polish my shoes, organize my ties, and wash the car. Sara counted and found that her dad had 6 pairs of shoes to be polished, 4 brown and 2 black. She found that he had 16 ties to be organized and that the tie rack had 6 hooks. There was only 1 car to wash. How many shoes did Sara have to polish?

## Relating Multiplication to Geometry

A geometric model helps children broaden their understanding of multiplication. Students use tiles or cubes to investigate all the different (noncongruent) rectangles for the numbers from 1 to 30 and use squared paper to cut out the rectangles they find.

It is helpful to introduce this problem by having each student arrange twelve tiles or cubes into a rectangle. Have some describe the arrangements they make. Usually, all the different ones will be generated (fig. 10.1).

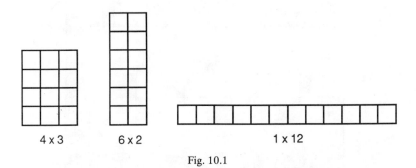

4 x 3          6 x 2                          1 x 12

Fig. 10.1

To verify that 4 × 3 and 3 × 4 rectangles are congruent, it is helpful to cut both out of squared paper to show that they match exactly in size and shape and therefore are not different. If no student suggests one of the arrays—for example, a 1 × 12 rectangle—the teacher should point this rectangle out.

Students work in pairs, investigating different numbers, cutting the rectangles out of squared paper, labeling them with the number of tiles or cubes they used, and posting them on the chalkboard. In this way, the students contribute to a class chart.

Students then investigate the cutout rectangles in various ways and create categories—rectangles that have 2 tiles or cubes on a side, 3 on a side, 4 on a side, and so on; numbers for which there is only one rectangle; numbers for which there are squares. For each category, students list the number of tiles or cubes in each rectangle and look for patterns in their lists. From a discussion of these patterns, the ideas of multiples, evens and odds, and prime numbers can be introduced.

## Patterns on the Multiplication Chart

Using copies of a 12 × 12 multiplication table, students work in groups to investigate the patterns of the multiples of 2, 3, 4, 5, 6, 7, 8, 9, 10, 11, and 12, each on a separate chart (see fig. 10.2). For each number, they first list all the multiples of that number up to 144, using a calculator if they wish, and then color in these multiples.

Multiples of 6

| 1 | 2 | 3 | 4 | 5 | 6 | 7 | 8 | 9 | 10 | 11 | 12 |
|---|---|---|---|---|---|---|---|---|----|----|----|
| 2 | 4 | 6 | 8 | 10 | 12 | 14 | 16 | 18 | 20 | 22 | 24 |
| 3 | 6 | 9 | 12 | 15 | 18 | 21 | 24 | 27 | 30 | 33 | 36 |
| 4 | 8 | 12 | 16 | 20 | 24 | 28 | 32 | 36 | 40 | 44 | 48 |
| 5 | 10 | 15 | 20 | 25 | 30 | 35 | 40 | 45 | 50 | 55 | 60 |
| 6 | 12 | 18 | 24 | 30 | 36 | 42 | 48 | 54 | 60 | 66 | 72 |
| 7 | 14 | 21 | 28 | 35 | 42 | 49 | 56 | 63 | 70 | 77 | 84 |
| 8 | 16 | 24 | 32 | 40 | 48 | 56 | 64 | 72 | 80 | 88 | 96 |
| 9 | 18 | 27 | 36 | 45 | 54 | 63 | 72 | 81 | 90 | 99 | 108 |
| 10 | 20 | 30 | 40 | 50 | 60 | 70 | 80 | 90 | 100 | 110 | 120 |
| 11 | 22 | 33 | 44 | 55 | 66 | 77 | 88 | 99 | 110 | 121 | 132 |
| 12 | 24 | 36 | 48 | 60 | 72 | 84 | 96 | 108 | 120 | 132 | 144 |

Fig. 10.2

After students have colored in the eleven charts for all the multiples, they should collectively investigate the patterns. Writing statements to describe what they notice gives students the opportunity to reflect on what they have done, clarify their thinking, and share their thoughts.

## Investigating Multiples Using Interlocking Cubes

Working in pairs, students make a number line from 1 to 24, large enough for the interlocking cubes to fit on each number. They stack cubes on the number line in the following way:

A red cube on each number that is a multiple of 2
A blue cube on each number that is a multiple of 3
A brown cube on each number that is a multiple of 4
A white cube on each number that is a multiple of 5
A black cube on each number that is a multiple of 6
A green cube on each number that is a multiple of 7
An orange cube on each number that is a multiple of 8
A purple cube on each number that is a multiple of 9
A yellow cube on each number that is a multiple of 10

Students then write statements about what they notice. A class discussion should deal with questions such as the following:

- Which is the tallest stack? Why is this so?
- Which stacks have only one cube? What can you say about these numbers?
- Which stacks are the same height?
- How could you predict how many cubes you would have placed on the number 30 if your number line had gone that high? Try it.

Ask students to remove all the stacks, keeping them intact, and then try to figure out which stack belongs on each number.

### Another Investigation of Multiplication in Contexts

Problem situations such as the following can engage students in computing mentally and using the distributive property:

If I promised to give each student in the class 5 markers, how many markers would I have to buy?

The following process can be used to investigate this problem. First the number of students in the class needs to be determined. Suppose there are twenty-seven. A way to make the problem easier is to break the 27 into parts that are easier to consider mentally—20 + 7 or 10 + 10 + 7. It is easier to multiply each of these numbers by 5 than it is to multiply 27 by 5. The class does these simpler multiplications mentally and then adds to calculate how many markers to buy. Also, it is useful to break 27 into 10 + 10 + 5 + 2 and verify that the result will be the same.

Other problems can also be used:

- If a company manufactures 75 tricycles a day, how many wheels a day are needed?
- If you will each get 3 tickets for our class play, how many tickets will our class use all together?

- If 22 teams are participating in a volleyball tournament, how many players will play in the tournament?

Students can make up similar problems and present them for the class to solve. As they become more proficient, the students can try the same sort of problems with larger numbers. For example, if a company has 12 buses that seat 42 people each, how many passengers can travel at one time? This is a way to build some beginning understanding of the partial products of the standard multiplication algorithm with two-digit multipliers.

### Exploring the Algorithm through a Problem-solving Approach

Rather than teaching the multiplication algorithm through demonstration, teachers can give students a problem-solving opportunity—inventing their own ways to record multiplications. Solving problems such as those suggested in the previous activity is extended from finding answers mentally to recording the processes they use. Students report their written methods to the class for discussion. They try one another's methods and compare their ease and efficiency.

It is after experiences like this one that it is appropriate to introduce the standard algorithm as one that has been commonly used. It is the sense of the methods rather than the learning of the steps in the procedure that needs to be stressed.

### Extending the Exploration of Rectangular Arrays to the Multiplication Algorithm

Extending their earlier work with rectangular arrays, students can use base-ten blocks and squared centimeter paper as visual models for the multiplication algorithm. For a multiplication problem such as $27 \times 3$, for example, students outline a 27-by-3 rectangle on the centimeter paper (fig. 10.3). Using the base-ten blocks, they cover the rectangle with 6 tens in 2 rows of 3 each, and then 21 units in 7 rows of 3 each. The $27 \times 3$ rectangle can be split into a $20 \times 3$ rectangle and a $7 \times 3$ rectangle, which represent partial products that are easier to figure.

Problems involving two-digit multipliers can be modeled in the same way. For $24 \times 13$, for example, hundreds, tens, and units blocks are used to fill in a $24 \times 13$ rectangle (fig. 10.4). This rectangle can be split into four pieces to find the product by figuring the value of the hundreds ($20 \times 10$), the two groups of tens ($20 \times 3$ and $4 \times 10$), and the units ($3 \times 4$). Again, the goal of this activity is to build an understanding of the logic of the algorithm, not to develop computational proficiency.

## WHAT ABOUT COMPUTATIONAL PROFICIENCY?

The activities suggested above are ways to build student understanding.

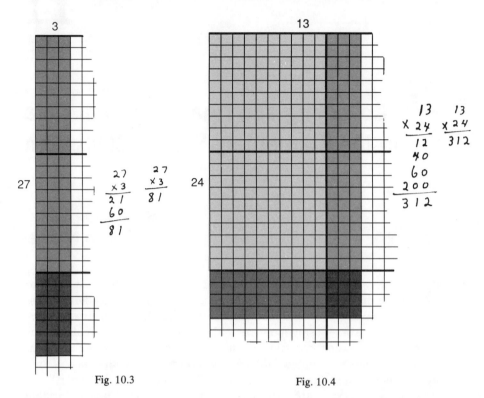

Fig. 10.3

Fig. 10.4

They do not promise to help children become facile and proficient paper-and-pencil calculators. A great deal of practice in one method is required for that skill to become well rooted and automatic. However, the pressure for making children into human calculators must continue to diminish and finally be replaced with more appropriate mathematical goals for children.

Do we really want children to be able to compute the answer to a complicated multiplication example when they cannot figure the tip for a meal in their heads? Are we satisfied that they come to truly understand multiplication by the rote learning of rules? (For example, when they carry in multiplication, they multiply and then add "the little number," yet they can't explain why they don't add "the little number" on first and then multiply.) Can we say that the solution to students getting absurd answers to problems and neither noticing nor seeming to care can be corrected by more drill and practice?

Student understanding of mathematics must not be sacrificed for mastering procedures that are often learned by rote and that are more efficiently done with a calculator. Teachers need classroom suggestions that will help them see the mathematical power that students can exhibit when helped to think and reason, not merely to do.

# 11

# Collecting and Analyzing Real Data in the Elementary School Classroom

Susan Jo Russell
Susan N. Friel

**B** ECAUSE we live in an age of information, we need to know how to manage the large amounts of information that bombard us daily. Much of this information is quantitative and is often described statistically. Consequently, statistics—using numbers to describe and interpret reality—has assumed an increasingly central place in desicion making in our society. Real users of numbers are familiar with many ways of working with data—picturing data using tables, graphs, and diagrams; describing what is "typical"; or showing how data vary, are distributed, or are related—and are comfortable with calculators and computers as critical tools.

Current mathematics textbooks are beginning to respond to the need for developing these skills. However, our analysis of several leading elementary school textbook series found that work in data analysis still consists overwhelmingly of exercises requiring students to *find* information in a table or graph preconstructed from hypothetical data. Interpretation is rarely called for, and the collection of original data is infrequently required.

We shall present four important areas in teaching data analysis: the selection of problems and data sets; the critical concepts underlying the process of data analysis; the development of pupils' facility with a range of representations, including the role of technology; and the management of data analysis activities in the classroom.

The staff of the *Used Numbers* project has been deeply involved in formulating and implementing the ideas and activities on which this article is based. Besides the authors, Rebecca Corwin, Antonia Stone, and Tim Barclay have been the primary developers of the *Used Numbers* curriculum. Members of the Used Numbers Advisory Board have also contributed to the development of the ideas expressed in this article. For more information about the *Used Numbers* project, contact the authors at the Technical Education Research Centers, 1696 Massachusetts Avenue, Cambridge, MA 02138.

## REAL PROBLEMS IN DATA ANALYSIS

A dynamic approach to teaching statistics is required if students are to develop the understandings and insights they will need. Students need to be actively involved with real problems in data analysis. A real data analysis problem has the following characteristics:

• Real data are either collected by the students or obtained from real-world sources. Real data are, by their very nature, "messy." More data might be available than are needed to solve the problem being considered. Unusual characteristics of the data might necessitate many attempts at selection, sorting, and representation in an effort to make sense of them.

• The collection of the data requires decisions to be made about what is needed and how to get it. Before any data are collected, data analysis begins with decisions about what constraints and freedoms will guide the collection process. These decisions profoundly affect the later stage of interpretation.

• The set of data provides information that is useful or of interest. One teacher noted her own and her students' dissatisfaction with a science unit in which students counted and graphed the increasing population of reproducing organisms: "But there's no problem!" she lamented. Collecting and organizing data had become divorced from their purpose.

• The data are examined, interpreted, and analyzed using multiple representations. Students move between table and graph, between one kind of graph and another, between spreadsheet and database, between database and graph. They use a range of technologies—from Unifix cubes to colored dots to electronic spreadsheets and graphing software. Students need time to browse in and through data sets in ways that are analogous to how they browse through a book. Juxtaposing different ways of organizing and representing the same data can spark questions, provide surprises, and encourage conjecturing.

• Discussion and disagreement about data interpretation are stressed. The data are examined for what they show and do not show. Differing interpretations are encouraged.

• Students deal with multiple and extended uses of data and their representations. Too often, data are collected, graphed, and posted as a one-time answer to a single question ("When are our birthdays?"). Data that have been collected and organized should be used to generate new questions, not just to obtain "answers." Students should come back to the data for comparison and use them as a resource to solve other problems.

A real problem in data analysis involves a series of processes, including problem formulation; data collection, organization, and representation; and summarization and interpretation. Each of these processes has its own complexities and difficulties and involves a wide range of possible approaches. Further, this series of processes can be iterative. Once the data are collected and organized, we might find that they are inadequate or incomplete for solving a particular problem; organizing and summarizing the data might send us back to collect more data or even to formulate the problem more carefully. Data analysis activities need to be built around considerations about what is developmentally appropriate, yet challenging and compelling, to the students. Figure 11.1 indicates the range of approaches within each process that students should become familiar with in the elementary grades.

New materials to help students in grades K–6 learn how numbers can be used to describe, interpret, and make predictions about real phenomena are being developed by Technical Education Research Centers (TERC) and Lesley College with funding from the National Science Foundation. The project, Used Numbers: Collecting and Analyzing Real Data, is designing curriculum modules that bring together work in measurement, estimation, graphing, and statistics and make appropriate use of computers and calculators as mathematical tools. The classroom activities in this article have been drawn from the project's work. Finding real problems that are manageable yet lead to interesting investigations in the classroom has been a primary emphasis in the project's work.

One simple but effective experience in data analysis is a study of family size, an introductory activity that we have used with students at a variety of levels, from third graders to adults. This topic is inherently interesting to almost everyone and does not require an initial problem or question to get things started.

Generally we start this activity with a known fact about family size, for example, the average size of families in the local community. This information is very easy to obtain—most towns have data from the last census that they will be happy to share. In one small city, the average (mean) family size was 3.03. We used this fact to begin a discussion with a mixed class of third and fourth graders. The information was modified to fit their level of understanding. Here are excerpts from the teacher's and the students' comments, taken from a much longer discussion.

*Teacher:*   I called up City Hall the other day and asked them what the typical family size in our town is. They looked it up and told me it was about three. What do you think they meant by this?

*Student 1:*   That three was the most.

*Student 2:*   Yeah, that usually it's about three.

*Teacher:*   How do you think they figured that out?

*Student 3:*   Well, the health clinic knows all that about my family. Maybe they go to the health clinic and find out.

| Grade | K | 1 | 2 | 3 | 4 | 5 | 6 |
|---|---|---|---|---|---|---|---|
| **Type of collection** | Observation | | | | | | |
| | Direct measurement | | | | | | |
| | | Surveys | | | | | |
| | | | | Experiments | | | |
| | | | | | Compiled data | | |
| | | | | | | Sampling | |
| | | | | | | Simulation | |
| **Type of analysis** | Counting | | | | | | |
| | Classification | | | | | | |
| | Comparison (bigger/smaller) | | | | | | |
| | | Looking for patterns (overall shape of the data — functions, correlation) | | | | | |
| | | | | | Comparison (fractions, percent, ratio) | | |
| | | | | | Central tendency and range (informal measures — mode, median, mean) | | |
| | | | | | | Prediction, trends | |
| | | | | | | | Indices |
| **Type of representation** | Concrete objects | | | | | | |
| | Pictures | | | | | | |
| | Picture bar graphs | | | | | | |
| | | Bar graphs | | | | | |
| | | Tables (one dimensional) | | | | | |
| | | Timelines | | | | | |
| | | Tallying | | | | | |
| | | | Stem and leaf | | | | |
| | | | Venn diagrams | | | | |
| | | | | Maps | | | |
| | | | | Tables (two dimensional) | | | |
| | | | | | Pie graphs | | |
| | | | | | Histograms | | |
| | | | | | | Line graphs | |
| | | | | | | | Box and whiskers |
| **Type of tool** | Calculator | | | | | | |
| | Unifix cubes, centimeter cubes, etc. | | | | | | |
| | | | Databases and database templates | | | | |
| | | | | Graphing software | | | |
| | | | | Spreadsheets and spreadsheet templates | | | |
| | | | | | | Simulation and modeling | |

Fig. 11.1. Data analysis activities in grades K–6

*Student 4:* Maybe they ask all the people who come to City Hall.

*Student 5:* Well, my mother just had my new brother. So they wouldn't have the right number for me.

*Teacher:*   That's interesting. Actually, these data were collected in 1980. How many years ago was that?

*Student 6:*  Seven years.

*Teacher:*   Hmm, I wonder if things have changed since then.

*Student 7:*  Wouldn't it be weird if a whole lot of people had been born and a whole lot of people died—and it was exactly the same!

*Teacher:*   Do you think that's likely?

This initial discussion highlights important issues in data analysis. Any of the students' remarks could have been (and, in many instances, were) pursued further: Where do data come from? How old are they? Are they still reliable? How might they be changing? What is the relationship of a "typical," representative, or average family size to the population it represents?

The next part of the activity is based on two more questions: Do you think the typical family size for our class might be the same as for the town as a whole? How would we find out? Students are always interested in comparing something about themselves to data from the outside world. But figuring out what data should be collected and how to organize, display, and interpret them are complex issues, even with this very simple data set.

## CRITICAL CONCEPTS IN DATA ANALYSIS

Three critical processes are fundamental to all quantitative data analysis activities at every grade level:

- Characterizing the overall shape of the data
- Summarizing the data
- Interpreting the data

Our classroom experience suggests that an emphasis on specific objectives often undermines the meaningfulness of work in data analysis unless the objectives are grounded in these critical processes. Finding the median, for example, can become an end in itself rather than a step toward a better understanding of the data set as a whole. When these three critical ideas are emphasized throughout an activity, particular skills can be built on a solid foundation.

### Clumps, Bumps, and Holes: Characterizing the Shape of the Data

Characterizing the shape of the data, as if you were going to sculpt this shape with clay, is a prerequisite to summarizing and theory building. Paying attention to the shape of the data may be the most important idea we can communicate to students about data analysis. When you look at a table or graph, what strikes you about the data? Where are the data clumped? Is there more than one clump? Are there bumps of data in surprising places? Are there holes that contain no data? For example, look at figure 11.2, which shows the number of raisins in each of 18 miniature boxes. As the students who collected these data pointed out, the data clump between 33 and 37; most boxes (almost half) contained 35 raisins; two bumps of data were unconnected to the major clump (one box contained 39 raisins and one had 43), and no data at all (a hole) were between 39 and 43. We advocate an explicit focus on these clumps, bumps, and holes as a way to help students integrate the individual features of the data with the whole set and develop a picture of the reality the data represent.

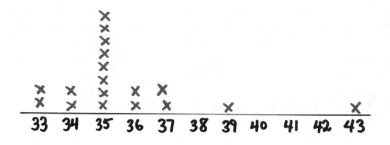

Fig. 11.2. Number-line representation for boxes of raisins

## What Is Typical? Summarizing the Data Numerically

Once students have experience in characterizing the overall shape of their data sets, they can learn about descriptive statistics that summarize the data more succinctly and characterize what appears to be typical or representative in their data. The range, mode, median, and mean can be introduced during the elementary grades, but these ideas must be built carefully on students' own informal descriptions of their data.

Measures of central tendency—mode, median, and mean—are difficult for elementary school students to understand and use appropriately. Our classroom experience and research indicate that although the calculation of these measures is deceptively easy—requiring only counting, ordering, addition, and division—understanding what they convey about a set of data is very complex.

The *mode* of a set of data is easily found by first and second graders (although they need not learn to use the term *mode*). However, upper elementary students, and even adults, often do not distinguish between a mode that is interesting, in the context of the data's overall shape, and one that is not. For example, in the distribution of the colors of twenty-five tulips, seven tulips were red, six were white, seven were violet, and five were pink. A group of upper elementary school students reported the modes as red and violet, ignoring the fact that the colors are almost as evenly distributed as they possibly could be.

The *median* might be the most important of the three measures of central tendency for upper elementary students. It is less subject to unusual values in the data; the mean is easily shifted by the presence of unusually large (or unusually small) values and may not be representative of the data as a whole. The idea of median is not intuitively difficult because students already have well-developed notions of "middle." However, students' ideas about a "middle" do not necessarily lead easily to an understanding of median. Teachers should expect that initially some students will be confused about exactly what middle is being discussed. Some students, given a simple vertical bar graph, find the middle of the horizontal axis rather than the middle of the *data*. Some students find the middle of the range of the data without taking into account how the data are distributed. Others looking at a collection of raw data find the middle without first ordering them! These confusions must be taken seriously; an understanding of median as the point that divides the set of ordered data in half is not straightforward but develops over time and through many experiences.

The arithmetic mean, which is what generally is meant by the word *average,* might be the most common descriptive statistic that students encounter in current events, in conversation, or in their science or social studies curricula. However, the *mean* is the most difficult and abstract of the three measures of center for elementary school students. Although it is commonly taught as early as fourth grade, its use should be postponed until at least fifth grade, when it should be given a more thorough treatment than the usual isolated teaching of the "add up the $n$ numbers and divide by $n$" algorithm.

If students have a strong foundation in the meaning and use of mode, median, and range, they will have some context in which to place this very different measure. Unlike the mode and median, which can be easily related to students' own experience with the ideas of "most" and "middle," the mean appears to be a more arbitrarily constructed notion. It can be developed by the following manipulation: If all the values in a set of data were "evened out" by taking excess amounts from the large values and adding them to small values, this constructed value is the arithmetic mean. For example, if we lined up all the sixth graders in a class and removed "bits" of the tallest students and glued them onto shorter students until everyone was the same height, that height would be the mean height in the class (this is a somewhat gruesome but much loved and memorable example for upper elementary students). Only after many experiences with a variety of data sets and discussions of what the mean does and does not show about the data are students ready to use the standard algorithm for finding the mean.

### Theory Building: Interpreting the Data

The third process fundamental to work with quantitative data is interpretation. Interpretation is an attempt to understand the meaning of the data in terms of the reality it represents. Interpretation involves coming to conclusions, developing theories, and posing new questions. Teachers must allow their students to grapple with their understanding of their results rather than try to pull from them what they *should* see in their data. When we have the outcome of interpretation too clearly in mind before we even start, we tend to channel or shape students' observations to emphasize predetermined teaching points. The following discussion about Friday-night bedtimes leads to theory building and further investigation:

*Student 1:*  Most boys went to bed later. The median time for boys was 10:30. The girls' median was 9:00.

*Teacher*  [to the class as a whole]:  Any theories about that?

*Student 2:*  Maybe boys eat more sugar.

*Student 3:*  Boys can sleep late and maybe their favorite show is on.

*Student 4:*  Girls are soft, so as soon as their parents say "Go to bed," they go.

*Student 5:*  Maybe girls get up earlier, too.

*Teacher:*  You're suggesting that maybe boys and girls are actually getting the same amount of sleep? We'd have to do another survey to see about getting up.

*Student 6:*  Why don't we ask right now?

Such theory building is an iterative process. Interpretation can lead students back to data collection or to presenting the data differently to better understand the information they have collected. Encouraging this rethinking and revision process helps students understand the importance of questioning and representing their data from a variety of perspectives.

Examining data, finding patterns in them, asking questions about them, and reflecting on them are essential processes in mathematical problem solving. To deal with data effectively, students must be encouraged to develop habits of thinking that focus on wondering and predicting. Such habits include the following:

• *Questioning:*  Do the data make sense? Are the data appropriate to their intended use? Do the data tell me what I want to know? Is the information reasonable? Is it reliable? Where and how were the data collected? What does this information tell me? What *doesn't* it tell me? Can I represent the data differently and get a different message?

• *Conjecturing:* Perhaps this means that. . . . If . . . then. Suppose. . . . What if . . .? What other questions do the data suggest?

- *Seeing relationships:* What do I already know that the data relate to? What other work has been done—by me, by others, or by the class—that applies here? Does this result have anything to do with the fact that all the people surveyed were in sixth grade, were boys, or lived in the same town? Does one variable have anything to do with another variable?

- *Withholding judgment:* I wonder why these data don't fit with what I already know? Have I tried enough samples? Does my idea work in all cases? How do I know or what don't I know? How else might I think about the problem and the data I need? What further information is needed?

- *Building theories:* I can generalize the following from what the data show. . . . I can prove that. . . . One theory that would explain the shape of these data is. . . , but an alternative theory might be. . . .

If these habits of analysis are to be nurtured, students must be able to view the data easily and use clear, multiple representations to illuminate their various aspects. In the next section, we describe the range of technologies with which students need to be familiar in an age of information.

## FROM UNIFIX CUBES TO COMPUTER GRAPHS: TECHNOLOGY FOR REPRESENTING DATA

Graphing is often taught as an art of presentation. A graph is used as the endpoint of the data analysis process, a means for communicating what has been done. Certainly graphs, pictures, and charts *can* be used to show data to an audience once the data have been collected, summarized, and analyzed. A pictorial representation is an effective way to make a point. However, a real user of statistics employs pictures and graphs as tools to understand the data *during the process of analysis.* We would like to adopt the following definition as the primary reason for teaching students about data representations:

*Representing data in a picture, table, or graph is a way to discover the features of the data, to array the data so that their shape and relationships among aspects of the data can be seen.*

If these purposes for picturing data are taken seriously, then the use of graphs in the classroom only as a product at the end of a data analysis activity must change. Although some representations might never be shown to anyone else and some might be of little use, they do help to uncover and elaborate the story of the data, to find out if the information collected is adequate for solving the problem, and to determine whether the data suggest other interesting problems and relationships.

Two principles should guide students' use of pictorial representations of data:

- A picture of the data is a beginning, not an end.
- More than one representation of the data should always be used.

We want students to gain facility with creating representations that offer a quick first look at the data. Students should be encouraged to create quick diagrams, tables, and graphs to get a feel for the data. Final representations are made after students have decided what they want to communicate about the data.

Students need to look at more than one representation of the data. Different students can see relationships in the data more clearly using particular kinds of representations, and different representations can illuminate different aspects of the data. For example, students who had collected data on the number of hours their classmates had watched television during one weekend looked at the information in an ordered table (using an electronic spreadsheet) and in a bar graph, with a bar for each student. In the graph, students who had watched no television were indicated by empty spaces, whereas in the ordered list, the zeros were grouped together at the beginning of the list. Students viewing the data noticed a striking number of nonwatchers when they looked at the ordered list, although they had not been struck by this information when they looked at the bar graph. The use of several representations underlines the need for representations that can be constructed and changed quickly and easily.

In our work with elementary school students, we have found several techniques and materials for creating representations of data that are easy to use, require small amounts of time and dexterity, and create representations that can be modified with little trouble. These techniques include concrete, pictorial, and numerical modes of representation and span a range of technologies, from Unifix cubes to pencil and paper to computer graphics. In the following sections these representations are grouped into categories that move generally from concrete to abstract. Whereas younger children would use more representations in the first two categories and children in the upper elementary grades would more often use representations in the latter categories, we use all types of representations in all grades. Unifix cubes and other concrete representations continue to be powerful for fourth and fifth graders, and simple numerical representations, such as the stem-and-leaf diagram, have been used successfully by first graders. The approaches listed here have proved versatile, clear, easy to use, and flexible in a variety of data analysis activities.

## Concrete Representations

Unifix cubes and centimeter cubes are essential materials in our representational repertoire. They have the advantage of being individual units that can be connected in some way to represent data. Because these representations are movable and embody the relative quantities, they naturally lead to ordering. For example, when students use Unifix cube towers to model the family size of each member of the class, we have never seen a group that did not order the bars without any prompting from teachers. As one fourth grader said when students looked at the twenty-four towers representing their class, "It's like a bar graph on the floor." Unifix cubes can be used in all the grades, even by older children, who do not see them as childish when they are used for sophisticated purposes.

### Flexible Unit Graphs

For generations, teachers of young children have been using a variety of objects, matchboxes, index cards, or other large items to make representations of categorical data. For example, students in kindergarten each take off a shoe and place them on the floor in rows to show types of shoes, such as sneakers or sandals. To make a birthday chart, students in a first-grade class draw pictures of themselves on index cards and tack them on the bulletin board under signs indicating the months of the year. On these unit graphs, one item represents each piece of data. Although these charts are similar to standard bar graphs, they differ from colored-in squares on graph paper because each item clearly represents an individual, identifiable piece of data and because the data can be easily rearranged and recategorized.

Post-its™ are an excellent material for constructing unit graphs. A small group of students trying to find the typical family size for their class used a row of such "stick on" notes for each student, for example, four stick-ons for Joe's family and three for Maria's, and so forth. They could easily move the stick-ons to determine how many people would be in each family if they were rearranged to have the same number of members, thus illustrating the mean of this set of data. After the redistribution, they cut the remaining stick-ons and distributed the fractional parts.

### Numerical Representations

Number lines and stem-and-leaf diagrams can be used to organize data to get a first look at its "shape." For example, if students have just collected data on the number of raisins in a box, a number-line representation for eighteen boxes of raisins might look like that in figure 11.2. Because this is a *working representation* of the data, a title, label, or vertical axis is not necessary.

For data distributed over a larger range, the stem-and-leaf diagram offers a quick way to organize and display the data. A set of data showing how long each of twenty-one children can hold her or his breath is recorded in a stem-and-leaf diagram in figure 11.3(a). In this situation, the stem-and-leaf shows the shape of the data better than a number line, on which the data would appear very scattered (fig. 11.3(b)).

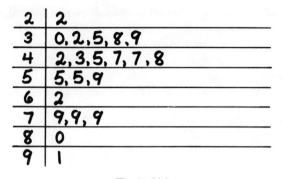

Fig. 11.3(a)

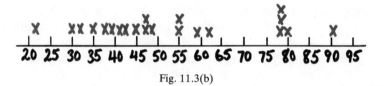

Fig. 11.3(b)

Notice that these representations are more condensed and abstract than the other two categories, but they give an easily organized overview of the range and distribution of the data. Are there any obvious concentrations of data? Are the data distributed evenly or unevenly? Are they distributed in a pattern? Do parts of the range contain no data?

Besides allowing for data ordering and organization, these representations also retain the original individual pieces of data in some form. This is important for two reasons. First, *the representations can be used to record data directly*—a student puts an index card on a chart to show her birthday month or the teacher writes an "x" on a number line to record each student's family size. Second, *a direct correspondence exists between the original data and the indicators on the representation.* Although any representation is a form of abstraction—a Unifix cube tower showing the number of peas in a pod is certainly not the peas themselves—the representations recommended here involve *minimal transformations* of the data. Even a simple bar graph can be, for many students, a long way from the original data.

## Using Technology for Organizing and Displaying Data

Once the data are gathered, graphing software offers a variety of opportunities for "what if" experimenting, which promotes a more extensive understanding of the power of a display of data for conveying information. Beyond this, the quality of the presentations makes using the software truly exciting for students.

Educationally, graphing programs should be introduced as part of a sequence of activities to teach students about collecting and analyzing data. Teachers need to consider the amount of precomputer experience that students should have in constructing their own graphs or other visual displays. Graphing software can be viewed as "magic" for those students who do not possess the conceptual understandings that develop, in part, from precomputer activities.

Another instructional component is the way that graphing software raises conceptual issues and concerns about the display of data. Since software creates a variety of graphs, students need to understand what graph(s) are appropriate to represent the given data. Because all graphs cannot communicate all kinds of information, students need to understand the nature of the data being used and think about the best ways to present them visually.

Other questions cannot be easily raised without the use of graphing software—questions that concern the presentation and interpretation of data. Scaling is important in creating bar or line graphs. A scale can be used to help clarify data, to create a "message," or to provide perspective in interpreting data. As an example, students in a fifth-grade class surveyed their classmates to find out the number of hours of television each member of the class watched over a weekend (48 hours). Figure 11.4 shows two bar graphs displaying the data. In the first graph, in figure 11.4(a), the scale has been automatically set by the software. Since the maximum hours of TV watched was 8 hours, the scale range is 0–10 hours. Because several students watched no TV, in several places no bar appears. What stands out for

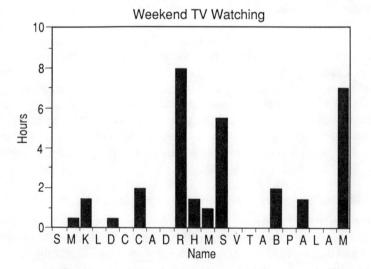

Fig. 11.4(a)

students when they first consider this graph is the three "tall" bars. The scale does not give a context for understanding what this amount of time actually means within an entire weekend. However, if the graph is rescaled for 0–48 hours (see fig. 11.4[b]), it is easier to consider the impact of TV viewing on each child's total weekend time.

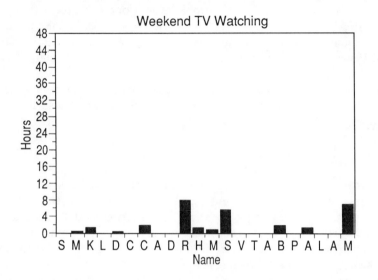

Fig. 11.4(b)

The use of graphing software permits a deeper exploration of the analysis and interpretation of data. The "what if" experimentation possible with such software permits data to be manipulated in ways not easily done by hand. Because of this capability, however, a greater understanding is required of concepts such as scaling, which have not received the attention they deserve because of "manipulation" requirements.

## MANAGING DATA ANALYSIS IN THE CLASSROOM

Although the complexity of data analysis problems offers a rich learning environment for the application and use of mathematics, they can also overwhelm students and teachers. For example, when data were collected about students' heights, the teacher found that many of the students had difficulty with the basics of linear measurement. She could not go on to the representation and interpretation of the data until they could be collected more reliably. Using demonstrations of height measurement, she led students to consider more carefully how they were making their measurements, what units they were using, and how accurate their measurements should be.

The discussion led to a more careful definition of height and an agreement on guidelines for measurement so that the data would be comparable. The class spent twice the amount of time the teacher planned on the data-collection phase of the problem, but as a result, the students grappled with two critical questions: How do you make sure the data collected are comparable? What degree of accuracy is appropriate for a given problem?

Data analysis problems are not problems that one can expect to move through step by step in an uninterrupted, linear fashion. Rather, the value of these problems lies in reflection and reevaluation made by students at many stages. However, teachers must also cope with the reality of limited class time and the management of complex activities. Although any data analysis problem can take many class sessions, we recommend that teachers balance data analysis problems with well-defined boundaries and those that are more open-ended.

## CONCLUSION

Skills in understanding and using large amounts of information are becoming increasingly important. Students need many varied experiences in collecting, describing, analyzing, presenting, and interpreting data. To address these needs, educators need to consider several issues as part of the instructional design process. In this paper, we have highlighted some of these issues, which have surfaced in our own research, to help educators begin to think about the underlying concepts and pedagogy that will produce more effective instruction.

# 12

# Developing Measurement Sense

## Jean M. Shaw
## Mary Jo Puckett Cliatt

**M**EASUREMENT is an important, useful topic that deserves a prominent role in the mathematics curriculum. Facility with measurement is valuable because people use it almost daily throughout their lives as they cook, give and receive directions, and participate in sports and hobbies. Many people also use measurement on the job.

The focus of elementary school measurement should be on the development of concepts and understanding rather than on separate and narrow skills. Students must gain insights and intuitions about measurements and the process of measuring. This emphasis promotes the development of "measurement sense," a highly useful outcome of measurement instruction.

Measurement sense has several interrelated components. Children and adults who have measurement sense have a *knowledge of the units appropriate for a task.* They have formed useful mental pictures representing measurement units. For example, mental images of units help people decide whether centimeters, meters, or kilometers are the most appropriate unit for measuring the distance from a student's home to the school. A student with good mea-  surement sense knows that although it is possible to measure such a distance in centimeters (or even millimeters), a larger unit such as meters or kilometers is easier to work with and communicate to others.

Measurement sense also involves a *knowledge of the measurement process.* Quantities are compared to standard or nonstandard units. Numbers are attached to units in the measurement process. Tools are often used: rulers, tapes, scales, clocks, thermometers, spoons, and cups are measurement tools with which elementary school children should be proficient.

Students with measurement sense have the *ability to decide when to measure and when to estimate.* When deciding how to dress for the day, most people want only a general idea of what the temperature will be. They are not ordinarily concerned with whether the temperature will be 20°C or 22°C, but rather that the temperature will be in the "low 20s." However, when someone is seriously ill, a single degree of temperature may be carefully monitored and measured.

Finally, measurement sense involves a *knowledge of strategies for estimating* lengths, temperature, volumes, masses, and time. Good estimators know several strategies and choose the one most applicable to a situation. According to Lindquist (1987), good estimators use at least three strategies: referents, chunking, and unitizing. With *referents,* a child might use a known quantity—her own weight of about 40 kilograms, for example—to estimate whether another person's mass is about the same as, greater than, or less than her own and by how much. With *chunking,* a quantity is broken into workable parts. In estimating the area of the floor of a classroom, a student might mentally break (or chunk) the area into three parts—the area of the chalkboard and the teacher's desk, the area of the students' desks, and the area of the small vestibule. The student would combine estimates of these three areas for an estimate of the total area of the room. With *unitizing,* a student divides a quantity into smaller, equal parts. To estimate the volume of a pitcher, a student might mentally divide the pitcher into "glassfuls" of 250 milliliters each, then work with the number of glassfuls to arrive at an estimate for the total volume.

Educators must teach measurement in appropriate ways. Children need repeated opportunities to work with measurement to develop the concepts and skills necessary for building measurement sense. The following introductory and follow-up activities give children chances to develop and refine their skills and deepen their understanding of measurement.

## PRINCIPLES FOR DEVELOPING MEASUREMENT SENSE

Several principles can guide educators when they work with children to develop measurement sense. These principles can help educators select a balance of measurement experiences to enhance and refine children's knowledge of measurement.

1. *Provide hands-on, "involving" experiences.* Children learn by doing. As they participate, children learn to measure rather than learn about

measuring. Hands-on experiences enhance children's mental images of measurements. As children handle and read measurement tools, they directly compare quantities to units. They see that measurements can be expressed many different ways. For example, the weight of a pencil can be described as "about 10 grams," "about 0.01 kilograms," or "much less than a kilogram."

2. *Make verbal and written language integral parts of measurement experiences.* Children must talk about what they are doing. Language complements and clarifies thought. Written records of data can be referred to and can help children keep from forgetting data. Often pairs or small groups of children can compile data and then bring this information to the entire class for discussion, comparison, and analysis. As children discuss and compare measurement results, they see that measurements can be expressed

in many different but correct ways. As they discuss their recorded data, students often pick out their own errors without an adult's prompting. For example, a group of students can weigh books of a set of encyclopedias and record their masses: 2 kg, 1.5 kg, 0.8 kg, 2 g, and 1800 g. The 2-g measurement "sticks out" as "way too little" to a group of children with a sense of what 2-g and 2-kg masses feel like.

3. *Compare and estimate, then measure.* When students routinely perform comparing and estimating steps before they measure, they are more careful with the measuring step than if they thoughtlessly pick up and use a measuring tool. Comparing and estimating take just a few moments, but they encourage thought about each problem and create interest in outcomes. These processes also develop sensitivity to the units being used and the number of units in the object being

measured. For instance, if students are using pieces of string as units for measuring the length of a work counter, they can first think about whether the string is longer or shorter than the counter. If the string is shorter, they can next try to visualize how many strings it would take to make the length of the counter. Finally, students will lay the string along the counter, each string-unit length beginning where the last one ended, and count the number of string-units in the counter.

4. *Have children make some of their own measurement tools.* Children can make inexpensive but useful measuring tools to supplement commercially made and teacher-made tools. Child-made measuring tools can also be taken home without a cumbersome check-out system for equipment. Chil-

dren usually take pride in creating and "owning" their own measuring equipment and are motivated to use them. Making tools contributes to children's measurement sense. They must decide what units are appropriate for the tool and its purpose and mark and label the tool with these units. As children make their own measuring tools, they typically handle units several times, thus increasing their familiarity with the units (Shaw 1983).

5. *Enhance home-school communication with measuring assignments.* Concerned, informed parents support school programs and contribute to their children's achievement. Creative homework activities are opportunities for building home-school communication and for strengthening measurement sense. For instance, third graders might use measuring tapes they have made to estimate, then measure, the lengths of family members' feet. The next day at school the children can report the different lengths, compare and order them, and find total lengths for their families. The ranges of foot lengths will probably be wide and generate much discussion!

MY FAMILY'S FEET

| person | estimate | actual length |
|--------|----------|---------------|
| Mama | 20cm | 25cm |
| Jorge | 16cm | 12cm |
| Juanita | 5cm | 7cm |
| Me! | 20cm | 24cm |

by Pacita

## ACTIVITIES TO DEVELOP MEASUREMENT SENSE

The following activities offer different types of measurement experiences and incorporate some or all of the suggested principles for teaching measurement. Because they are versatile and flexible, these activities can be adapted for different settings and levels.

- *"Show me" lengths.* Children with strong mental images of lengths can demonstrate different lengths with their hands. Practice with several "show me" activities will help to strengthen mental images in children who have trouble visualizing lengths. A kindergarten or first-grade teacher might show the children a new pencil, then "hide" the pencil and have the children illustrate how long it was. She can bring the pencil back out and let the children "check" the lengths they showed. Next she might ask that children show the length of a new crayon, their own shoe, or other familiar objects. Many sixth graders will be able to deal with "show me" tasks involving fractional parts and conversions: "Show me 0.3 meter," "Show me 0.5 of a meter," "Show me 80 millimeters," for example. The sixth graders can verify lengths by looking at the ruler. As students work with "show me," it is OK for those who are less secure to look at their classmates' hands for guidance. Observing classmates' answers is a legitimate way of verifying or modifying one's own answers during a practice session.

• *How many smaller ones make a larger one?* This versatile question prompts many different investigations. Kindergartners and first graders might explore the question at a "waterplay table" using small containers to fill a larger one. They might also make investigations using a balance scale and classroom objects. For example, young children can try to see how many crayons balance a pair of scissors. Second or third graders might use a fishing pole with a magnet for bait to catch paper fish with pins or paper clips attached to them. They could see how many fish make a meter length. Elementary students of any age might work with

several sizes of plastic containers and see how many smaller ones will fill a larger one. Pouring water or "solid fluids," such as sand, cornmeal, or birdseed, from one container to the other to verify estimates makes this a sensory, motivating activity. Teachers can challenge children to make their own problems and solve them by manipulating physical objects and tools.

• *Body measurements.* Making body measurements is appealing because the process is so personalized. Children can use body parts as nonstandard measures or can relate body parts to standard measures. Young children can "step off" the lengths of such classroom objects as rugs or chalkboards by using their feet as handy nonstandard units of measurement.

Children may have read about how ancient peoples used the length of a forearm as a measurement unit called a cubit. They might investigate to see whether a distance like 20 cubits is longer than their chalkboard, shorter, or about the same length. Children can compare 20-cubit distances laid out by several classmates and see the slight variations due to differences in the lengths of arms. To enhance mental images of standard measures of length, children can find body parts that are close to 1 centimeter, 1 decimeter, or 1 meter. These images will vary; 1 meter may be about the distance from the floor to the waist of one fifth grader but "hit" a shorter classmate in the middle of the chest.

An intriguing project for children of almost any age is recording different body measurements in a "Metric Me" booklet (Shaw 1984). The booklet can be just two to four pages. Each child can record  estimates and actual measures of such vital statistics as height, mass, head circumference, the length of a smile and the length of a "serious" mouth, axillary body temperature, and the length of a foot. After individual measurements are made, the children might also examine a single measurement such as foot length. They can pool their measurements, order them, see the range, and pick the median of the set of data. Older children can figure the mean length on their calculators. Each child can compare his or her foot length to the mean: Is it close to the mean? Longer? Shorter? By how much?

Interesting comparisons can emerge from body measurements. Children might work in groups to investigate questions such as these:

How does the length of an upper arm compare to that of a lower arm?

How does the length of a lower arm compare to a person's foot?

How does a person's arm span compare to height?

- *Scavenger hunts.* In this activity children find objects that fit given categories. A teacher might start by asking young children to find something on the playground that is longer than their hands or heavier than a rock. The children can compare and perhaps order all the objects they bring back. Second graders might cut out ten-centimeter-long strips of paper and "scavenge" at home for five objects each about a decimeter long. The objects can be displayed on a "sharing table" in the classroom. Fifth graders might work in groups to find, estimate, and then measure temperatures in ten different locations in the school on a temperature scavenger hunt. Scavenger hunts either with verbal instructions or with a list of items to collect are versatile, involving, and fun!

- *Seasonal measurements.* To keep measurement skills alive throughout the year and to quantify the observations that children routinely  make, teachers can make use of seasonal measurements, which can be interesting and valuable. For instance, children might record and compare indoor and outdoor temperatures for a week at the beginning of school, in mid-winter, and in early spring. They can measure and weigh fall fruits and vegetables that are available. Cooking seasonal dishes is always a popular activity and enhances children's understanding of measures of volume: as they prepare foods like whipped topping or popcorn, they can see dramatic changes in volumes. Children might also compare the masses (weights) of food before and after cooking.

For other seasonal activities, children might make measurements as they construct geometric and free-form shapes for decorations for a holiday tree or a bare branch. (Of course they would estimate and measure the height of the tree or the length of the branch, too.) Children might estimate and measure the lengths and widths of several Valentine cards, then pursue different strategies to get "good" answers for their areas. As spring growth emerges or after children plant seeds, they can keep track of the heights of new plants. Alert teachers will find many seasonal opportunities to develop and reinforce measurement sense and to encourage parents to engage in measurement activities at home.

## BIBLIOGRAPHY

Lindquist, Mary Montgomery. "Estimation and Mental Computation: Measurement." *Arithmetic Teacher* 34 (January 1987): 16–17.

Shaw, Jean M. "IDEAS." *Arithmetic Teacher* 32 (December 1984): 20–24.

———. "Let's Do It: Student-made Measuring Tools." *Arithmetic Teacher* 31 (November 1983): 12–15.

Trimble, Harold C. "Teaching about 'About.'" In *A Metric Handbook for Teachers,* edited by Jon L. Higgins, pp. 100–104. Reston, Va.: National Council of Teachers of Mathematics, 1974.

# 13

# Teaching about Fractions: What, When, and How?

Nadine Bezuk
Kathleen Cramer

L EARNING about fractions is one of the most difficult tasks for middle and junior high school children. The results of the third National Assessment of Educational Progress (NAEP) show an apparent lack of understanding of fractions by nine-, thirteen-, and seventeen-year-olds. "The performance on fractional computation was low, and students seem to have done their computation with little understanding" (Lindquist et al. 1983, p. 16). Similar trends were observed in the first, the second, and the recently completed fourth National Assessments (Carpenter et al. 1978, 1980; Post 1981; Dossey et al. 1988). Even though operations on fractions are taught as early as grade 4, the second NAEP showed that only 35 percent of the thirteen-year-olds could correctly answer the test item $3/4 + 1/2$.

The difficulty children have with fractions should not be surprising considering the complexity of the concepts involved. Children must adopt new rules for fractions that often conflict with well-established ideas about whole numbers. For example, when ordering fractions with like numerators, children learn that $1/3$ is less than $1/2$. With whole numbers, however, 3 is greater than 2. When comparing fractions of this type, children need to coordinate the inverse relationship between the size of the denominator and the size of the fraction. They need to realize that if a pie is divided into three equal parts, each piece will be smaller than when a pie of the same size is divided into two equal parts. With fractions, the *more* pieces, the *smaller* the size of each piece.

---

The preparation of this article was supported in part by the National Science Foundation (NSF DPE 84-70077). Any opinions, findings, conclusions, and recommendations are those of the authors and do not necessarily reflect the views of the National Science Foundation.

Another difficulty is that the rules for ordering fractions with like numerators do not apply to fractions with like denominators. In this situation, children can use their already learned ideas about counting. For example, a student might reason that the fraction 5/7 is greater than 2/7 because 5 is greater than 2.

When adding or subtracting fractions, children may have ideas about whole numbers that conflict with their ideas about fractions. An estimation item from the second NAEP reveals this phenomenon. Students were asked to estimate the answer to 12/13 + 7/8. The choices were 1, 2, 19, 21, and "I don't know." Only 24 percent of the thirteen-year-olds responding chose the correct answer, 2. Fifty-five percent of the thirteen-year-olds selected 19 or 21—they added either the numerators or the denominators. These students seem to be operating on the fractions without any mental referents to aid their reasoning.

Clearly, the way fractions are taught must be improved. Because of the complexity of fraction concepts, more time should be allocated in the curriculum for developing students' understanding of fractions. But just more time is not sufficient to improve understanding; the emphasis of instruction should also shift from the development of algorithms for performing operations on fractions to the development of a quantitative understanding of fractions. For example, instruction should enable children to reason that the sum of 12/13 and 7/8 is about 2 because 12/13 is almost 1 and 7/8 is almost 1. Children should be able to reason that 1/2 + 1/3 cannot equal 2/5 because 2/5 is smaller than 1/2 and the sum must be bigger than either addend. Further, they should realize that 3/7 is less than 5/9 not because of a rule but because they know that 3/7 is less than 1/2 and 5/9 is greater than 1/2. Students who are able to reason in this way have a quantitative understanding of fractions.

To think quantitatively about fractions, students should know something about the relative size of fractions. They should be able to order fractions with the same denominators or same numerators as well as to judge if a fraction is greater than or less than 1/2. They should know the equivalents of 1/2 and other familiar fractions. The acquisition of a quantitative understanding of fractions is based on students' experiences with physical models and on instruction that emphasizes meaning rather than procedures.

This chapter presents suggestions for changes in the content and pace of instruction to help children develop both a quantitative understanding of, and skill in operating with, fractions. Specific suggestions are presented for what, when, and how fractions should be taught.

## RECOMMENDATIONS FOR CHANGE

Many current textbooks introduce fraction concepts as early as grade 2, though the main work on them begins in grade 4. The scope and sequence of the topic in grades 4, 5, and 6 are remarkably similar. The naming of fractions and the ideas of order and equivalence are briefly presented at each grade level; the most instructional time is allocated to operations with fractions. Addition and subtraction of fractions with like and unlike denominators are initially taught in grade 4 and repeated in grades 5 and 6. Multiplication and division of fractions are introduced in grade 5 and repeated in grade 6.

The result of this repetitious scope and sequence is that none of the topics is taught well. We suggest that by postponing most operations with fractions at the symbolic level until grade 6 and using instructional time in grades 4 and 5 to develop fraction concepts and the ideas of order and equivalence, teachers will find that their students will be more successful with all aspects of operations with fractions and will have a stronger quantitative understanding of them.

We shall present our recommendations in two ways: (*a*) general recommendations applicable to instruction at all grade levels and (*b*) specific changes for the primary and intermediate grades.

### General Recommendations

1. The use of manipulatives is crucial in developing students' understanding of fraction ideas. Manipulatives help students construct mental referents that enable them to perform fraction tasks meaningfully. Therefore, manipulatives should be used at each grade level to introduce all components of the curriculum on fractions. Manipulatives can include these models: fractional parts of circles, Cuisenaire rods, paper-folding activities, and counters (see fig. 13.1).

2. The proper development of concepts and relationships among fractions is essential if students are to perform and understand operations on fractions. The majority of instructional time before grade 6 should be devoted to developing these important notions.

3. Operations on fractions should be delayed until concepts and the ideas of the order and equivalence of fractions are firmly established. Delaying work with operations will allow the necessary time for work on concepts.

4. The size of denominators used in computational exercises should be limited to the numbers 12 and below.

### Specific Recommendations

*Primary grades.* The major purpose of initial fraction-concept activities is to offer students experiences that will allow them to develop strong mental images of fractions. These images are the basis for quantitative understanding. Specific suggestions for early experiences with manipulatives in the primary grades are listed below.

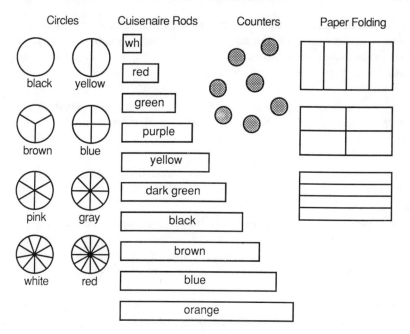

Fig. 13.1. Fraction manipulatives

1. Instruction should be based on the part-whole concept using first the continuous model (circles, paper folding) and then the discrete model (counters). The discrete model should be introduced by relating it to the circles.

2. Include activities that ask students to name fractions represented by physical models and diagrams. Unit and nonunit fractions with denominators no larger than 8 should be used. Also include activities that ask students to model or draw pictures for fraction names or symbols.

3. Use words (three-fourths) initially and then introduce symbols (3/4).

4. Introduce "concept of unit" activities, that is, activities in which students name fractions when the unit is varied. For example, with the fraction circles in figure 13.1, state that each yellow piece is 1, rather than having the whole circle as the unit. Then ask students the value of the other pieces.

*Intermediate grades.* If the abstraction of fraction operations proceeds too quickly, the result may be a rote application of rules. Algorithms for the addition and subtraction of fractions with unlike denominators and the multiplication and division of fractions should be postponed until grade 6. Instruction in grades 4 and 5 should extend students' concepts of fractions, establish intuitive ordering strategies, and develop the idea of equivalent fractions. More specific suggestions for experiences with fractions in the intermediate grades are listed below.

1. Fraction-concept activities from the primary grades can include fractions with denominators no larger than 12 and problem-solving activities that extend students' concept of unit. For example, if a blue circular piece is called 1/3, then students can be asked to find the value of other circular pieces.

2. Fraction concepts can also be extended to new physical models (number lines or Cuisenaire rods) and to a new interpretation (e.g., the quotient model—3 pizzas shared by 4 people).

3. Activities for generating equivalent fractions should be introduced with manipulatives, then with diagrams. In particular, equivalent forms of such common fractions as 1/2, 1/3, 1/4, and 3/4 should be stressed, with the greatest emphasis placed on 1/2.

4. Comparisons of fractions with like denominators (2/7 and 3/7) and like numerators (2/4 and 2/8) should be developed with manipulatives. Children should be able to verbalize a rule for ordering fractions with like numerators that does not rely on changing them to equivalent fractions with like denominators.

5. Ordering pairs of fractions by comparing them to 1/2 or 1 should be included. For example, 3/10 is less than 2/3 because 3/10 is less than 1/2 and 2/3 is greater than 1/2. (Notice that although this pair of fractions has unlike numerators and unlike denominators, an ordering decision can be made without finding equivalent fractions with the same denominator).

6. The initial goal of instruction for addition and subtraction of fractions should be to model these operations with manipulatives and diagrams. Instruction should emphasize estimation and judging the reasonableness of answers.

7. Addition and subtraction of fractions at the symbolic level is appropriate in grade 6. Multiplication and division of fractions can also be introduced, but the goal should not be to calculate the answer, since it can easily be obtained using whole number ideas, with no conceptual understanding. Children should demonstrate an understanding of multiplication and division by modeling a problem with manipulatives or by naming the problem for the manipulative model. Students should be able to create story problems for a multiplication or division sentence or write a multiplication or division sentence for a story problem.

Specific teaching activities for some of the suggested curricular changes conclude this chapter. The activities are in three categories: (*a*) the concept of unit, (*b*) ordering, and (*c*) addition of fractions.

### How to Teach Fractions

*Concepts and ordering.* As previously stated, an understanding of fraction concepts and order and equivalence relations is a prerequisite for success in computation with fractions. Behr, Lesh, Post, and Silver (1983) recommend using a variety of manipulatives to develop fraction concepts. The use of more than one manipulative enhances students' understanding and promotes abstraction of the concept from irrelevant perceptual features of a manipulative, such as color, size, or shape.

The following topics should be included in the teaching of fraction concepts, order, and equivalence: (*a*) modeling fractional amounts with more than one manipulative and naming unit and nonunit fractions; (*b*) generating equivalent fractions; (*c*) performing concept-of-unit activities; (*d*) ordering fractions. The following section describes sample activities for the last two topics. Post and Cramer (1987) and Bezuk (1988) present examples of activities for modeling fractions and generating equivalent fractions.

## Concept-of-Unit Activities

Concept-of-unit activities require students to name fractional parts when the unit is varied. These activities strengthen their understanding of fraction concepts and reinforce mental images created in introductory activities with manipulatives. Figure 13.2 shows examples of activities with circles, counters, and Cuisenaire rods; in each case students are asked to name the fractions as the whole unit varies.

Teachers can extend concept-of-unit activities by including more difficult questions in which children are asked to reconstruct the whole given a unit or

---

A. Use fraction circles to solve these problems:

The black circle is 1. What is the value of each of these pieces?

　　　　1 blue　　　3 grays　　　1 pink　　　3 yellows

(Change the unit: The yellow piece is 1. Now what is the value of those pieces?)

B. Use counters to solve these problems:

Eight counters equal 1. What is the value of each of these sets of counters?

　　　　1 counter　　　2 counters　　　4 counters　　　6 counters

(Change the unit: Four counters equal 1. Now what is the value of those sets of counters?)

C. Use Cuisenaire rods to solve these problems:

The green Cuisenaire rod equals 1. What is the value of each of these rods?

　　　　red　　　black　　　white　　　dark green

(Change the unit: The dark green rod is 1. Now what is the value of those rods?)

---

Fig. 13.2. Concept-of-Unit Activities

nonunit fraction. For example, if the blue circular piece is 1/2, what is the value of one pink piece? Or, if six counters equal 3/5, what is the value of two counters?

These questions reinforce the idea that, for example, two halves equal one whole, three thirds equal one whole, and so on. They also reinforce the notion that nonunit fractions are iterations of unit fractions (3/5 = 1/5 + 1/5 + 1/5).

## Ordering

Many pairs of fractions can be compared without using a formal algorithm, such as finding a common denominator or changing each fraction to a decimal. Children need informal ordering schemes to estimate fractions quickly or to judge the reasonableness of answers. They can be led to discover these relationships if they have had experiences in constructing mental images of fractions. Figure 13.3 shows four categories of fractions that can be compared without a formal algorithm.

---

1. Pairs of fractions with like denominators:
       1/4 and 3/4           3/5 and 4/5

2. Pairs of fractions with like numerators:
       1/3 and 1/2           2/5 and 2/3

3. Pairs of fractions that are on opposite sides of 1/2 or 1:
       3/7 and 5/9           3/11 and 11/3

4. Pairs of fractions that have the same number of pieces less than one whole:
       2/3 and 3/4           3/5 and 6/8

---

Fig. 13.3. Comparing fractions with mental images

The first two types of comparison problems are fairly straightforward when developed with manipulatives. Children have more difficulty with the second category because of the inverse relationship between the number of pieces the whole is divided into and the size of the denominator. Manipulatives are crucial in the development of an understanding of this relationship.

The last two categories of ordering problems were described to the authors by fourth-grade students who had used manipulatives to learn fraction concepts for several weeks. These strategies were not taught to the students and seemed to be self-generated. The fact that the students could create these two ordering procedures clearly demonstrates the power of using manipulatives to develop quantitative understanding of fractions.

The fractions in the third category are on "opposite sides" of a comparison point. Students order such fractions by comparing each to a known fraction, such as 1/2, and combining these results to make a final decision. One fourth-grade student compared 3/7 and 5/9 in the following manner (Roberts 1985): "Three-sevenths is less. It doesn't cover half the unit. Five-ninths covers over half." Notice that the child's reasoning is based on an internal image constructed for fractions.

The last type of comparison problem concerns pairs of fractions for which the difference between the numerator and denominator is the same. These pairs can be compared by determining how much less than a whole each fraction is. The remaining portion of the whole will represent fractions with the same numerator. Students then compare these fractions and reverse their decision for the answer. A fourth-grade student compared 6/8 and 3/5 in this way (Roberts 1985): "Six-eighths is greater. When you look at it, then you have six of them, and there'd be only two pieces left. And then if they're smaller pieces like, it wouldn't have very much space left in it, and it would cover up a lot more. Now here [3/5] the pieces are bigger, and if you have three of them you would still have two big ones left. So it would be less."

All four types of comparison problems can readily be solved with mental images developed by using manipulatives. Figures 13.4 and 13.5 present

---

*Exploring fractions with the same denominators*

Use circular pieces. The whole circle is the unit.

A. Show 1/4.          B. Show 3/4.

Are the pieces the same size? _____
How many pieces did you use to show 1/4? _____
How many pieces did you use to show 3/4? _____
Which fraction is larger? _____

---

*Exploring fractions with the same numerator*

Use your circular pieces. The whole circle is the unit. Take out the pieces listed in each problem; then answer the questions.

| Pieces | How many cover 1 whole circle? | Which color takes more pieces to cover 1 whole? | Which color has the smaller pieces? |
|---|---|---|---|
| 1. Brown | 3 | | |
| Pink | 6 | √ | √ |
| 2. Blue | | | |
| Yellow | | | |

Fig. 13.4. Activities for ordering fractions

*Comparing fractions to 1/2 or 1*

Use circular pieces. The whole circle is the unit.

A. Show 2/3.          B. Show 1/4.

Which fraction covers more than one-half of the circle? _____

Which fraction covers less than one-half of the circle? _____

Which fraction is larger? _____

Compare these fraction pairs in the same way.

| 2/8  3/5 | | 1/3  5/6 | | 3/2  2/3 |
|---|---|---|---|---|

*Comparing fractions by deciding how close each fraction is to 1*

Use your circular pieces. The whole circuit is the unit. Take out the pieces listed in each problem, then answer the questions.

| Pieces | How much more is needed to make 1 whole? | Which piece is bigger? | Which display shows more? |
|---|---|---|---|
| 2/3 | 1/3 | √ | |
| 3/4 | 1/4 | | √ |
| 4/5 | | | |
| 6/8 | | | |

Fig. 13.5. More activities for ordering fractions

ordering activities by which teachers can lead students to discover rules for ordering fractions.

## Addition of Fractions

The initial goal for instruction on operations with fractions should be to have pupils add and subtract fractions using a manipulative. Fraction circles are excellent materials for modeling the addition and subtraction of fractions. An addition problem with like denominators, $1/6 + 4/6$, for example, can be demonstrated like this: One pink piece (1/6) can be placed on the unit circle, followed by four pink pieces (4/6). The sum is represented by the fraction of the whole circle that is covered.

To add fractions with unlike denominators, children should understand why both fractions are converted to those with like denominators. To demonstrate this idea, first model sums of fractions with unlike denominators using fractions that have equivalences that students already know. For example, model $1/2 + 1/4$ by placing a yellow piece and blue piece on a unit circle. Children can easily see that three-fourths of the circle is covered. To discuss the need for a common denominator, ask such questions as "How is this problem different from adding fractions like 1/8 + 5/8?" "How can you know for sure that 3/4 is covered if the circle has two different colored pieces on it?" "Can you show an equivalent problem using pieces of the same color?"

Whether they are adding fractions with like or unlike denominators, it is important to have students estimate the size of the sum before they model the problem with manipulatives. Such questions as "Is the answer greater than 1/2 or less than 1/2?" "Greater than 1 or less than 1?" force children to think quantitatively about fractions. To answer these questions, students can draw on their earlier use of manipulatives in naming and ordering fractions.

Reflecting on a frequently given incorrect sum is also important. For example, by asking if the sum of 1/6 and 4/6 could be 5/12, which is less than 1/2, the teacher can make students aware of the unreasonableness of adding numerators and denominators. With the concrete experiences recommended here, a student should be able to respond that since 5/12 is less than 1/2, it cannot be the correct answer. This observation is correct, since one of the addends (4/6) is greater than 1/2. Notice how a student giving this response uses the ordering strategies developed previously.

The next step in finding the sums of fractions with unlike denominators is to use pairs of fractions whose sums are more difficult to see from the model, for example, 1/3 + 3/6 or 1/3 + 1/4. The steps for modeling the sum of 1/3 and 1/4 with circular pieces are described below:

Estimate the answer first: "Is the answer greater than 1/2? Less than 1/2? Greater than 1? Less than 1?" Now demonstrate the problem with the circular pieces: place the blue piece and the brown piece in the unit circle and reflect on the accuracy of the estimates. Now ask, "Can you show 1/4 as an equivalent fraction using the brown pieces? Can you show 1/3 as an equivalent fraction with the blue pieces?" Since neither fraction can be shown with the other color, set aside time for students to use the circular pieces to find all the fractions equal to 1/4 and all those equal to 1/3 until they find one color that they can use to show both 1/4 and 1/3. Figure 13.6 illustrates this procedure.

By laying the pieces side by side, children can see that both 1/4 and 1/3 can be shown with the red pieces. One blue (1/4) equals three reds (3/12); one brown (1/3) equals four reds (4/12). Exchanges can be made with the circular pieces and the sum found.

Students should also reflect on why 2/7 is an unreasonable answer to this problem. They should be given opportunities to solve many sums with the circular pieces. When students are ready for work at the symbolic level, teachers can help them see the link between their physical actions with the fraction circles and the algorithm they will be taught.

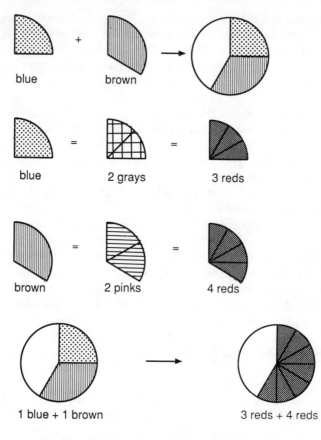

Fig. 13.6. Using fraction circles to model 1/3 + 1/4

## CONCLUSION

We encourage teachers and schools to implement more appropriate objectives for teaching fractions in elementary school. We encourage teachers to use an instructional approach that emphasizes student involvement, the use of manipulatives, and the development of understanding before beginning work with formal symbols and operations.

### REFERENCES

Behr, Merlyn J., Richard Lesh, Thomas R. Post, and Edward A. Silver. "Rational Number Concepts." In *Acquisition of Mathematics Concepts and Processes,* edited by Richard Lesh and Marsha Landau, pp. 91–126. New York: Academic Press, 1983.

Bezuk, Nadine S. "Fractions in the Early Childhood Mathematics Curriculum." *Arithmetic Teacher* 35 (February 1988): 56–61.

Carpenter, Thomas P., Terrence G. Coburn, Robert E. Reys, James W. Wilson, and Mary Kay Corbitt. *Results of the First Mathematics Assessment of the National Assessment of Educational Progress.* Reston, Va.: National Council of Teachers of Mathematics, 1978.

Carpenter, Thomas P., Mary Kay Corbitt, Henry S. Kepner, Mary Montgomery Lindquist, and Robert E. Reys. "Results of the Second NAEP Mathematics Assessment: Elementary School." *Arithmetic Teacher* 27 (April 1980): 10–12, 44–47.

Dossey, John A., Ina V. S. Mullis, Mary M. Lindquist, and Donald L. Chambers. *The Mathematics Report Card: Are We Measuring Up? Trends and Achievement Based on the 1986 National Assessment.* Princeton, N.J.: Educational Testing Service, 1988.

Lindquist, Mary Montgomery, Thomas P. Carpenter, Edward A. Silver, and Westina Matthews. "The Third National Mathematics Assessment: Results and Implications for Elementary and Middle Schools." *Arithmetic Teacher* 31 (December 1983): 14–19.

Post, Thomas R. "Fractions: Results and Implications from National Assessment." *Arithmetic Teacher* 28 (May 1981): 26–31.

Post, Thomas R., and Kathleen Cramer. "Research into Practice: Children's Strategies in Ordering Rational Numbers." *Arithmetic Teacher* 35 (October 1987): 33–35.

Roberts, Mary Pat. "A Clinical Analysis of Fourth- and Fifth-Grade Students' Understandings about Order and Equivalence of Rational Numbers." Master's thesis, University of Minnesota, 1985.

# 14

# The Calculator as a Tool for Instruction and Learning

## Barbara J. Reys

**M** UCH has been written and said about the role of the calculator in the mathematics classroom. A great deal of the research conducted on this topic for the past fifteen years has been narrowly focused. The situation is aptly described by Hembree and Dessart (1986, p. 84): "Much research has focused on the likelihood of [calculators] harming basic skills, but little effort has been accorded to *enhancing* student achievement through a systematic use of calculators." Today, however, research, professional dialogue, and classroom practice are beginning to shift to questions regarding the role of the calculator in teaching, learning, and assessment—most important, how does the use of a calculator as a computational tool alter curricular emphasis and teaching methods?

## CHANGES IN TEACHING METHODS

This article will explore changes in teaching approaches and methods associated with using calculators. The changes in curricular emphasis associated with calculator use are explored in Coburn's discussion elsewhere in this yearbook (see chapter 4). The basic premise of this discussion is that *using the calculator as a computational tool provides teachers and students the time necessary to focus student effort and concentration on conceptual understanding and critical thinking.* Several activities will illustrate ways in which calculator use can help attain this new focus.

### Focusing on Conceptual Understanding and Critical Thinking

Suppose you are a fifth-grade teacher. Your mathematics objective for the day's lesson is to introduce the concept of *mean*. In the past, when paper and pencil were the only available computational tools, students spent a considerable amount of time adding lists of numbers and then dividing to find the mean. Because of the amount of time and energy spent on the calculation (and searching for errors), attention was often distracted from the objective. Consider the difference the calculator can make: since all the computation can be performed on a calculator, the students can concentrate on the concept rather than the tedious computation. Students will still make computational errors (often keystroking errors), but doing the calculations over again is not a chore, not something the students are unwilling to do. For a teacher, this approach provides the additional time needed to bring meaning to the concept and helps retain students' interest in the concept. For example, a greater variety of examples and different kinds of data can be considered, and more realistic data sets can be examined. Original data can be generated by the class and explored (e.g., What is the average height of students in the class? The average family size? The average home team basketball score?). The focus of attention in this example is directed at understanding the concept of mean rather than simply computing the mean.

Many other topics and concepts can be more effectively dealt with by allowing the calculation to be done by a calculator—percents, the manipulation of formulas, and problem solving are only a few. Traditionally, each of these topics is troublesome. They are acknowledged to be "tough to teach" by most veteran teachers because, to some extent, of the level of computation involved. It should be stressed that simply allowing students to use calculators will not solve all the problems. Indeed, each of these topics is complex and takes some time to develop fully. The strength of the calculator is that it focuses student attention directly on the concept.

## Developing Topics in New Ways

The calculator's computational power also *allows the teacher to approach and develop topics in new ways.* For example, consider a topic from the intermediate grades—the area of a triangle. Suppose you, the teacher, have developed the formula for finding the area of a triangle. You want your students to have practice using the formula with a variety of types of triangles. Consider, then, activity 1 (fig. 14.1). The principal instructional features of this activity are as follows:

- Students practice using the formula (they use the formula three times for the same triangle).
- Students have an opportunity to use measuring skills (which highlights the efficiency of the metric system).
- Accuracy in measure is rewarded (the three approximations of area will be only as close as the accuracy of each measure).
- The meaning of base and height in a triangle is reinforced.
- A discussion of the notion of error in measurement is permitted.

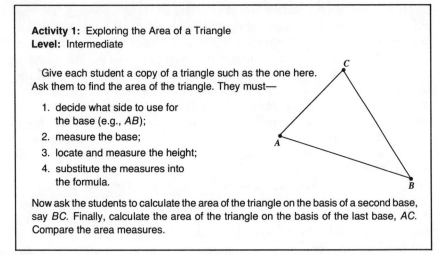

**Activity 1:** Exploring the Area of a Triangle
**Level:** Intermediate

Give each student a copy of a triangle such as the one here.
Ask them to find the area of the triangle. They must—

1. decide what side to use for
   the base (e.g., *AB*);
2. measure the base;
3. locate and measure the height;
4. substitute the measures into
   the formula.

Now ask the students to calculate the area of the triangle on the basis of a second base,
say *BC*. Finally, calculate the area of the triangle on the basis of the last base, *AC*.
Compare the area measures.

Fig. 14.1

This activity is enhanced by using the calculator to do the computation. In fact, the calculator actually promotes more careful measuring (it wouldn't pay to measure too precisely if the calculations had to be done by hand!). Again, the calculator is used as a tool so that more time and effort can be engaged in other important features of the concept. It is true that this activity could be done without a calculator, but the whole point would be lost— students would spend a majority of their time doing tedious computation. Using the calculator frees them to explore, compare, and experience.

### Exploring Problem-solving Strategies

The calculator also *promotes the natural exploration of problem-solving strategies and the application of intuitive processes.* The following problem was recently given to a sixth-grade class:

> I now have $63.00. I plan to save $7.00 a week. In how many weeks will I have enough money to buy a $175.00 used motorcycle?

The intent was to impress on the students that even though they had a calculator to help them, the real problem solving would have to be done by them before using the calculator. It was anticipated that students would use a standard approach to this problem: subtract 63 from 175 to determine how much was needed and then divide by 7 to determine the number of weeks. As the approaches to this problem were being discussed, it became obvious that many students had used a different approach, one that the calculator made easily available. One student described his solution process this way:

"I entered 63 into the calculator, then pressed + 7 =. Then I just kept pressing = [adding 7s] until I reached 175, counting the number of 7s [weeks] it took." In this instance the calculator allowed the student to explore an approach that was intuitively obvious to him.

## Generating Data

*The power of the calculator to generate many examples quickly can help students develop conceptual understanding.*

In much the same way that primary-grade children develop an understanding of whole numbers through a variety of counting activities, middle-grade children should also explore decimals through counting activities. For example, most inexpensive calculators have a constant addend feature, which is used in activity 2 (see fig. 14.2).

---

**Activity 2:** Counting with Decimals
**Level:** Intermediate

Ask students to key in 0 + .1 and then continue to press the equal (=) key, naming each number before it appears (e.g., "one-tenth, two-tenths, three-tenths, etc.). Notice what happens when they reach 0.9—what is next? Many students will say "ten-tenths." Take this opportunity to highlight the different forms of ten-tenths (as a fraction and in its efficient decimal form of 1). Have students continue this counting aloud as they bridge several whole numbers.

Next, ask them to count by hundredths (0.01) and name each number displayed. Which is faster, counting by tenths to 10 or counting by hundredths to 1?

---

Fig. 14.2

The principal instructional features of this activity are as follows:

• The relationship among 0.01, 0.1, and 1 is reinforced.
• An opportunity is given for students to get quick feedback on each number named.
• The opportunity is given to see patterns in the base-ten system as well as "hear" these patterns.

The calculator's ability to provide quick feedback can help students develop an understanding of multiplication when one factor is near 1. The objective of the game of TARGET (see fig. 14.3) is to help students understand what happens when a number is multiplied by a number near 1 (either more than or less than 1). Only one calculator is needed—an overhead calculator is especially effective.

Activity 3 takes only a few minutes, students enjoy it, and they learn

**Activity 3:** Exploring Factors near 1
**Level:** Intermediate

Give students a target range—for example, **2000–2100**—and a start value—say, **36.**

Enter 36 into the calculator, press ×, and ask for a volunteer to estimate a factor that when multiplied by 36 will produce a product within the target range. Here's an example of how the game might go:

Try 60 . . . 36 × 60 = 2160—just over the target range.

Students must now work with the new display, 2160. What number can be multiplied by 2160 to produce a product (display) in the target range?

Try 0.9 . . . 2160 × 0.9 = 1944—just under the target range.

Students must now work with the new display, 1944. What number can be multiplied by 1944 to produce a product in the target range?

Try 1.05 . . . 1944 × 1.05 = 2041.2. That did it!

Fig. 14.3. The TARGET game

valuable ideas about numbers around 1 and how they affect the multiplication of whole numbers.

*The calculator can quickly generate data to be studied.* The constant addend feature of the calculator can be used in activity 4 by primary-grade teachers to study patterns and begin the development of the notion of multiples (fig. 14.4).

**Activity 4:** Patterns in Skip Counting
**Level:** Primary

Give each student or pair of students a calculator and a recording sheet with a set of four hundred-charts on it. Students use the constant addend feature of their calculator to skip count by 2s, 3s, 4s, and 5s (or whatever number the teacher chooses). For each count, the numbers displayed are recorded on one of the hundred-charts. The sample here shows the pattern of skip counting by 4s.

| 0 | 1 | 2 | 3 | 4 | 5 | 6 | 7 | 8 | 9 |
|---|---|---|---|---|---|---|---|---|---|
| 10 | 11 | 12 | 13 | 14 | 15 | 16 | 17 | 18 | 19 |
| 20 | 21 | 22 | 23 | 24 | 25 | 26 | 27 | 28 | 29 |
| 30 | 31 | 32 | 33 | 34 | 35 | 36 | 37 | 38 | 39 |
| 40 | 41 | 42 | 43 | 44 | 45 | 46 | 47 | 48 | 49 |
| 50 | 51 | 52 | 53 | 54 | 55 | 56 | 57 | 58 | 59 |
| 60 | 61 | 62 | 63 | 64 | 65 | 66 | 67 | 68 | 69 |
| 70 | 71 | 72 | 73 | 74 | 75 | 76 | 77 | 78 | 79 |
| 80 | 81 | 82 | 83 | 84 | 85 | 86 | 87 | 88 | 89 |
| 90 | 91 | 92 | 93 | 94 | 95 | 96 | 97 | 98 | 99 |

Fig. 14.4

When a hundred-chart is completed, the teacher can direct attention to the different patterns highlighted on the chart. One idea for extending this activity is to have students record counting patterns for 3s in yellow and 4s in blue. When completed, which numbers are colored green (a combination of yellow and blue)? What patterns are represented in these green numbers?

Another example of how the calculator helps in exploring a concept by generating many examples is in the development of the concept of square root. Consider activity 5 in figure 14.5.

---

**Activity 5:** Developing the Concept of Square Root
**Level:** Intermediate

Using a simple calculator (preferably one without a square root key), ask students to find the square root of 7569. Students are to "guess and test" until they find the square root. Encourage them also to estimate and use any clues available to them (e.g., since the ones digit is 9, if the square root is an integer value, it must have a ones digit of 3 or 7).

---

Fig. 14.5

Students will likely make several attempts before finding the square root. This exploration is valuable and serves to reinforce the concept. For example, every time a guess is tested, the value will have to be entered into the calculator and multiplied by itself, thereby reinforcing what a square root is.

## SUMMARY

The calculator offers teachers and students a rich learning aid. Its potential is great and as yet untapped both in developing concepts and in developing positive attitudes and persistence in problem solving. As stated in NCTM's *Curriculum and Evaluation Standards for School Mathematics,* "the thoughtful and creative use of calculators greatly improves the quality of the curriculum and the quality of children's learning" (1987, p. 21). We must not lose sight of our primary goal in teaching mathematics: to develop conceptual understanding of mathematical ideas. The calculator can help us achieve this goal if we take advantage of its computational power.

### REFERENCES

Hembree, Ray, and Donald J. Dessart. "Effects of Hand-held Calculators in Precollege Mathematics Education: A Meta-Analysis." *Journal for Research in Mathematics Education* 17 (March 1986): 83–99.

National Council of Teachers of Mathematics. *Curriculum and Evaluation Standards for School Mathematics.* Working Draft. Reston, Va.: The Council, 1987.

# CHILDREN WRITE ABOUT MATHEMATICS

*Submitted by Marilyn Burns*

Grace Rubenstein
June 8 1988 ①

What I Learned
This Year in Math
I learned that math is
not just numbers. It is life.
The reason I say that
is because math can be made
from anything; art, music, clothes
clothes, ice cream, even the
ceiling. I could go on forever.
Math is also thinking out
things that confuse you.
We need math. Without
decimals, everybody would go
bankrupt!
I learned that it doesn't
matter how old you are or what

Grace Rubenstein
June 8, 1988 ②

grade your in, you can learn
anything if you really put your
mind to it.
If math is taught
right, it is fun and easy
to remember.

**4156**

Name: Cathleen
Grade: 2-Bova

*Submitted by Barbara Reys*

DEAR FRIEND,

THIS YEAR IN SCHOOL I USED A CALCULATOR IN MATH CLASS. FOR ME, THE CALCULATOR . . . Was very fun to use. You half to press buttons to make it work. We did something neat with it we Colunted by ones, 2s, 4s, 9 tens. It was very fun., We leard how to go down more in numbers, Like you have o ther is more you half to go down like one blow, 0 2 blow 3 blow o ther is a lot more we leared how to play spin the web.

SINCERELY,

P.S. NEXT YEAR I HOPE THAT . . . We get to use them.

---

Anri ̶ ̶ ̶ ̶
Jar 15/92.

What does geometry help you learn about mathmatics?

Geometry helps me learn that that there is more then one kind of math, at first I thought there were only one kind of math the adding and subtracting kind but I just leaned that there is more than one kind of math and geometry is one kind of math.

Geometry also helps you think and do better in mathematics.

*Submitted by Marilyn Burns*

grade 1

problem solving is my best.
problem solving is
problem solving is
fun. problem
solving is ezy.
I like all the
valentines problems.
problem solving
problem solving
makes me feel smrt.
only got a
cupl rong. I have it in
hope
sekind grad. I hope so too!

Do you like to show the class
your                          solutions? __YES__

*Submitted by Randall Charles*

---

1. What does it mean when your teacher asks you to estimate an answer?

To round off

It means ro ~~Fand~~ round.
The number.

Round off a number to a tens or hundreds place.

To round the number and not
to give the exact answer.

If a number is around your right answer
like      estimate Answers
          400      423

to make a logical guess, or to round to the
right number.

not to work the problem
out exactly but give an approximate
answer.

Make a answer that is
close to the real answer

*Submitted by Barbara Reys*

# 15

# Making Mathematics Come Alive through a Statistics Project

Alison S. Claus

ONE of my responsibilities in a K–4 school is teaching a small group of fourth-grade children who participate in the advanced mathematics program. In our weekly sessions we explore and discuss a wide variety of mathematical ideas and applications. One of my objectives is to involve the pupils in actively doing mathematics.

One topic in the program is statistics, in which we gather, represent, analyze, and interpret data on a relevant question. As I started to explain one day a project I had planned—investigating characteristics of fourth graders—Amanda raised her hand and said, "You know what I *really* want to know? How many people really like fruit bars better than ice cream." "Yeah," Tom added, "maybe we could persuade Mr. Best to give us back our ice cream."

A little gentle questioning elicited that the principal had replaced ice cream with frozen fruit-juice bars in the school lunchroom to encourage healthy eating habits. These students were upset with this decision. They liked ice cream and had not been consulted. When asked what other questions they had about the lunchroom, the questions flew thick and fast: Why didn't they have hot lunches? Could they have special lunches, like hot-dog day, more often than one or twice a year? What about having a wider choice of foods to buy than just fruit-juice bars? I realized that we had the topic for our statistics project. This would be a great opportunity for students to use mathematics to investigate an issue that really concerned them.

Class ended at this point, and my students went home to think up more questions about the school lunchroom. I went to get the principal's approval for our project—after all, it was his decisions and policies we wanted to survey. He cautioned that the children must understand that he probably would not change his opinions or decisions but agreed that the project would be a wonderful learning experience.

The children's excitement was remarkable! They stopped me in the hall throughout the week to ask if the principal had said we could go ahead with the project. During our next class, we considered additional questions and revised and consolidated them. We also made decisions about gathering data. For the project to be manageable, the scope of our investigation needed to be limited. We also needed to determine our sample. We brainstormed and decided to ask only six questions about the lunchroom but to survey all students who ate in the lunchroom, first through fourth graders. (Kindergarten students were not included, since they did not eat there.)

Next we discussed the mechanics of conducting the survey. Several questions arose: How do you ask the questions? How do you interrupt a class? Do you go by yourself or with a friend? How do you record the data you collect? We agreed on a form for our survey (see fig. 15.1). The form included a short introductory paragraph that students could read or paraphrase to the class being surveyed. We agreed on the classroom each student would go to. We decided it was more appropriate to make an appointment with each teacher rather than just "drop in." I agreed to send a letter to each of my colleagues explaining the project and requesting their cooperation.

By our next meeting all the data had been collected, so we began to organize them. One student or a pair of students worked with the data from one question. Since over three hundred students were surveyed, using calculators was clearly in order—it would help the work go more quickly and increase accuracy.

The data were organized first by grade and then for the total population. Organizing the data provided good experience in making and using tables. When this task was completed, we turned our attention to constructing graphs to represent the data visually. Although computer programs that construct graphs are available, I thought it was important at this time for my fourth graders to construct their own graphs. They needed experience with such tasks as determining the scale, labeling the axes, and laying out the graph. Again, each student or pair of students graphed the data for one question by grade and by the whole school. Much discussion about the scales and layout of the graphs ensued. Typical questions were these: How wide

Teacher _____ Room # _____

**Fourth-Grade Survey Sheet**

My name is _____. Our fourth-grade math enrichment class is doing a survey to test people's opinions about the lunchroom. I have six questions I would like to have you answer for me. Please vote by raising your hand when I ask.

1.  Do you buy milk in the lunchroom?
    How many people buy milk
    every day _____       sometimes _____       never _____

2.  Which would you rather buy for lunch: fruit bars or ice cream?
    How many people like     fruit bars _____       ice cream _____

3.  Would you like to have a special lunch like McDonald's or a hot-dog day once a month?

    Yes _____       No _____

4.  If you would like a special lunch day, which kind do you like best?

    McDonald's _____       Pizza _____       Hot-dog day _____

5.  If the lunchroom sold hot lunches, would you buy one?

    Yes _____       Maybe _____       No _____

6.  If the lunchroom sold the following items, would you buy them?

    How many people would buy—

    Fun Fruits _____                Chips _____

    Juice Boxes _____               Candy Bars _____

    Granola Bars _____              Pop _____

Thank you very much for helping us. We will report the results of our survey to you when it is completed.

Fig. 15.1

should the bars be? How much space should be left between them? How should the scales be numbered? My role was that of a facilitator, providing guidance and helping the children resolve problems as they arose.

When the visual displays of the data were completed, we analyzed the data. The children noted several things:

• Older children tended to prefer "junk" food over "healthy" food, although they liked milk and pizza better than younger children.

• A majority of students would buy a special lunch once a month, especially if it were pizza or hamburgers from a fast-food restaurant.

- A majority of students would prefer to purchase a hot lunch rather than carry a bag lunch to school every day. (The results of *this* question interested our superintendent, who was conducting his own survey on that topic with parents.)

The discussion of the graphs led to other questions:

- Why did fewer first graders buy milk than fourth graders?
- What would happen if fourth graders could buy anything they wanted for lunch? (They tended to prefer pop, chips, candy bars, and ice cream.)
- Why did first and second graders vote for hot-dog day, whereas third and fourth graders preferred pizza?

When the data had been thoroughly discussed and we thought our graphs were ready to be presented, we invited the principal to our class. There was a marvelous discussion between him and the students. He examined the data with them and reviewed some implications of the results. Then he talked to them about the costs of hot lunches and other items that were sold in the lunchroom. He had them roughly calculate the costs to the school and their parents as taxpayers. Most student did not realize that the school district subsidized their purchases. When the class was over, the principal had a greater respect for the students' ability to apply themselves to a project that had meaning to them, and the students had gained respect for how decisions are made. They also understood some of the factors that influence the decisions for which a principal is responsible.

Our concluding activity was making a huge display of our graphs on one wall of a central hallway. We hoped that children and adults who saw the display would be attracted by it and stop to study the graphs. These hopes were more than fulfilled.

Fruit bars were still sold in the lunchroom the rest of the year, but Amanda and Tom and the others didn't complain. Although they still prefer ice cream, they have become much more knowledgeable about the entire lunchroom procedure, as well as students' likes and dislikes with respect to healthy foods. I think they are also very proud of their efforts in gaining that knowledge.

As I reflect on the project, the following points seem important:

1. Data collection and processing have an important role in the curriculum. They allow children to apply techniques and skills they have learned in school to a real-world situation of importance to them. In the course of this investigation, these children used their skills in adding, counting, comparing, estimating, and constructing tables and graphs to help them.

2. Applying mathematics is important. The students began to sense the usefulness of mathematics in solving a problem that at its inception seemed

nonmathematical. It was important for them to recognize that mathematical processes could help with their project. I think probably many problems of real concern to children outside of mathematics are appropriate for data collection and analysis. What better way to learn the importance of mathematics in solving real-world problems?

3. Projects like this one allow the teacher's role to shift from knowledge dispenser to facilitator in creating a climate for promoting exploring, testing, and discussing ideas. I became a co-learner and a resource for making decisions about what was appropriate, and I provided examples of good technique and how to assemble and process the final product.

4. The importance and usefulness of calculators were evident. Children have difficulty, for example, in adding long columns of multidigit numbers accurately, and computation should not be the focus of a project like this in any event. Calculators were available for students to use whenever they wished. The children used them in a manner very similar to adult usage. When computation became awkward or the lack of accuracy became frustrating, they picked up a calculator and used it, much as they also used paper-and-pencil computation or mental computation for simpler calculations.

5. The cooperation of the school staff is very important when conducting a project such as this one. Without the help of every classroom teacher, it would have been very difficult to collect the data. Without the principal's support, the impact of the project would have been far less.

This school year, changes have been made in the lunchroom procedure: Fruit bars are no longer sold, ice cream is for sale, hot lunches are offered to the whole school once a week, and pizza and hot dogs are among the weekly offerings. The decision makers claim that these changes were determined by parent and teacher requests. I like to think that our little survey raised the consciousness of, and perhaps influenced, those adults. These results alone would have made the project rewarding, but even more good things have happened. When the school nurse surveyed the students about health habits and menus of healthy foods this fall, she brought the data to my class for processing and interpretation. After reviewing her data, my students decided to produce their own survey to follow up her results, which they felt were very idealistic. They are seeking to determine whether the children were actually bringing in their lunches the food that they indicated to the school nurse would make healthy menus. My students feel they were not. This survey lends itself to learning about the random selection of a sample population, collecting data over a period of time, and once again an analysis of data in tabular and graphical form. When we finish, the school nurse plans to use our results as follow-up lessons, using my students as her experts. What will grow from this project next year? It will be exciting to see!

# 16

# The Power of
# Mathematical Investigations

### David J. Whitin

O NE OF my most rewarding days as a principal occurred the time I substituted in the fifth-grade classroom of our school. I decided to interject a mathematics lesson of my own, testing out an idea that I had recently read about in a textbook. I was intrigued by the notion that if one took a four-digit number, reversed its digits, and subtracted that number from the original number, the difference would always be 6174. I tried it:

| | | |
|---|---|---|
| 8532 | 9643 | 7861 |
| − 2358 | − 3469 | − 1687 |
| 6174 | 6174 | 6174 |

It worked! I was eager to share this discovery with children not only because the problem was a bit mysterious but also because it would give them some practice in subtraction. Little did I realize that this aim would be the least of the benefits. We were about to embark on a mathematical venture that would consume our energies for two hours and would carry us far beyond the narrow walls of simple subtraction practice.

### THE BEGINNING

After introducing the problem to the children, I encouraged them to select their own examples.

"Hey, mine doesn't work," said Gail.

"Mine doesn't either," said Jeff.

I soon realized that I had not tested enough samples.

"Can anyone find one that *does* work?" I asked.

"I have one," offered Darren.

I wrote each problem on the board, and we checked them together.

$$\begin{array}{r} 8721 \\ -\ 1278 \\ \hline 7443 \end{array}\ \text{No!} \qquad \begin{array}{r} 4251 \\ -\ 1524 \\ \hline 2727 \end{array}\ \text{No!} \qquad \begin{array}{r} 8642 \\ -\ 2468 \\ \hline 6174 \end{array}\ \text{Yes!}$$

These results forced me into the role of a learner, and we launched an investigation together. I posed some other questions: "Has anyone found any other numbers that work?" "Has anyone discovered any other numbers that do not work?" "How can we keep track of our findings?"

## THE INVESTIGATION

Several children came to the chalkboard and began to make a list of their discoveries while others continued to test additional numbers at their desks.

| Numbers That Work | Numbers That Do Not Work |
|---|---|
| 8642 | 8721 |
| 8532 | 4251 |

I encouraged children to work with a partner or in a small group if they wished to do so. Together they began raising their own questions and offering their own conjectures.

Jason suggested, "I think that all four numbers [digits] have to add up to be an even number." The two answers that we had so far followed that rule. Would we find others? Jason found one that worked—9533:

$$\begin{array}{r} 9533 \\ -\ 3359 \\ \hline 6174 \end{array} \qquad \begin{array}{l} \underline{\text{Sum of Digits}} \\ 9 + 5 + 3 + 3 = 20 \end{array}$$

However, he also found many combinations that did not work; for example:

$$\begin{array}{r} 7313 \\ -\ 3137 \\ \hline 4176 \end{array} \qquad \begin{array}{l} \underline{\text{Sum of Digits}} \\ 7 + 3 + 1 + 3 = 14 \end{array}$$

Lee noticed that the digits of his first answer, 8642, were all even numbers. Would a numeral with all odd digits work? He found one:

$$\begin{array}{r} 7311 \\ -\ 1137 \\ \hline 6174 \end{array}$$

If he used other odd digits, it did not work; for example:

$$\begin{array}{r} 3751 \\ -\ 1573 \\ \hline 2178 \end{array}$$

Libby also wondered if odd and even numbers would be helpful clues in unlocking the mystery. She noticed that the second four-digit combination that I tried was composed of two odd and two even numbers (8532). She created other four-digit numerals that contained two odd and two even digits to see if such combinations would work each time; sometimes it worked and sometimes it did not:

$$
\begin{array}{r}
9643 \\
-\ 3469 \\
\hline
6174
\end{array}
\qquad
\begin{array}{r}
5324 \\
-\ 4235 \\
\hline
1089
\end{array}
$$

Holly shared with the class that before we subtract the second number from the first number, we must be sure that in the original number the ones digit is less than the thousands digit. Otherwise, the reversed number will be larger than the original number. Her example was a good illustration:

$$
\begin{array}{r}
4327 \\
-\ 7234 \\
\hline
\end{array}
$$

Each conjecture was uncovering more information. Although we had no general rule for predicting a pattern, we were nevertheless asking good questions, generating some information, and persisting in our efforts.

Gail asked, "Can you repeat a digit?" The class agreed that such answers would be acceptable, and Gail found one such example:

$$
\begin{array}{r}
8862 \\
-\ 2688 \\
\hline
6174
\end{array}
$$

Would we find others? Gail set out to see.

At this point I asked, "Has anyone found a number that has a zero as one of its digits? If not, is it possible to have a zero in the original number?" Terri was the first person to discover an example:

$$
\begin{array}{r}
6310 \\
-\ 0136 \\
\hline
6174
\end{array}
$$

The question about zeros intrigued Libby as well. After Terri shared his discovery, Libby also began working on possible combinations. A little later she shared her own insight into this problem. She made a chart (fig. 16.1) and claimed that 6 was the only number that could be paired with 0 to work, using this particular frame: 6 _ _ 0.

She reasoned that other combinations would produce a difference either too large or too small:

$$
\begin{array}{r}
9730 \\
-\ 0379 \\
\hline
9351
\end{array}
\qquad
\begin{array}{r}
5320 \\
-\ 0235 \\
\hline
5085
\end{array}
$$

$$
\left.\begin{array}{l}
9 \ \_ \ \_ \ 0 \\
8 \ \_ \ \_ \ 0 \\
7 \ \_ \ \_ \ 0
\end{array}\right\} \text{ will produce an answer greater than 6174}
$$

$$
6 \ \_ \ \_ \ 0 \ \Big\} \text{ will work}
$$

$$
\left.\begin{array}{l}
5 \ \_ \ \_ \ 0 \\
4 \ \_ \ \_ \ 0 \\
3 \ \_ \ \_ \ 0 \\
2 \ \_ \ \_ \ 0 \\
1 \ \_ \ \_ \ 0
\end{array}\right\} \text{ will produce an answer less than 6174}
$$

Fig. 16.1

Libby had found one other number with a 0 in it that worked: 6530. In studying this answer, she reasoned further that if 0 was left in the ones place and 6 in the thousands place, then the two middle numbers could not be the same. If they were the same, one would have to rename the 6 while subtracting and then the difference would be too small, in the 5000s. For example:

$$
\begin{array}{r}
6440 \\
- \ 0446 \\
\hline
5994
\end{array}
$$

More numbers that worked were discovered with this new information. Somehow we felt we were getting closer to a final solution but were still unable to detect an overall pattern.

I asked, "Can we rearrange our answers in some way to see if they reveal some kind of pattern?" Our recent investigation with 6 _ _ 0 led us to the following table:

$$
\begin{array}{c}
6640 \\
6530 \\
6420 \\
6310 \\
6200
\end{array}
$$

Darren suggested that perhaps the difference between the first and last digits must always be 6. This idea held true for the 6 _ _ 0 pattern; for example:

$$
6530
$$
$$
6 - 0 = 6
$$

What about the other numbers that we had already found to work, 8532 and 8642? Yes, we also found a difference of 6 for them:

$$
8532 \qquad\qquad\qquad 8642
$$
$$
8 - 2 = 6 \qquad\qquad\qquad 8 - 2 = 6
$$

With this new piece of information, the number hunt was resumed with renewed alacrity. Libby sensed the progress we were making and commented: "We started off just bungling any four numbers, but now we're getting somewhere!"

Indeed we were! In viewing the answers for the 6 _ _ 0 pattern, Sarah also noticed that the difference between the two middle numbers was always 2 and that the hundreds digit was always the larger of the two middle digits; for example:

| 6420 | and | 6640 |
|---|---|---|
| 4 − 2 = 2 | | 6 − 4 = 2 |

"I'll work on the seven thousands," remarked Sarah. Other pupils sought to find solutions for numbers in the 8000s and 9000s. It was not long before we produced a more complete list. Color is used here to highlight the constant differences that we discovered. Red indicates a difference of 6 between the thousands digit and the ones digit; gray represents a difference of 2 between the hundreds digit and the tens digit:

| | | | |
|---|---|---|---|
| 9973 | 8862 | 7751 | 6640 |
| 9863 | 8752 | 7641 | 6530 |
| 9753 | 8642 | 7531 | 6420 |
| 9643 | 8532 | 7421 | 6310 |
| 9533 | 8422 | 7311 | 6200 |
| 9423 | 8312 | 7201 | |
| 9313 | 8202 | | |
| 9203 | | | |

We were all quite satisfied with the progress we had made, but still we wondered, "Are those all the numbers that worked? How can we be sure?" Then we made the following conjectures:

1. What if the two interior digits had a difference of 3? Jeff investigated that suggestion but did not find any numbers that worked:

| 9743 | 8852 | 6520 |
|---|---|---|
| − 3479 | − 2588 | − 0256 |
| 6264 | 6264 | 6264 |

However, the solution was the same in every instance, 6264, and he continued to pursue that pattern on his own.

2. What if the difference between the two interior numbers was 2 but the tens digit was the larger of the two numbers? Holly discovered that although the difference would not be 6174, the number 6814 kept appearing as the difference:

| 7571 | 8352 |
|---|---|
| − 1757 | − 2538 |
| 6814 | 6814 |

3. What if the hundreds digit was greater than the thousands digit? Would 6174 still be the difference? We tried some problems together and found that it was:

$$
\begin{array}{r}
7861 \\
- \ 1687 \\
\hline
6174
\end{array}
\qquad
\begin{array}{r}
7971 \\
- \ 1797 \\
\hline
6174
\end{array}
$$

Our final list of numbers was this:

| 9973 | 8972 | 7971 | 6970 |
|------|------|------|------|
| 9863 | 8862 | 7861 | 6860 |
| 9753 | 8752 | 7751 | 6750 |
| 9643 | 8642 | 7641 | 6640 |
| 9533 | 8532 | 7531 | 6530 |
| 9423 | 8422 | 7421 | 6420 |
| 9313 | 8312 | 7311 | 6310 |
| 9203 | 8202 | 7201 | 6200 |
| 8 numbers | 8 numbers | 8 numbers | 8 numbers |

Lee and Jason created a chart to show the number of times each numeral appeared in an answer. Although finding a pattern in their results was difficult, they continued to check their table, hoping to find a clue that would give us further information, and came up with the following:

| Numeral | 0 | 1 | 2 | 3 | 4 | 5 | 6 | 7 | 8 | 9 |
|---------|---|---|---|---|---|---|---|---|---|---|
| Number of times it appears | 12 | 12 | 16 | 16 | 8 | 8 | 16 | 16 | 12 | 12 |

## LESSONS LEARNED

My involvement in this mathematical investigation gave me numerous insights into my role both as a principal and as a teacher. First, as an administrator, I learned two important lessons:

1. Allow teachers to be flexible with their scheduling. Although the teacher's plans called for a forty-five-minute mathematics period, our search for patterns occupied us for two hours straight. When children are engaged in a mathematical investigation, they must be allowed the time to pursue it. Teachers must learn to sense and sustain enthusiasm as it builds. As an administrator I must be careful not to restrict a teacher's freedom by requiring an inflexible schedule. The next English lesson can wait until tomorrow. Years later children will not remember that their teacher dutifully followed a set schedule and never missed a single English class; instead, they will remember the joy of a mathematical discovery because their teacher ignored the clock and nurtured their spirit of inquisitiveness.

2. Look beyond "time on task" requirements. Some principles are pressured to ensure that children work on tasks for a required number of minutes. However, in trying to document this time requirement, principals sometimes do not consider the quality of the experience. From this mathematical investigation I learned that true time on task was an unmitigated desire to find a pattern, to unlock the mystery of these numbers at all costs. Genuine time on task cannot be counted by minutes on the clock but is to be measured by the incessant hum of purposeful activity. It cannot always be documented by the number of workbook pages completed but rather by the learner's knowledge that he or she persisted, took some risks, ventured some guesses, uncovered some dead ends and partial solutions, and experienced the joy of a mathematical discovery.

As a teacher I learned some valuable lessons as well:

1. Allow children the opportunity to solve problems in their own way. I had no preconceived notion of how the problem ought to be solved. I helped support the investigation through open-ended questioning and positive recognition of efforts, believing that children would be creative and flexible in their thinking and would devise solutions that were meaningful to them. Nothing builds a more positive atmosphere for learning than trust. Children sense it in the problems that are posed, the questions that are asked, and the choices that are offered. It is difficult to mark off this trust on any checklist, but it is there in the air, and it sets the tone and creates the climate that says all things are possible.

2. Value the process. As Libby stated so aptly, we began by just "bungling any four numbers together." However, it was in this "bungling" that some of the most important learning occurred: children were offering conjectures, testing hypotheses, and revising hunches. Schools need to promote more "bungling."

3. Remember that learning is a social event. Too often, mathematics time is a silent time. However, in this activity children learned from each other by asking questions, challenging assumptions, and building on each other's ideas. Children of all abilities need opportunities to work together.

4. Mathematical investigations can create a sense of accomplishment and cooperation. Yes, mathematics, of all subjects, has the power to draw people together and create a positive classroom atmosphere. As the problem began to unfold, different children began to take on different tasks. Lee and Jason started to create their numeral chart; Libby and two others began investigating odd and even numbers. Terri sought a number with a zero. All shared their findings willingly and tested each other's conjectures. In the end we all felt a special pride about the patterns we discovered because everyone had contributed to their attainment.

5. Teachers are learners, too. One of the advantages of mathematical investigations such as this one is that teachers are forced into the role of learners. I, too, became caught up in the excitement to uncover the pattern for this problem. It is important that teachers experience this joy of discovery because, as Polya remarks, "Nobody can give away what he has not got. No teacher can impart to his students the experience of discovery if he has not got it himself" (Polya 1980, p. 2). The enthusiasm and fascination for numbers that I gained through this activity will stay with me as I make other forays into the world of numbers.

### REFERENCE

Polya, George. "On Solving Mathematical Problems in High School." In *Problem Solving in School Mathematics*, 1980 Yearbook of the National Council of Teachers of Mathematics, pp. 1–2. Reston, Va.: The Council, 1980.

# 17

# Hidden Mathematics Lessons

## Anita S. VanBrackle

I N EVERY classroom mathematics is always around us, not just on a textbook page or worksheet or even in the lesson that is planned; rather, many activities throughout the school day are sources of wonderful experiences for applying mathematical concepts and solving problems. Let's uncover some of these "hidden" mathematics lessons.

### ALL-IN-A-DAY MATHEMATICS ACTIVITIES

Consider a typical day in a primary classroom. Where's the mathematics? It begins with those repetitive administrative tasks—attendance, lunch count, and lunch money. Before taking attendance, don't miss the opportunity to have students count off. Then have one student tell you how many children are absent; develop awareness and memory skills by having another student name those who are absent. This activity takes only three or four minutes, and it lets the children become involved with their environment. Soon each student will be especially eager to help you with the attendance.

Similar techniques can be used for lunch counts, especially if your students have to make choices for lunch. This is an excellent opportunity to discuss and use counting and comparison ideas. The class must determine if each child made one choice and if the total number matches the number of students present on that day. Mathematics is everywhere—just look for it!

Collecting lunch money is often the next daily duty. This activity takes a little longer, but it is time well "spent." Let each child identify his or her coins and tell you the value of each one. As the year progresses, becoming aware of each coin's value will help the pupils determine if they have the correct amount of lunch money. Don't "short change" your students; what better time do you have to make the topic of money relevant?

Twenty minutes of the school day have passed by now, but you have already informally used such mathematical ideas as addition, subtraction, counting, comparing numbers, and money—all in a real-world context. Not bad for a beginning!

What's next? Well, the calendar usually plays a part in the morning activities. This is a great time to locate today's date on the calendar, as well as the dates before and after. Identifying and sequencing numbers are just a portion of this lesson. The pupils can clap or jump to show the number represented by the date. Later in the year you can ask them to tell the date of special events, such as library, music, or art classes. Let the pupils find the dates. Weekends, school vacations, or holidays require more calculations and really get the children involved in analyzing and solving a relevant problem.

Mathematics progresses with you throughout the day, even into your reading groups. Listen to your directions—"Open your books to page 27"—there's a number, so use it! Although some children might have difficulty finding the page, *don't* find it for them. Show them the number 27, find it on a number board, and decide if it is before or after another specific number. Will 27 be closer to the beginning or the end of the book?

Even a class break does not have to be lost instructional time! Make a large number line, up to fifty, on your classroom's floor. When your students line up, assign each a specific number on which to stand (fig. 17.1). Or tell them to stand on the number before, after, or equal to an addition or subtraction fact. Each child can be given a problem appropriate to his or her achievement level. This activity is individualized instruction in action, and we haven't even had our math lesson.

Time concepts and clock-reading skills can also be emphasized throughout the school day. A cardboard clock can be placed near the real clock. Set the hands of the cardboard clock to show an important time during the day and write the time next to the clock. Let the children watch the hands on the real clock move as the targeted time approaches. When children are aware how a clock's hands move as time passes, it is much easier to have a meaningful lesson about minutes and hours. A simple comparison of the two

Fig. 17.1. The class lines up on numbers at breaktime.

clocks takes only a few minutes, and awareness of time becomes real and meaningful for the pupils.

A mathematics lesson can also be lively and exciting. Bring place value to life by placing chairs at the front of the classroom to represent the ones and tens places. Have a child sit in each place and hold the number of objects he or she represents (fig. 17.2). It's amazing how quickly the tens place becomes the more popular place to sit. This simple lesson shows how the ones place changes to 0 when a set of ten is transferred to the tens place. Children seated in the tens place are eager to get more tens and so will watch carefully so they can inform the child in the ones place when it is time to pass them a set of ten. As the study of place value expands to include hundreds, thousands, and so on, the most popular place to sit changes as the children's understanding develops. This activity is also helpful for showing renaming in addition and subtraction.

After thoroughly discussing place value, conduct a simple counting activity. Divide the class into groups of four or five students and place a large number (50–99) of objects in the middle of each group for its members to count. The directions are simple: "Please count these objects. Remember to think about what we have learned." With four or five students in the group, this task becomes more than a counting problem. The groups must organize themselves and decide on the best solution to the problem. If a child counts out his or her own small collection, remind the students that they must count all the objects together, and have them begin again. After considerable moaning and groaning, someone in the groups will remember that they have been studying sets of tens. The group can then count the objects in sets of tens and quickly and accurately find the total. A simple counting problem has become one requiring group cooperation, application of place value, and analytical skills. The excitement on the children's faces as they discover the ease of counting by tens is worth the time this activity takes.

Geometry, measurement, and graphing are other topics readily adaptable for instruction throughout the day. Learning geometric concepts includes

Fig. 17.2. "Place-value chairs" reinforce the idea of ones, tens, and hundreds.

not only visually recognizing shapes but also developing the vocabulary of geometry. Use geometric and other mathematics vocabulary as part of your instructions throughout the day. Refer to the *rectangular* table, the *square* desk, the *circular* clock, and so on. Encourage the children to use the same words. On the playground, point out the triangular supports for the swings or the square shapes of the jungle gym. When the class forms lines for relay races, help them compare the lines and tell you if they are "equal in number" or if one line has "fewer" or "more" children. Listen for their mathematical vocabulary. When your students are using mathematical vocabulary in conversational speech, you can be confident that they are on their way to understanding basic concepts. Help the children see and verbalize the mathematics around them.

Any teacher of a class who has had its picture taken knows the relevance of the terms *shorter* and *taller* as the members of the class are lined up by height. If time permits, let some pupils line up others in the correct order. Let them take turns "playing teacher" to decide where one of their classmates should stand in line.

Introducing graphing is natural in classrooms with desks in rows. Assign numbers to the rows and to the desks in each row; for example, one desk becomes row 3, desk 4. Illustrate the arrangement on the chalkboard or a laminated poster board (fig. 17.3). Let each child locate his or her own desk. Use the chart as a method of indicating any child who is absent for the day by having a student examine the chart and circle any desks that do not have a

Fig. 17.3. The concept of graphing can be introduced with a seating chart.

name written on them. The student then fills in the names of the children who are absent and reports that information to the teacher. With a quick glance over the classroom the teacher can verify the accuracy of the child's report.

When the children are familiar with numbering desks and rows to indicate relative position, make use of the floor tiles as "living" graphs. Move the desks and draw a graph on the floor with chalk, letting each tile represent one unit. Graph such things as birthdays in each month or hair or eye colors, or, for advanced students, combine measurement and graphing. Have the children measure each other's heights or weights and then stand on the appropriate tile in the graph. Of course, the class must decide on the graph's categories and labels and reach a consensus.

## CONCLUSION

Innovative ideas are important to the future of mathematics in our schools. However, we live in the present and need to look around us for ways to bring mathematics to life. Often, such ideas are right in our classrooms. Don't be afraid to be creative or to put mathematics in the hands of your students. Let them feel, think, observe, and experience the wonder of true understanding.

# DRAWING PICTURES AND WRITING STORIES FOR EQUATIONS

There were 3 boys. Each of them had 2 markers. How many in all. 3×2=6

Marc C.

Erica
Becky

15 Tomato plants.
5 plants in each row.
How many rows in all?
15 ÷ 5 = 3

Submitted by Sandra Adrian

# 18

# Connections between Psychological Learning Theories and the Elementary Mathematics Curriculum

Diana Lambdin Kroll

**D**URING the first two-thirds of this century the teaching of mathematics in American elementary schools passed through three major phases: the *drill and practice* phase, the *meaningful arithmetic* phase, and the *new math* phase. Each of these phases is worthy of attention because each corresponds to a period when American education in general was going through radical and fundamental changes, and each introduced new and innovative practices to mathematics education.

In fact, the existence of these historical phases would seem to belie the old cliché that there's nothing new under the sun. The field of education seems to be continually passing through cycles of change. On closer examination, however, many educational innovations are actually recycled in slightly modified forms. Not only is it difficult for newcomers to the profession to tell which aspects of mathematics education are recent innovations and which represent established practice, but it is often difficult for veteran teachers as well to recognize old ideas when they come around again, perhaps in new clothing. Thus, another reason for looking back at the three major phases of mathematics education during this century is to discover the extent to which certain contemporary practices have their roots in the educational changes of yesteryear.

Finally, and most importantly, through historical analysis we may gain some perspective on the forces and issues that contribute to change in education. Historical perspective helps us avoid tunnel vision about the uniqueness of the educational problems we face today and suggests options to be considered as we ponder their solutions.

During any era, numerous diverse factors play a part in directing and influencing educational practice. Indeed, the factors surrounding the emergence of the drill and practice, meaningful arithmetic, and new math phases were complex: a constellation of mathematical, political, psychological, and sociological elements. This article discusses the influence of one significant factor—psychological learning theories—both on these three earlier phases in the teaching of mathematics and on the teaching of elementary school mathematics today. Although during each phase numerous strands of psychological theory and educational practice can be discerned, a major psychological trend is also recognizable, and the work of particular theorists can be considered central. Table 18.1 provides a brief overview of each of the three phases, including their main theorists, classroom focus, and primary teaching methods.

TABLE 18.1
Relationships between Phases of Mathematics Education
and Psychological Learning Theories

| Phase | Main Theorists | Focus | How Achieved |
|-------|---------------|-------|--------------|
| Drill & practice (approx. 1920–1930) | Thorndike | Facility with computation | Rote memorization of facts and algorithms<br>Break all work into series of small steps |
| Meaningful arithmetic (approx. 1930–1950s) | Brownell (Gestalt psychologists) | Understanding of arithmetic ideas and skills<br>Applications of math to real-world problems | Emphasis on mathematical relationships<br>Incidental learning<br>Activity-oriented approach |
| New math (approx. 1960–1970s) | Bruner (Piaget) | Structure of the discipline | Study of mathematical structures<br>Spiral curriculum<br>Discovery learning |

## THE DRILL AND PRACTICE PHASE

In the early years of this century, drill and practice, which had long been a component of mathematics instruction, became its primary focus. Prior to

1900 the aim of schooling had been to confront students with difficult mental exercises to build up their powers of reasoning and thought. However, implicit faith in "mental discipline" as a theory of learning had begun to wane by the beginning of this century, when Edward Thorndike proposed a new theory—a theory that became known in its various forms as "connectionism," "associationism," or "S-R bond theory." Thorndike claimed that learning is the formation of connections or bonds between stimuli (events in the environment) and responses (reactions of an organism to the environment). His theory maintained that, through conditioning, specific responses are linked with specific stimuli.

In 1922 Thorndike published *The Psychology of Arithmetic*, in which he demonstrated how his theory applied to the teaching of arithmetic. He explained that teachers needed to recognize and make explicit the essential bonds that constitute the subjects they teach. As an example of what he meant by bonds, Thorndike listed seven separate S-R bonds in "simple two-column addition of integers." Among the list were bonds such as "learning to keep one's place in the column as one adds," "learning to add a seen to a thought-of number," and "learning to write the figure signifying units rather than the total sum of a column." The list concluded with the statement that "learning to carry also involves itself at least two distinct processes" (1922, p. 52). According to Thorndike, the teacher's aim was to arrange for students to receive the right type of drill and practice on each of the right bonds for the right amount of time.

That Thorndike's theory did, in fact, influence mathematics education can be seen by examining yearbooks of professional societies and textbooks of the time. For example, in the introduction to the 1930 Twenty-ninth Yearbook of the National Society for the Study of Education (entitled *Report of the Society's Committee on Arithmetic*), the editor presents the overall perspective of the volume: "Theoretically, the main psychological basis is a behavioristic one, viewing skills and habits as fabrics of connections" (Knight 1930, p. 5). As another example, figure 18.1 shows a portion of a page from Thorndike's (1924) arithmetic text for third graders, a page showing drill on basic addition facts. Since Thorndike did not provide any prior instruction to encourage pupils to relate the basic facts to one another, pupils working on this page would probably view the exercise 3 + 1 as totally unrelated to the exercise 1 + 3.

In fact, one major effect of Thorndike's theories was the segmentation of the mathematics curriculum into many disjoint bits. Teachers attempted to be certain that an entire collection of individual bonds was established and exercised in order for each higher-level skill to be mastered. Since each bond was believed to exist in isolation, it was thought that mixed, unorganized drill was perhaps even more effective than practice on a systematic arrangement of facts; with mixed drill the problem of interference between similar bonds

## 8. Addition

Read these lines. Say the right numbers where the dots are:

| | | |
|---|---|---|
| 2 and 3 are  .... | 5 and 3 are  .... | 4 and 3 are  .... |
| 1 and 3 are  .... | 6 and 3 are  .... | 7 and 3 are  .... |
| 4 and 4 are  .... | 5 and 4 are  .... | 6 and 4 are  .... |
| 3 and 1 are  .... | 6 and 1 are  .... | 2 and 1 are  .... |
| 7 and 1 are  .... | 4 and 1 are  .... | 8 and 1 are  .... |

### 9.

Add and say the sums:

| 2 | 3 | 4 | 2 | 1 | | 4 | 1 | 2 | 4 | 4 |
|---|---|---|---|---|---|---|---|---|---|---|
| 3 | 4 | 2 | 1 | 6 | | 3 | 5 | 7 | 4 | 1 |

| 1 | 2 | 2 | 4 | 1 | | 3 | 3 | 3 | 3 | 5 |
|---|---|---|---|---|---|---|---|---|---|---|
| 8 | 6 | 2 | 5 | 4 | | 3 | 1 | 6 | 2 | 1 |

| 3 | 3 | 1 | 2 | 4 | | 2 | 1 | 2 | 1 | 4 |
|---|---|---|---|---|---|---|---|---|---|---|
| 5 | 7 | 2 | 4 | 6 | | 8 | 3 | 5 | 1 | 2 |

Fig. 18.1. A portion of a page from a 1924 third-grade text: Thorndike's *The Thorndike Arithmetics.*

was avoided. Another effect of connectionist theory was the prescriptive teaching methods that it encouraged. Teachers tended not to permit unorthodox algorithms or novel solutions, since the most efficient way to direct pupils to form correct bonds was to carefully keep them from forming incorrect bonds. Thus, in the curriculum of the drill and practice era, mathematics was taught by concentrating on drill with skills that had been segmented into small, distinct, easily mastered units.

Although reformulated types of drill and practice continue to be used to this day, in the years immediately following the drill and practice era the focus of mathematics education shifted considerably. Parents and educators of the 1930s and 1940s began to question the extreme emphasis on drill for drill's sake, and to wonder whether the arithmetic that children were learning was of any practical use. The focus of instruction during those years—the progressive era—became an attempt to ensure that the skills children had mastered constituted "meaningful" arithmetic.

## THE MEANINGFUL ARITHMETIC PHASE

From approximately 1930 to 1950, when the progressive education movement was influential in the United States, there was a new emphasis on "learning for living." The major change in mathematics education was a shift from an emphasis on drill for drill's sake to a focus on attempting to develop arithmetic concepts in a "meaningful" way. This vague term meant different things to different educators of the progressive era.

For some progressives, arithmetic was meaningful when it was encountered in the context of practical activity. Arithmetic was learned for social utility—to acquire the tools for dealing with problems that would be encountered in later life. These educators recommended an activity-oriented approach. Some believed that children would learn all the mathematics they needed—and learn it better—through incidental experience rather than by systematic teaching. As a writer in the 1935 NCTM Tenth Yearbook commented:

> A large part of the most efficient learning is incidental, that is, learning a special subject with reference to some broader interest or aim without realizing it: Learning number relationships in connection with telling time or making change; learning baseball averages (without effort) through sheer interest in big league contests. (Wheeler 1935, p. 239)

However, incidental learning was often haphazard, slow, and time consuming, and according to William Brownell—a psychologist and influential mathematics educator of the time—the arithmetic learned under such circumstances was "apt to be fragmentary, superficial, and mechanical" (1935, p. 18). When children were left to do whatever they felt like, their experiences were often so diverse and unstructured that they were unable to relate the different bits and pieces.

As a result, many mathematics educators of the era debated the merits of incidental learning for teaching meaningful arithmetic. They proposed a different interpretation of "meaningful arithmetic," claiming that "to learn arithmetic meaningfully it is necessary to understand it systematically" (McConnell 1941, p. 281). In a 1938 *Mathematics Teacher* article, Buckingham attempts to clarify this view of meaningful arithmetic by emphasizing what he saw as an important distinction between the significance and the meaning of arithmetic. For him, the *significance* of number was functional: "its value, its importance, its necessity in the modern social order," whereas the *meaning* of number was mathematical—embodied in the structure of the number system (p. 26). In general, although proponents of this type of "meaning theory" acknowledged the motivating and enriching value of number experiences that emanate from student-initiated activities, they emphasized as well the notion of "arithmetic as a closely knit system of understandable ideas, principles, and processes" (Brownell 1935, p. 19). This emphasis on mathematical relationships is clearly illustrated in figure 18.2, a reproduction of a page from Buswell, Brownell, and Sauble's (1959) third-grade text. In introducing basic subtraction facts to pupils, these

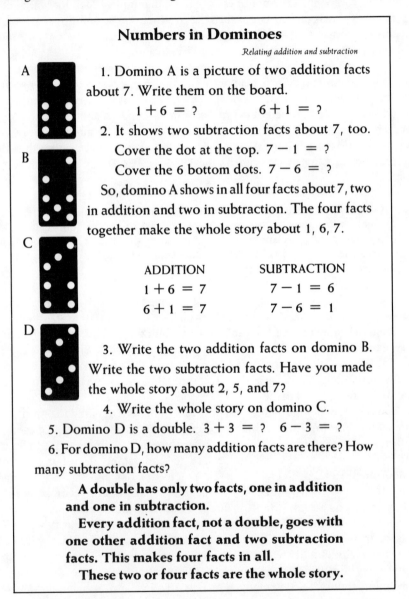

**Numbers in Dominoes**

*Relating addition and subtraction*

A　1. Domino A is a picture of two addition facts about 7. Write them on the board.

$$1 + 6 = ? \qquad 6 + 1 = ?$$

2. It shows two subtraction facts about 7, too.

Cover the dot at the top. $7 - 1 = ?$

B　Cover the 6 bottom dots. $7 - 6 = ?$

So, domino A shows in all four facts about 7, two in addition and two in subtraction. The four facts together make the whole story about 1, 6, 7.

C

| ADDITION | SUBTRACTION |
|---|---|
| $1 + 6 = 7$ | $7 - 1 = 6$ |
| $6 + 1 = 7$ | $7 - 6 = 1$ |

D　3. Write the two addition facts on domino B. Write the two subtraction facts. Have you made the whole story about 2, 5, and 7?

4. Write the whole story on domino C.

5. Domino D is a double. $3 + 3 = ?$　$6 - 3 = ?$

6. For domino D, how many addition facts are there? How many subtraction facts?

**A double has only two facts, one in addition and one in subtraction.**

**Every addition fact, not a double, goes with one other addition fact and two subtraction facts. This makes four facts in all.**

**These two or four facts are the whole story.**

Fig. 18.2. A page from a 1959 third-grade text: Buswell, Brownell, and Sauble's *Arithmetic We Need.*

textbook authors emphasized the relationship of the subtraction facts to previously learned addition facts, explicitly pointing out the "whole story" involving two different addends, a "story" in which the student relates two addition facts and two subtraction facts into one coherent whole.

Another important factor in the emergence of the new meaning theory of arithmetic was the introduction to this country of the "Gestalt" or "field" theory of learning (Fehr 1953). The central idea of field psychology is expressed in the German word *Gestalt,* which means an organized whole in contrast to a collection of parts. Gestalt psychologists regarded learning as a process of recognizing relationships and of developing insights. They believed that it is only when the relationship of a part of a situation to the whole situation is perceived that insight occurs and a solution to a problem can be formulated. Rather than drill on individual skills that in sum might lead to the solution of a problem (as a connectionist would), the field psychologist would try at the start to bring all the elements of a problem together.

A writer in the 1941 Sixteenth Yearbook of the NCTM rejected the connectionist theories of the earlier era as he explained the relationship of field psychology to the new meaning theory of arithmetic. Arguing that "meaning inheres in relationships," he claimed that the connectionists had "mutilated" arithmetic by decomposing it into numerous unrelated facts and by emphasizing "discreteness and specificity" (McConnell 1941, p. 275). The new "meaning theory," however, emphasized "understanding and relating the many specific items which are included [in our decimal number system]" (p. 280).

The meaning theory of arithmetic attempted to combine the progressive idea of activity learning with the ideas of the Gestalt psychologists. Teaching meaningful arithmetic demanded a very different kind of instruction from what had been the norm during the earlier drill and practice phase. Rote memorization was de-emphasized, and activity-based discovery was used to help children see connections among the many discrete skills and concepts they were learning. A new era in mathematics education was born. In fact, one important aspect of the new math—a focus on clarifying mathematical structures—might be seen as a refinement and an extension of the meaningful arithmetic programs initiated during the progressive era.

## THE NEW MATH PHASE

The profound and far-reaching changes that took place in the new math curriculum during the 1960s were stimulated by severe criticism of American education in the years following the Second World War. In an article in the *Saturday Review,* an education writer blamed outdated teaching methods for the students' difficulties:

> In many classrooms teachers still rely exclusively on the drill-and-memory system of the past. Others teach arithmetic "incidentally," as it is needed in other subjects and school activities. (Dunbar 1956, p. 54)

In response to such criticisms, mathematicians, educators, and psychologists joined together for the first time in a massive effort to restructure the teaching of mathematics.

In September 1959, thirty-five scientists, scholars, and educators gathered at Woods Hole on Cape Cod to discuss how science and mathematics education might be improved. A major theme for the Woods Hole conference was that a knowledge of the fundamental structures of a discipline was considered crucial. The conference participants believed that "an understanding of fundamental principles and ideas . . . appears to be the main road to adequate 'transfer of training'" and that the learning of "general or fundamental principles" ensures that individuals can reconstruct details when memory fails (Bruner 1960, p. 25).

Thus, in the early 1960s at least a dozen curriculum development projects were established to write new mathematics texts. The new texts differed considerably from traditional texts both in organization and in content. A major innovation was the attempt to introduce abstract but fundamental ideas early in the curriculum (in modified form when necessary) and to return continually to these ideas in subsequent lessons, relating, elaborating, and extending them. In the elementary school curriculum, lessons were included on such previously unheard-of topics as sets, numeration systems, intuitive geometry, and number theory, and these new topics were related to more familiar content through a spiral organization of unifying strands. For example, figure 18.3 illustrates how the notions of subsets, take-away subtraction, and the writing of equations are all intertwined on one page from a third-grade new math text (School Mathematics Study Group 1965).

It was a bold undertaking to attempt to design materials that would help children understand the underlying structure of a subject as abstract and complex as mathematics. And the notion that young children could profit from lessons on topics (such as set theory) that had previously been studied only at the college level seemed incredible to many. Although the educators and mathematicians who cooperated to write the new texts may not have relied heavily on any specific learning theory to guide their efforts, one psychologist is closely associated with the new math movement: Jerome Bruner (Resnick and Ford 1981, p. 111).

Bruner (1960) supported two major recommendations for the new math curricula: the idea of a spiral curriculum and the idea of discovery learning. Grounding his psychological theory in part in the stage-theory work of Piaget, Bruner claimed that children move through three levels of representation as they learn. The first is the "enactive level," where the child directly manipulates objects. In the second, or "ikonic level," the child

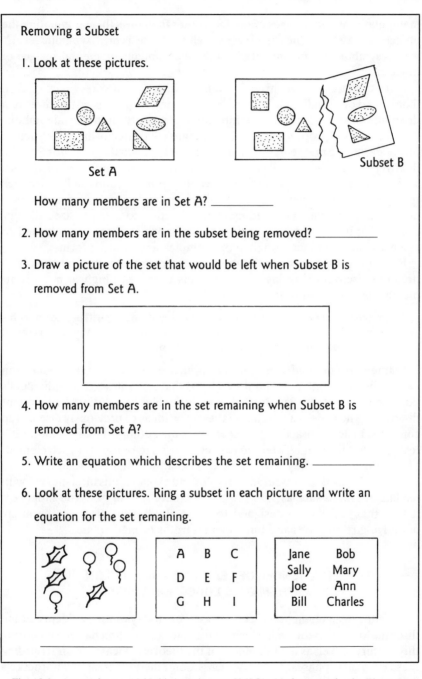

Removing a Subset

1. Look at these pictures.

Set A

Subset B

How many members are in Set A? _____

2. How many members are in the subset being removed? _____

3. Draw a picture of the set that would be left when Subset B is removed from Set A.

4. How many members are in the set remaining when Subset B is removed from Set A? _____

5. Write an equation which describes the set remaining. _____

6. Look at these pictures. Ring a subset in each picture and write an equation for the set remaining.

| A | B | C |
| D | E | F |
| G | H | I |

| Jane | Bob |
| Sally | Mary |
| Joe | Ann |
| Bill | Charles |

_____    _____    _____

Fig. 18.3. A page from a 1965 third-grade text: SMSG's *Mathematics for the Elementary School.*

manipulates mental images of objects rather than directly manipulating the objects themselves. The final level the child attains is the "symbolic level," where symbols are manipulated rather than objects or mental images of objects.

Just as children evolve through levels in which they use first enactive, then ikonic, and eventually symbolic representations, so the basic structures of a discipline can be represented manipulatively, visually, or in formal symbolic language. Many proponents of the new math advocated using this structure in the design of mathematics curricula: teachers should first promote the discovery of mathematical concepts through the manipulation of blocks, sticks, or chips; then present these concepts pictorially; and finally introduce the appropriate mathematical symbolism. In other words, during the new math era, mathematicians and mathematics educators emphasized the notion of a spiral curriculum—a curriculum in which ideas are returned to again and again in increasingly more complex and abstract forms.

Bruner's second recommendation for the new math curriculum was to promote discovery learning. Of course, discovery learning was not a completely new idea, but it has been said that

> more than any one man, Bruner managed to capture its spirit, provide it with a theoretical foundation, and disseminate it. Bruner is not the discoverer of discovery; he is its prophet. (Shulman 1970, p. 29)

Mathematicians had considerable influence on mathematics education during the new math era, and they agreed that regardless of an individual's developmental stage, intellectual activity involves a continual process of discovering new ideas and relating these new ideas to previously discovered concepts. In actual practice, however, since the authors of most "new math" texts felt that it was inefficient to expect children to rediscover each element of the curriculum, they wrote textbooks that adopted a guided discovery approach. Texts that presented examples and explanations interspersed with leading questions such as "Do you believe that . . .?" or "Do you suppose it is true that . . .?" were designed to guide children to discover the many underlying regularities and fundamental truths of mathematics.

## INFLUENCES OF LEARNING THEORIES ON MATHEMATICS EDUCATION TODAY

A visitor to an elementary school classroom today can see evidence of the three major phases through which mathematics education has passed during this century as well as the influences of the theories of learning undergirding these curricular phases. In today's classroom, the influence of Thorndike's S-R theory can be seen, for example, in behavioral objectives, in individualized learning packages, and, most recently, in many computer-based instructional systems. In all these, the aim is to break the material to be learned into small units and to maximize the effectiveness of reinforcement. In these more refined forms, drill and practice is still a focus of mathematics education today.

The recent concern for problem solving in mathematics can be seen as an extension of the influence of the Gestalt psychologists on the formulation of a meaning theory of arithmetic during the progressive era. We are currently experiencing a rebirth of interest in helping children to develop insights and to consolidate the skills they have learned into a meaningful whole. Furthermore, an important component of problem-solving instruction is the opportunity it gives children to experience the use of arithmetic skills in real-life situations. In this aspect of the contemporary curriculum we see the continued influence of the activity approach that dominated the progressive era.

In spite of the fact that the new math curriculum projects of the 1960s failed to fulfill the optimistic dreams of their originators for universal and massive curriculum reform, the projects have, in fact, effected certain fundamental changes both in the content and in the organization of today's mathematics curriculum. One of the major aims of mathematics instruction today is—as during the new math era—to help children understand the structure of mathematics. Important ideas such as properties of numeration systems or fractions are now introduced quite early in many texts and returned to again and again in later years (although some critics of today's curriculum would argue that most of today's middle-grade texts return to the same topics year after year at precisely the *same* level of development rather than spiraling to higher, more abstract levels with advancing years).

Interestingly, it is possible to detect in mathematics education today not only the influences of psychological theories of days gone by but also profound influences of educational psychology today. In recent years, mathematics educators have linked their work with that of learning theorists in investigating important questions about how children learn mathematics. Piaget's work sparked a great deal of research in mathematics education, and this research has no doubt influenced the strong interest in activity-based mathematics education programs today. The work of cognitive psychologists, in particular those who study information processing, has close links to much of the work of certain mathematics educators and program developers today. In recent years it has become more and more evident that many current developments in teaching mathematics are heavily grounded in psychological learning theories.

In fact, although it is always hard to recognize a historical phase until it has become well established, there are those who believe that we may currently be on the verge of a fourth major phase in mathematics education in this century—a phase heralded by the publication of the standards report of the

National Council of Teachers of Mathematics (1987). The report points out the importance of considering not only what mathematics itself is and why various mathematical concepts are important to know but also—perhaps most important—how students learn mathematics. In this respect, the report quite clearly reflects the influence of a recent psychological theory known as "constructivism." Students are no longer being viewed as "passive absorbers of information, storing it in easily retrievable fragments as a result of repeated practice and reinforcement"; rather, constructivist theory would claim that "individuals approach each new task with prior knowledge, assimilate new information, and construct their own meanings" (NCTM 1987, p. 8).

Does the publication of the NCTM's curriculum and evaluation standards herald a new phase in mathematics education in this century? How innovative are the ideas? How unique? How practical? How are we—as mathematics educators—to respond? How should we evaluate the ideas of the report? How can we make any predictions about which ideas will be absorbed into general practice and which will probably fall by the wayside? Can we recognize any of the recommendations as a reiteration of established practice? Is it possible to tell what's new and what's not?

This study of the recent influences of learning theories on mathematics education should make it clear that many educational practices and catch phrases that today seem quite current actually have their roots in bygone eras. Too often, however, we use such practices and phrases without perspective, without some appreciation for the contexts that gave them birth. According to the historian Morris Cohen, this can lead to an "exaggerated idea of our own originality and of the uniqueness of our own age and problems" (1961, p. 277). In addition, Cohen continues, without historical perspective we may "fail to see all that is involved in the issues of the day" (p. 277). History gives us clues to factors that may still be in operation today, to currents and forces that move our discipline, and to motives and conflicts that shape it. Most important, a knowledge of the past empowers us to speak with more authority and to make better-informed decisions about contemporary educational practices. In particular, when we become aware of their historical roots, it is clear not only that a number of psychological theories are very influential in the elementary mathematics curriculum of the 1980s and 1990s but also that we must think more critically about the relevance of those theories—and the practices they engender—for today's problems in mathematics education.

## REFERENCES

Brownell, William A. "Psychological Considerations in the Learning and the Teaching of Arithmetic." In *The Teaching of Arithmetic,* Tenth Yearbook of the National Council of Teachers of Mathematics, edited by W. D. Reeve, pp. 1–31. New York: Teachers College, Columbia University, 1935.

Bruner, Jerome S. *The Process of Education.* Cambridge, Mass.: Harvard University Press, 1960.

Buckingham, B. R. "Significance, Meaning, Insight—These Three." *Mathematics Teacher* 31 (January 1938): 24–30.

Buswell, Guy T., William A. Brownell, and Irene Sauble. *Arithmetic We Need: Book 3.* Boston: Ginn & Co., 1959.

Cohen, Morris. *The Meaning of Human History.* 2d ed. LaSalle, Ill.: Open Court Publishing Co., 1961.

Dunbar, Ruth. "Why Johnny Can't Add." *Saturday Review,* 8 September 1956, pp. 28, 54.

Fehr, Howard F. "Theories of Learning Related to the Field of Mathematics." In *The Learning of Mathematics: Its Theory and Practice,* Twenty-first Yearbook of the National Council of Teachers of Mathematics, edited by Howard F. Fehr, pp. 1–41. Washington, D.C.: The Council, 1953.

Knight, F. B. "Introduction." In *Report of the Society's Committee on Arithmetic,* Twenty-ninth Yearbook of the National Society for the Study of Education, edited by F. B. Knight, pp. 1–8. Bloomington, Ill.: Public School Publishing Co., 1930.

McConnell, T. R. "Recent Trends in Learning Theory: Their Application to the Psychology of Arithmetic." In *Arithmetic in General Education,* Sixteenth Yearbook of the National Council of Teachers of Mathematics, edited by W. D. Reeve, pp. 268–89. New York: Teachers College, Columbia University, 1941.

National Council of Teachers of Mathematics. *Curriculum and Evaluation Standards for School Mathematics.* Working Draft. Reston, Va.: The Council, 1987.

Resnick, Lauren B., and Wendy W. Ford. *The Psychology of Mathematics for Instruction.* Hillsdale, N.J.: Lawrence Erlbaum Associates, 1981.

School Mathematics Study Group. *Mathematics for the Elementary School, Book 3.* Stanford, Calif.: SMSG, 1965.

Shulman, Lee S. "Psychology and Mathematics Education." In *Mathematics Education,* Sixty-ninth Yearbook of the National Society for the Study of Education, edited by Edward G. Begle, pp. 23–71. Chicago: University of Chicago Press, 1970.

Thorndike, Edward L. *The Psychology of Arithmetic.* New York: Macmillan Co., 1922.

————. *The Thorndike Arithmetics: Book One.* New York: Rand McNally, 1924.

Wheeler, Raymond H. "The New Psychology of Learning." In *The Teaching of Arithmetic,* Tenth Yearbook of the National Council of Teachers of Mathematics, edited by W. D. Reeve, pp. 233–50. New York: Teachers College, Columbia University, 1935.

# 19

# Mathematics Teaching and Learning: Meeting the Needs of Special Learners

Barbara Wilmot
Carol A. Thornton

- **What mathematics is appropriate for students who are learning-handicapped or gifted in mathematics?**
- **What factors contribute to nurturing significant mathematical growth for special learners?**
- **How can critical thinking skills be nurtured or extended among special learners?**
- **What opportunities can teachers provide for special learners to demonstrate their growth in mathematical insight?**

**R**ESEARCH and experience are continually offering new information about learning and instruction in mathematics for students at both ends of the learning continuum. Promising practices related to major issues such as those implied by the questions above are beginning to emerge.

In an attempt to clarify, summarize, contrast, and enlighten, important elements of the mathematics curriculum related to these issues will be considered for two distinct populations in the mathematics classroom, *mathematically gifted* students and *learning-handicapped* students. Even if "pull out" or resource programs are in place, regular classroom teachers usually interact with each of these types of students daily. Some of the desired elements are quite similar for both groups, but for different reasons; others are decidedly opposite. This article will focus on the four major components of mathematics instruction involving special students.

## APPROPRIATE MATHEMATICS CONTENT

The mathematics curriculum for *all* students should be broader than just arithmetic. Children with special needs are frequently deprived of an appropriate curriculum. Concern about curriculum content in mathematics has led to recommendations for major change in school mathematics programs. Computational skills (including mental computation), estimation, and calculators are essential content for both the mathematically gifted and the learning handicapped. But to limit mathematics to even this broadened view of computation is inadequate.

Placing greater emphasis on conceptual understandings, number relationships, and mathematical reasoning; on the collection and interpretation of data; and on neglected curriculum areas like geometry, measurement, and probability serves two broad instructional goals with special learners: (1) to provide opportunities to explore the "essence" of mathematics as a framework for appropriate decision making with quantitative data in and out of school, and (2) to promote positive attitudes toward mathematics and the learning of mathematics. The net result is a "broad and enriched view of mathematics in a context of higher expectation" (NCTM 1987).

When we consider the content of a program for mathematically gifted students, the first consideration has to be philosophical: Do we accelerate the learning process, enrich it with topics not usually covered in the classroom, or provide some combination of the two?

In the context of the typical school structure, the first emphasis should be enrichment, which comes with some degree of serendipitous accleration. Noncomputational areas that, if studied in depth, can achieve the identified instructional goals include probability, statistics, extended problem solving, transformational geometry, logic, spatial visualization, topology, number theory, computer science, and so on. The scope and sequence of enrichment options should offer depth in topics rather than a superficial covering of numerous areas. In addition, experiences should be planned so that students are allowed to see the interrelationships between the different branches of mathematics.

Sherry (sixth grade) remarked: "I've been so bored with fractions. . . . But using them while making tessellations with the pattern blocks is better. I really like having the turtle make my design, too."

Learning-handicapped students may have any combination of memory deficits, visual/auditory perception or discrimination deficits, abstract reasoning difficulties, or other difficulties that interfere with learning. These conditions tend to skew a teacher's perception of children's abilities and increase the tendency to limit mathematical experiences to paper-and-pencil computation.

A broader, more relevant, and more stimulating curriculum can be carried out with learning-handicapped students when one integrates (1) careful sequencing, (2) small step size, (3) active learning approaches, (4) systematic review, and (5) compensation techniques for dealing with the handicap. Too often it's the instructional approach that is inappropriate, not the content.

Terry (seventh grade, learning-disabled with memory and visual perception deficits) had just participated in a water-pouring "experiment" involving pyramids and prisms of like heights and bases. Kinesthetic involvement with discussion that allowed Terry to summarize his group's findings had been part of the planned activity. "It will be easy to remember that the volume of a pyramid is one-third the volume of a prism." Then, seeing the cones and cylinders on the desk, he asked: "Will we do another experiment to pour three cones into one cylinder?"

## NURTURING MATHEMATICAL GROWTH

A supportive classroom environment is necessary for all special students. Differentiated instruction is the key. Important aspects of this instruction include cooperative learning groups, a risk-free environment, question-response techniques, and teacher flexiblity.

Differentiated instruction involves responding in different ways to different students on the basis of their individual abilities, interests, and needs. So little can do so much!

Ms. Martin moves about her third-grade class during guided study after her lesson on area. Each child has a slip of paper taped to the desk top showing three number facts with answers. As she draws close to Sherri (borderline mentally handicapped), she whispers: "Cover!" She says one of the facts just covered by Sherri and waits for the child to provide the answer.

Then she approaches Paul, who will shortly leave the room to attend a pull-out class for gifted students. She says, "Cover!" and asks Paul to suggest a real-world situation that might involve knowing $70 \times 5$. To other students Ms. Martin presents $7 \times 5$ and asks for the "product, plus 7." This is differentiated instruction.

Mr. Mooney (sixth grade) is about to give a seatwork assignment. Instead of having students do all the odd-numbered problems on the page, he asks them to do only those problems whose sum is less than 5 1/2. "It's all right to do more problems. I'll just grade only those with sums less than 5 1/2."

He then moves quietly to Judy, the behavior-disordered student just mainstreamed back into the class, and directs her to do just those with sums less than 5 1/2 *in the first row.* "Bring them to me when you've found them, and I'll do a quick check before you continue." To Sally, the brightest student in the class, he gives a different target number (involving fewer written problems) and suggests project options to be completed, recorded in her log, and discussed during their "chat time" on Thursday—differentiated instruction again.

## Cooperative Learning Groups

There are times when whole-class activity and discussion are more productive after students have had the opportunity to interact with each other on a problem or task. Typically the constituency of cooperative learning groups is heterogeneous, for this type of interaction gives students opportunities to recognize and value their interdependence on one another. In such instances, accountability is promoted when teachers assign specific roles to be carried out by the groups in general and by individuals within each group. The teacher encourages students to "solve" their own problems and intervenes only when everyone in the group has the same unanswered question.

Mathematically gifted and learning-handicapped students alike profit from the interaction of heterogeneous learning groups structured in the way

described above. Both groups of special learners, however, also have homogeneous group needs.

Mathematically gifted students need time to interact with peers of similar abilities as well as with adults. They need time to explore their numerous questions, elaborate on their creative ideas, evaluate potential problem solutions, and learn to cope with the implications of their special gift. They also need to be able to brainstorm, share ideas, extend thoughts, and evaluate their own potential.

Jason (fourth grade) is chided by his classmates for always getting high scores on tests. He wants to do well and cannot understand why this is a source of criticism. Group discussions of various attitudes to learning and success can lead to an understanding and acceptance of our culture's love-hate relationship with outstanding individuals.

Sarah (fifth grade) has used her computer to generate a listing of the possible combinations and permutations of double-dip ice-cream cones sold by a store that offers thirty-seven flavors. She realizes that this program could be used for other similar situations and is anxious to share her insights with her peers. Most of her classmates find it difficult to understand her enthusiasm.

Learning-handicapped students also benefit from the attention of additional individual or small-group instruction. Extra time typically is needed to establish necessary prerequisites; to teach (or reteach) with smaller instructional steps, using more time for active, individual involvement; and to provide necessary overlearning.

Sometimes it is possible to provide extra instruction for these students just after the lesson development and guided seatwork when the teacher is assured that others generally are proceeding well. In other situations the teacher may choose to work with these students at the beginning of the next day's lesson while other students do a different task.

These small-group or individual sessions provide handicapped learners with the additional structure and support they need. They give teachers time to supply additional small steps to bridge the gaps of typical textbook instruction. These sessions are particularly valuable when they require students to use models to illustrate and check written work; when they call on students to explain mathematical concepts, patterns, and procedures in their own words; and when they emphasize techniques to accommodate the handicap.

On a "bad" day, Ed (fourth grade, with figure-ground deficits) looked at the shaded fraction bar on the board and said, "Half shaded." He was not able visually to distinguish the vertical division lines that had been shaded over in the drawing, and he missed one. Because of his visual problems he could not "see" that the shaded part was longer than the unshaded. Ed called it as he saw it: one part shaded out of two that appeared to be equal in size.

Like other learning-handicapped students in mathematics, Ed needs time and specific guidance to learn the limitations of his handicap in each new context and to learn how to compensate for that handicap. In this case, the marking illustrated in figure 19.1 would have been better for Ed than the customary shading (Bley and Thornton 1981).

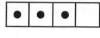

Fig. 19.1

## Question/Response Techniques

Learning-handicapped students characteristically are not good "risk takers"; mathematically gifted students vary in their willingness to take a risk. Some, tending toward perfectionism, fear offering an incorrect response; others blurt out intuitive answers. Some, having often been chastised for unexpected suggestions, have learned how to be "one of the regular kids."

The best way to help both types of learners is to help them learn to help themselves. They will not otherwise become independent thinkers. The teacher's attitude toward "right" and "wrong" answers and toward student response in general sets the stage for change.

One of the essential components of giftedness is creativity (Ridge and Renzulli 1981). In order to foster this creativity in mathematics, the student must feel free to suggest a pattern or relationship, a strategy, a hypothesis, or a direction to pursue for verification, even though it might be different from that of the instructor or appear to be totally unsuitable. This is not a time for evaluation. Instead, a nonjudgmental response such as "Could you explain that further?" or "What made you think of that?" or "Let's look at the pros and cons together" will increase their willingness to risk thinking novel thoughts and then sharing them. Society's problems need innovative solutions, and the classroom can be a good incubator for innovative thinking.

Chris (fifth grade) has been using the geoboard to find area generalizations for parallelograms and trapezoids. He now suggests that he wants to use the pattern blocks, tangrams, and graph paper to make sure he is correct. The instructor might judge this a waste of time, but Chris should be allowed to pursue the verification.

Because they have been told they are wrong so many times, learning-handicapped children often back off from responding, in the fear they may be wrong again. To help create a risk-free environment, the teacher might call on a second or third child, even when the correct answer is given, at least once in each lesson. The teacher has thereby provided time for the learning-handicapped child to process information and to be in a position to risk answering.

Mr. Martin holds a demonstration clock and asks for the time. He accepts the first correct answer and moves on. In the meantime Jack (second grade, learning disabled with short-term and sequential memory deficits) has had to grapple individually with silent questions: "What hand do I look to first? What number does this hand point to? Does it mean minutes or hours? What number does the other hand point to? How do I count by fives?" Jack does not attempt to respond, because there is no time for him to process the necessary information and he fears giving a wrong answer.

## Flexibility

Teacher flexibility in both content and methodology is very important when working with both mathematically gifted and learning-handicapped students. Teachers often must be willing to alter their plans or the materials with which they teach in order to meet the special needs of their students.

With mathematically gifted students, newness and variety will stimulate creativity and give a reprieve from what many students consider to be boring daily arithmetic tasks. New people, books, topics, places, ideas, experiences, and learning aids should be planned and offered frequently. Fortunately, mathematics has a wide variety of materials that provide excellent learning tools, such as attribute blocks, dominoes, geoboards, Cuisenaire rods, Miras, computers, pattern blocks, strategy games, tangrams, and graphs (Thornton and Wilmot 1986).

Even with careful short- and long-range planning, the spontaneous nature of these students suggests that teachers should make sincere attempts to quickly evaluate new potential directions and then adapt. This can extend the momentum created by the excitement of a new discovery or idea.

Nancy (first grade) has been using the pattern blocks to make larger equilateral triangles from the small green ones and larger squares from the orange square blocks. When trying to verify the same pattern with the hexagons, she not only discovered that it was impossible but also began to put various combinations of two and three colors together to make larger hexagons. Nice patterns emerged. The project then took several (unplanned-for) days to complete, but the teacher felt that the time reaped several benefits.

Learning-disabled students are consistently inconsistent. Some, like those with behavior deficits, are often controlled by emotions and moods that may interfere with learning. Each handicapping condition and every handicapped child has a specific learning style. A teaching style that caters to individual learning strengths while accounting for learning deficits is one that must be flexible. This flexibility sometimes affects the choice of teaching materials and the way they are used. Most often it affects the content one has planned to teach.

Keri (sixth grade, memory and visual perception deficits) is doing an independent seatwork example that involves multiplying 1 2/3 by 3 3/4.

When the teacher sees Keri rewrite the problem as $3/3 \times 6/4$, she realizes that Keri has simply added the whole number to the numerator each time. The teacher decides to reteach the renaming with fraction strips and pieces before Keri is allowed to proceed. This means replanning: "If I shift to measurement for two days I can find time to work on renaming with Keri. Then I can come back to the fraction chapter." Being flexible now will be more beneficial to Keri and allow the teacher to "keep the class together."

## PROMOTING HIGHER LEVELS OF CRITICAL THINKING

The primary goal of mathematics instruction for both mathematically gifted and learning-handicapped students should be to promote higher levels of critical thinking in problem situations.

Critical and creative thinking have always been emphasized in gifted education. Mathematically gifted students are capable of delving deeper into ideas—analyzing, synthesizing, and evaluating. As they learn to do this with the thoughts of others, they also begin to dissect their own insights and refine them. Individually or in small groups, these talented students often can make giant leaps, discover patterns, form generalizations, create nonexamples, or verbalize a newly uncovered mathematical property. Learning concepts and reasons, rather than merely memorizing facts, increases the likelihood that they will enjoy mathematics and assume responsibility for their own computational skills. Generally, they need much less drill and lecture. They respond well to a mixture of guided discovery and independent learning.

Three ways of extending the thinking and independent problem-solving attempts of these students are (1) using questioning techniques that increase the complexity of their thought processes; (2) continually striving to improve their insight into relationships and the forming of generalizations; and (3) neither confirming nor denying the "correctness" of a new discovery but instead requesting some citation of proof or evidence of reasoning.

Using these techniques will lead mathematically gifted students to become independent learners. Instead of being dependent on the teacher or answer book for verification, they will learn to hypothesize, test, and conclude. They will also look for possible exceptions or contradictions. Learning in this manner is very stimulating and exciting to these students; it builds their confidence and leaves them continually open to new puzzlements.

Tiffany's group (fourth grade), working with star polygons, has been exploring the relationship between the number of points on a circle, the number of points skipped, and relatively prime numbers. Acting as the spokesperson for her group, she asked, "Is this the right pattern?" The teacher's response might take the form of questions like these: "Can you show me that your table is correct?" "What was your first discovery?" "Why do you suppose that some are the same?" "What if there were an odd number of points?"

Critical thinking among learning-handicapped students frequently does not emerge "naturally," since these students tend to be inconsistent and approach learning in a disorganized manner. In addition to learning mathematical content, these students have to learn how to learn! The day-by-day requirements and reactions of the teacher do much to determine the pattern by which these children *expect* to learn: memorizing and imitating demonstrated methods versus thinking independently and critically.

Explicit intervention techniques are necessary to nurture the potential of learning-handicapped students for higher-level thinking and problem solving. The most important of these techniques include (1) suitably structuring activities that encourage experimentation, (2) helping students record and analyze results that lead to useful patterns and relationships, and (3) structuring questions and probes that extend children's thinking: "Can we do it another way?" "Using objects or finger counting takes a long time. Is there a pattern in the numbers?" "How do you know?" Visual, auditory, and kinesthetic/tactile methods also can help.

Ryan (second grade, learning disabled with visual perception problems) closed his eyes, felt, and counted the six eggs in each half-dozen container. "Six and six, that's twelve." He wrote the matching fact. He then repeated the procedure for the 6 + 7 fact: "There's one extra egg by the second carton— 6 + 7, that's 13." The "one more" number relationship was one Ryan learned well through activities like these. The unexpected (but welcome) transfer came during later work with other unknown addition and subtraction facts: 6 + 8 ("One more than 6 + 7, which I know"); 15 − 7 ("One more than 14 − 7").

## DEMONSTRATING GROWTH IN MATHEMATICAL INSIGHT

A wider variety of opportunities for expressing understanding should complement the traditional paper-and-pencil evaluations.

Evaluation should focus on assessing what has been learned, not on the number of problems completed correctly. An appropriate goal for all students is the mastery of the skills and concepts of the standard curriculum of their school. For the mathematically gifted, the focus should be on quality rather than quantity. Assignments for the able should be altered so that these students are required to complete only the most challenging exercises, not all of them. This approach accomplishes several desirable goals:

- Students realize they are responsible for the material and can learn to adjust the amount of practice required according to their own needs.
- Students are less likely to become bored.
- Students are allowed more time to pursue enrichment topics and in-depth projects.

Renzulli, one of the leading specialists in gifted education, strongly advocates the use of projects as products of learning, suggesting that gifted students spend approximately 50 percent of their learning time on them (Ridge and Renzulli 1981). These can be independent or small-group activities and should, if possible, arise from real problems and from students' interest in a particular branch of mathematics.

Examples of projects range from a complex computer program to a display created for a science fair to an extensive research paper. Often the demands of the classroom preclude more than one or two of these projects a year. Projects of a lesser scope can also be very beneficial—for example, constructing a spinner with unfair probabilities; filling in a $3 \times 3$ matrix with attribute blocks where each block horizontally and vertically differs by two values; creating scenarios so that other students can use logic tables to discover "Who Done It"; reporting on the accomplishments of famous female mathematicians; formulating predictions after gathering data, organizing the information, and constructing several different types of graphs to illustrate the information. With projects of any type, these students still need motivation, encouragement, and direction from the teacher (Short 1985). Even though they are highly able, they are not mature adults.

Because there is wide variation in the nature and degree of handicapping conditions, the "product" of learning in school mathematics for handicapped students ranges from survival-related concepts and skills to demonstrated understandings and competence prerequisite to success in pure mathematics. The common element in this range of goals is the ability to make appropriate decisions in situations involving numeric data.

Achieving minimal competency scores on written tests clearly falls short of the broader goal in the mathematics education of learning-handicapped students—the ability to *think* in quantitative situations. It is critical that they understand what they are doing and why they are doing it. Otherwise, inferences or transfer to new situations cannot be made.

Students can be made accountable for demonstrating their growth in mathematical understanding by using objects to illustrate or model a concept, procedure, or problem solution; using objects to show that a given response is correct; describing in their own words both the mechanics and appropriateness of a procedure; and identifying the pattern or number relationship that has been used. Teachers might create a checklist of one or two main points for each chapter covered. As the chapter progresses, students can be asked individually to demonstrate their understanding of the checklist items in one of the alternative ways.

## SUMMARY

Promising practices are beginning to emerge in mathematics instruction for special learners. A broader mathematics curriculum with differentiated expectations is essential. Teaching techniques that allow and encourage these students to understand concepts, recognize and use number relationships, solve problems, and apply knowledge are available and appropriate. The major goal—*thinking,* not just memorizing and calculating—is appropriate for *all* mathematics students.

Progress in this direction with both mathematically gifted and learning-handicapped populations involves an awareness of the characteristics of these special students, an understanding of their unique educational strengths and needs, and program modifications tailored to fit. This article, based on extensive experience with both special groups, has highlighted major issues in an attempt to increase both sensitivity and understanding and to offer specific instructional suggestions.

Understandably, change in any of these areas will come gradually and needs to be linked with professional development. Both teachers and administrators should cooperate to find viable alternatives to instruction that will allow and encourage all children to reach their fullest mathematical potential.

### BIBLIOGRAPHY

Bley, Nancy, and Carol A. Thornton. *Teaching Mathematics to the Learning Disabled.* Rockville, Md.: Aspen Systems Corporation, 1981.

Maker, C. J. *Curriculum Development for the Gifted.* Rockville, Md.: Aspen Systems Corporation, 1982.

National Council of Teachers of Mathematics. "Vertical Acceleration." *NCTM News Bulletin* 20 (September 1983): 4.

———. "Provisions for Mathematically Talented and Gifted Students." *NCTM News Bulletin* 23 (January 1987): 7.

Ridge, H. Laurence, and Joseph S. Renzulli. "Teaching Mathematics to the Talented and Gifted." In *The Mathematical Education of Exceptional Children and Youth,* edited by Vincent J. Glennon, pp. 191–266. Reston, Va.: National Council of Teachers of Mathematics, 1981.

Short, D. "From the Other Side of the Desk: How a Gifted Student Wants to Be Taught." *Gifted/Creative/Talented* 37 (March/April 1985): 19–21.

Thornton, Carol A., and Barbara Wilmot. "Special Learners." *Arithmetic Teacher* 33 (February 1986): 38–41.

Tuttle, F. *Gifted and Talented Students.* Washington, D.C.: National Education Association, 1983.

Wilmot, Barbara. "Mathematically Gifted Students: Who Are They? What Should Be Done for Them?" *Math Lab Matrix* [Illinois State University] 19 (Spring 1983): 1–3.

# 20

# Staff Development: Directions and Realities

## Arthur A. Hyde

I N THE second half of the 1980s, professional organizations and mathematics educators are promoting a greater emphasis in the mathematics curriculum on problem solving, mathematical thinking and reasoning, and linkages between conceptual and procedural knowledge. In this era of fundamental curricular change, teachers are urged to adopt a dynamic approach to instruction, to help their students construct mathematical knowledge through the active integration of ideas and experiences. This kind of instruction calls for dramatic changes in the teaching styles and behaviors of most teachers. If these substantial changes in curriculum and instruction are to occur, two areas of difficulty must be addressed: (1) the organizational features of schools that inhibit teachers' effectiveness and hinder substantial change and (2) the complex relationships among teachers' actions, knowledge, beliefs, and attitudes. These are discussed in the next section.

An examination of these two areas leads directly to a consideration of how to create effective staff development programs. Fortunately, a substantial body of literature exists on staff development in schools and on two related areas, organizational change and adult learning. This literature can direct our efforts to improve mathematics teaching.

## CONSTRAINTS ON EFFECTIVE MATHEMATICS TEACHING

### The School's Organization

Several organizational features of schools can create obstacles to effective mathematics teaching and staff development. Teachers generally operate with great autonomy and are isolated from their peers. They receive little support, assistance, or feedback to improve their teaching. At the building level, it is rare to find a person with either the knowledge or the specific role to improve mathematics teaching. The building principal is traditionally more concerned with teacher evaluation than with instructional improvement.

The typical approach to staff development taken by school districts is piecemeal and episodic. Teachers are exposed to an array of unconnected in-service sessions, speakers, and workshops. (See Moore and Hyde [1982].) Districtwide interest in mathematics teaching is expressed primarily when a new textbook series is adopted.

Most elementary school teachers are generalists who have a minimum of specialized knowledge in any one curricular area. In fact, many educators strongly support the notion of elementary school generalists who can integrate knowledge and thinking processes for their students. However, curricular guidelines, textbooks, mandated time allotments, and the like force clear, and sometimes rigid, demarcations among curricular areas.

School districts have rather specific expectations for the amount of material to be completed in mathematics at each grade level. Curricula are often keyed to particular objectives and standardized tests to ensure coverage and mastery. Although teachers may initially attempt to teach for conceptual understanding, after a relatively brief period of developmental instruction using models, examples, and so forth, they feel compelled by time pressures to complete the "coverage" of the topic. Thus, they move quickly to solidify an appropriate algorithm in their students' minds. What passes for conceptualization is all too often the memorized manipulation of symbols, devoid of meaning.

School district leaders who create policies and guidelines for the mathematics curriculum need to be thoroughly informed about current curricular reforms in mathematics. They should understand that the reforms are not merely adding more content or new topics to the curriculum. A fundamental shift in conceptualization and emphasis is occurring, one that has dramatic implications for teaching. Administrators and policy makers must understand the delicate balances that are required between mathematical concepts and reasoning, conceptual and procedural knowledge, developmental instruction and practice, and related issues.

## Teachers' Beliefs and Attitudes

Teachers are frequently criticized for their level of mathematical knowledge and teaching skills. However, this criticism is too simplistic. In some respects, teachers are as much victims as those they teach. Where mathematics is concerned, we have a truly remarkable cultural heritage of phobias and anxieties, misconceptions and myths, stumbling blocks and brick walls. Schools have transmitted this heritage—they merely mirror our culture and society.

Like most members of our society, elementary school teachers do not have extensive mathematical knowledge, and many have anxiety and negative feelings about mathematics. Yet, unlike others, they must teach the subject to children. Many teachers have misconceptions and erroneous beliefs about mathematics. They equate mathematics with arithmetic, particularly with symbol manipulation. Many believe that their main task is to teach rapid computation, that good problem solving is done quickly, that problems always have one right answer, and so on. With such a narrow view of mathematics, with little knowledge of the way children learn mathematics, and with a limited sense of the importance of mathematical thinking and reasoning, it is likely that they would emphasize the rote, the algorithmic, and the procedural. It is hardly the fault of these teachers—as students themselves they experienced little else.

In the past, many educators assumed that improvements in mathematics teaching would result from increasing the mathematical knowledge and technical skills of individual teachers. Programs and courses would be provided for the teachers, who would return to their classrooms and implement the new program or use the new approach. We have come to realize, however, that improving mathematics teaching is more complicated than merely offering a teacher additional mathematical or technical knowledge.

If teachers are to comprehend the nature of mathematics and mathematical thinking, they must experience *as learners* the kinds of mathematical knowledge and thinking that we expect them to teach. However, it is a serious mistake to assume that this learning is solely for the sake of knowledge. Equally important are teachers' beliefs, attitudes, and feelings about mathematics, their own mathematical thinking, and the teaching of mathematics. They must develop some level of confidence and competence in doing mathematics. They must believe that they and their students are capable of learning mathematics. They must experience good mathematics teaching as a model of what they themselves might do. Otherwise, we are asking them to teach in a way they have neither seen nor experienced.

## Implications

Staff development in mathematics for veteran elementary school teachers must be seen as a process of working with individuals within an organizational context. Whatever the vehicles for staff or instructional improvement, they must account for the district and building contexts in which the teachers work. Teachers need the support and encouragement of colleagues and principals in their efforts to try something markedly different from what they have been doing.

Within these organizational contexts, methods of helping individual teachers change or improve must address more than their knowledge. The change or improvement can be conceived as attitude change, which has three components: cognitive, behavioral, and affective. Simply stated, what teachers *do* in the classroom is a function of how they *think* about mathematics and how they *feel* about mathematics and its teaching. The knowledge component is clearly present, but it exists within the broader framework of attitudes, beliefs, feelings, and the school's organizational features.

It is crucial to consider teachers' willingness to confront their own knowledge limitations and their own anxieties about mathematics and its teaching. This willingness is extremely important, because the structure of schools, with their isolation and autonomy, does not promote development and improvement. Teachers are not required to take additional courses in mathematics or its teaching. Thus, we need to create structures and processes that foster a desire to improve mathematics teaching among elementary school teachers. We also need to recognize that any change in teaching behavior takes time and effort. How can we structure staff development to sustain over time this willingness to improve? How can we assist teachers so that they both can and want to approach teaching in new ways?

## STAFF DEVELOPMENT, ORGANIZATIONAL CHANGE, AND ADULT LEARNING

In the past twenty years, policy analysts and researchers have examined numerous efforts aimed at improving schools, enhancing teachers' performance, and so forth. These improvement efforts and the research had a variety of theoretical orientations that I shall address under three different, but related, rubrics: staff development, organizational change, and adult learning.

Although most staff development programs for veteran teachers are concerned with helping them improve, develop, change, or learn, well-articulated theories of adult learning and development are scarce. Sprinthall and Thies-Sprinthall (1983) reviewed relevant theories and research that could inform staff development. Their work suggests the following guidelines for facilitating a teacher's cognitive development:

1. Teachers should be exposed to significant, direct, and active role-taking experiences in which they must employ new models, not merely hear about, observe, or experience them vicariously.

2. These role-taking experiences must be appropriate for the teacher's state or stage of development; the potential learning should neither be "beyond the reach nor below the grasp" of the individual.

3. Careful and continuous guided reflection must accompany the experiences. Experiences and reflection must be balanced, since they are equally important.

4. Experience and reflection should be continuous processes, probably occurring over at least a one-year period.

5. Both personal support and challenge are necessary. To relinquish established systems of thought and action, a person has to be dissatisfied with existing modes and get assistance from sympathetic and supportive others in making the transition to new modes.

A landmark study of efforts to support educational change was commonly known as the Rand Change Agent Study (Berman and McLaughlin 1975, 1977). A seven-volume set of reports described findings from nearly three hundred projects. Subsequent work by McLaughlin and Marsh (1979) directly related the findings of this study to staff development. They suggested the following:

1. Staff development should not be conceived as "technology transfer," but rather "as ongoing program building in an organizational context" (p. 87).

2. Teachers often possess the "best clinical expertise available" on the practice of teaching and should be involved in identifying and solving problems (p. 87).

3. Professional learning must be related to ongoing classroom activities. However, any new approach or innovation will undergo substantial adaptation as it is implemented in local schools and individual classrooms.

4. Professional learning and implementation of an innovation is a nonlinear, multiyear process strongly influenced by such organizational factors as institutional leadership and school climate.

Two somewhat broader conceptions of educational change are presented by Sarason (1982) and Fullan (1982). Sarason examines features of school culture that dramatically inhibit substantive organizational change. One of his illustrative cases is the introduction of "new math" in the 1960s. Fullan's review of research gives a comprehensive overview of the processes of educational change at various organizational levels.

From the literature on staff development, one can discern several major points of consensus among researchers and practitioners. There is a recognition of the necessity to understand the specific district and school organizational contexts in which the teachers work and the staff development activities take place. (See Griffin [1983]; Schlechty and Whitford [1983]; and Fenstermacher and Berliner [1985].) Leaders of staff development programs should have expertise in using a new approach in actual classrooms so that their advice and assistance recognizes the constraints that teachers face. Effective leadership in staff development often means an ongoing collaboration with teachers in their classrooms to adapt the approach and to assist them in developing confidence and skill. (See Lieberman and Miller [1979] and Joyce and Showers [1983].) Collaborative and supportive interaction among peers is a necessary ingredient in staff development. This interaction seems most helpful when it occurs among a group of teachers in a particular school over an extended period. (See Lieberman and Miller [1979]; Courter and Ward [1983]; and Little [1981].)

## EFFECTIVE STAFF DEVELOPMENT IN MATHEMATICS TEACHING

As one looks at the literature on staff development, educational change, and adult learning, five interrelated areas seem most important to staff development in mathematics:

1. Rethinking what is needed
2. Using staff development leaders with special knowledge, skill, and sensitivity
3. Arranging sustained collegial interaction
4. Linking staff development and classroom practice
5. Involving school administrators in staff development

### Rethinking What Is Needed

Staff development often flounders because leaders assume that all teachers have to do is take what is presented in a staff development program and do it in the classroom. Some skills can be readily transferred from the training situation directly to the classroom. Joyce and Showers (1983) call this *horizontal transfer*. However, most complex teaching strategies are not readily transferred from training to practice.

Teaching requires an extraordinary amount of judgment and discretion; thousands of moment-to-moment decisions must be made about what is appropriate for particular students. An individual teacher chooses what to do and say with little supervision.

A teacher's repertoire of actions and strategies has been formed over time in the context of specific classrooms. Major changes in mathematics teaching, such as the adoption of new approaches for teaching mathematical thinking, cannot be implemented in the way implied by horizontal transfer. A more dramatic adaptation and modification of the existing teaching repertoire must occur. Further refinement and adaptation must continue over time before the new approach is fully incorporated and regularly used. This process is called *vertical transfer*. (See Joyce and Showers [1983].)

If teachers are willing to try a new strategy, how can it be used proficiently? Certainly, the teachers must understand the strategy conceptually and operationally, but they must also learn how to—

- adapt the strategy for particular groups of students;

- apply it to various areas of the mathematics curriculum;
- modify or create instructional materials to accompany it; and
- organize, group, and manage the students within it.

Therefore, the knowledge component of staff development must include more than a "knowing about" but also an applied knowledge, in which teachers work out these ideas, practices, and strategies in their own classrooms. This process is the essence of vertical transfer.

Both leaders and participants in staff development should realize that a different way of teaching mathematics involves substantial vertical transfer. Both groups should be honest about the need to address not only knowledge but attitudes and beliefs. Without overdramatizing these issues, staff development planners and leaders should readily acknowledge that there are no shortcuts to staff development; teachers should be encouraged to experiment, adapt, and try out new ideas. Vertical transfer is a developmental process. Difficulties, discomfort, frustration, and setbacks are to be expected. Figuring out how to make an idea work in one's own classroom takes time and effort.

### Staff Development Leaders

For teachers to achieve vertical transfer, leaders of staff development in mathematics need to understand classroom realities. They must be able to assist teachers in making the new ideas, techniques, and approaches meaningful, practical, and applicable to their own particular classrooms. They should have extensive experience in adapting a strategy to the classroom just as they are asking teachers to do.

Leaders must be thoroughly knowledgeable about both the practical and theoretical aspects of a new approach. As teachers successfully incorporate the approach, they become interested in learning not only what works but why—the principles that underlie the approach. If they understand the principles and have incorporated some of the approach into their repertoire, they become able to create their own variations that fit their classrooms.

An approach used successfully by several projects has been for college faculty to collaborate as staff development leaders with selected classroom teachers. Since the leaders had participated in extensive staff development programs and had incorporated the new approach themselves, they understood what the classroom teachers had to do in their classrooms to achieve vertical transfer.

### Sustained Collegial Interaction

Schools need to establish ways for teachers to participate in continual dialogues about teaching practice. To counteract isolation, the improvement of teaching requires open, nonjudgmental discussions among teachers about how they teach. *Collegiality, collaboration, cooperation,* and *companion-ship* are some of the terms used by educators studying staff development and school change (Joyce and Showers 1983; Lieberman and Miller 1984).

These concepts are especially important in the improvement of mathematics teaching, where affective factors are pronounced. Teachers need to realize that their feelings about teaching mathematics are not unique. They need nonevaluative assistance and reassurance from leaders and their peers that they can overcome difficulties and develop more effective teaching strategies.

If teachers are to make fundamental changes in how and what they teach, this collegial dialogue on mathematics teaching must be sustained. They need support while they are trying to make these changes. Successful staff development projects in mathematics should feature regular sessions (probably weekly) during the school year to assist teachers in understanding the new approaches and adapting them to their own classrooms.

Continuity of teachers and leaders greatly facilitates this collegial interaction. When the same ten to twenty teachers meet with the same leaders during the year, the support and assistance received can be significantly more personal and specific than in a series of workshops where the composition of the group changes regularly. Having the same leaders and participants can bring both continuity and coherence to the discussion of ideas, issues, and techniques as the teachers develop and refine their practices over time.

## Linking Staff Development to Classroom Practice

For teachers to accomplish vertical transfer and adapt new approaches to their own classrooms, staff development leaders must provide activities that shift from trying out new teaching ideas to collegial reflection and back again. Thus, a staff development effort might include sessions with teachers and leaders discussing, presenting, and sharing ideas or practices as well as leaders and teachers interacting in classrooms.

The main purpose of collaboration in the classroom is to give teachers feedback to help them develop and incorporate an approach into their repertoire of teaching techniques. However, feedback is not evaluation. It includes encouragement, support, listening, and suggestions rather than judgments and statements of what was done wrong. Feedback requires interpersonal sensitivity from the leaders and a climate of trust in the collegial group.

The difficulties some teachers have in implementing new approaches have as much to do with classroom management as with mathematics. For instance, allowing pupils to work with manipulatives can threaten a teacher's sense of control. He or she might not have developed procedures to handle small groups of students working cooperatively at a table or might not be able to tolerate the added noise of a lively discussion. Demonstration lessons by leaders in a teacher's own classroom can serve as a concrete illustration of how to handle such concerns. A number of staff development programs in mathematics now include direct work in small-group projects, cooperative learning, and other classroom structure and climate concerns.

A major advantage of collegial interaction over time is the continuing dialogue that can focus on affective areas. Teachers engage in mutual reflection with leaders and peers as they struggle to incorporate new approaches. Ongoing collaboration allows teachers to share frustrations and successes, check their perceptions and beliefs, and receive reassurance that difficulties are a normal part of developing proficiency.

In these collegial sessions the leaders should deal with teachers' attitudes toward mathematics and teaching to fully incorporate new approaches into the classroom. Influencing attitudes, emotions, and the like requires many varied experiences in mathematics with extensive group interaction and open expression. (See Tobias [1978] and Buxton [1981].) For instance, in some staff development projects, small groups of three or four teachers engage in collaborative problem solving. After the groups reach solutions, they discuss the mathematical content of the problem and analyze the mathematical thinking they used. Next, teachers explicitly address how they felt about this work. They are asked to discuss their past experiences as students. Teachers describe and analyze how they wish they had been taught and what was successful in helping them. Frequently, they express the view that small-group problem solving is less threatening than the performance pressure of working as an individual.

When such activities are done in a collaborative support group, teachers are more willing to talk about their possible feelings of inadequacy concerning mathematics and, perhaps most important, become more willing and able to do mathematics. This combined affective and cognitive development can greatly enhance the vertical transfer of teaching approaches into the classroom.

## Involving School Administrators in Staff Development

Staff development leaders must understand the organizational context of their efforts. They must ask, What is essential for administrators to understand and value concerning this new approach if the work is to be successful? Although it may be rare to find administrators who want to participate fully in teachers' training, it is valuable to include them in some way because they have the formal authority to facilitate staff development. They can authorize teachers to observe one another's classes, making substitute teachers available. They can reschedule events to allow teachers to hold planning discussions during the school week. They can allocate funds for materials. Besides providing resources and time, administrators can integrate staff development into the ongoing life of the schools.

It is important that administrators' teacher-evaluation processes recognize that difficulties will emerge as new strategies are attempted. Also, administrators should fully understand the implications of instructional changes. For instance, teachers may spend more time discussing concepts and using manipulatives than they did previously.

## CONCLUSION

Many teachers truly desire to be effective in teaching mathematics. Whether or not they openly admit feelings of inadequacy, many want to be more effective; they want practical, usable methods and materials and effective techniques, strategies, and approaches. However, any new way of operating must hold the promise of actually working in their own classroom, not in an idealized setting with students who are young Polyás.

If staff development programs are to have the long-term impact and effectiveness needed to revamp elementary school mathematics teaching, the willing participation of large numbers of teachers is essential. This participation is more likely to occur if we are honest about the amount of time and effort required; if we have sensitive and knowledgeable leaders who can work collegially over time with groups of teachers; and if we offer activities that allow teachers to help each other gain knowledge, change beliefs and attitudes, overcome negative feelings, and apply, adapt, modify, and develop versions of an approach that fits their classrooms. Finally, we can improve mathematics teaching if we weave our staff development efforts into the fabric of the schools by facilitating understanding in administrators.

### REFERENCES

Berman, Paul, and Milbrey W. McLaughlin. *Federal Programs Supporting Educational Change,* vol. 4. *The Findings in Review.* Santa Monica, Calif.: The Rand Corporation, 1975.

———. *Federal Programs Supporting Educational Change,* vol. 7. *Factors Affecting Implementation and Continuation.* Santa Monica, Calif.: The Rand Corporation, 1977.

Buxton, Laurie. *Do You Panic about Maths?* London: Heinemann Educational Books, 1981.

Courter, R. Linden, and Beatrice A. Ward. "Staff Development and School Improvement." In *Staff Development,* Eighty-second Yearbook of the Society for the Study of Education, edited by Gary A. Griffin, pp. 185–209. Chicago: University of Chicago Press, 1983.

Fenstermacher, Gary D., and David C. Berliner. "Determining the Value of Staff Development." *Elementary School Journal* 85 (Jan. 1985): 281–314.

Fullan, Michael. *The Meaning of Educational Change.* New York: Teachers College Press, 1982.

Griffin, Gary A. "Implications of Research for Staff Development Programs." *Elementary School Journal* 83 (March 1983): 414–25.

Joyce, Bruce R., and Beverly Showers. *Power in Staff Development through Research on Training.* Washington, D.C.: Association for Supervision and Curriculum Development, 1983.

Lieberman, Ann, and Lynne Miller. *Teachers: Their World, Their Work.* Washington, D.C.: Association for Supervision and Curriculum Development, 1984.

————. "The Social Realities of Teaching." In *Staff Development: New Demands, New Realities, New Perspectives,* edited by A. Lieberman and L. Miller, pp. 54–68. New York: Teachers College Press, 1979.

Little, Judith W. *School Success and Staff Development: The Role of Staff Development in Urban Desegregated Schools.* Boulder, Colo.: Center for Action Research, 1981.

McLaughlin, Milbrey W., and David D. Marsh. "Staff Development and School Change." In *Staff Development: New Demands, New Realities, New Perspectives,* edited by A. Lieberman and L. Miller, pp. 69–94. New York: Teachers College Press, 1979.

Moore, Donald M., and Arthur A. Hyde. *Making Sense of Staff Development.* Washington, D.C.: National Institute of Education, 1982.

Sarason, Seymour. *The Culture of the School and the Problem of Change.* 2d ed. Boston: Allyn & Bacon, 1982.

Schlechty, Phillip C., and Betty Lou Whitford. "The Organizational Context of School Systems and the Functions of Staff Development." In *Staff Development,* Eighty-second Yearbook of the Society for the Study of Education, edited by G. A. Griffin, pp. 62–91. Chicago: University of Chicago Press, 1983.

Sprinthall, Norman A., and Lois Thies-Sprinthall. "The Teacher as an Adult Learner: A Cognitive-Developmental View." In *Staff Development,* Eighty-second Yearbook of the Society for the Study of Education, edited by G. A. Griffin, pp. 13–35. Chicago: University of Chicago Press, 1983.

Tobias, Sheila. *Overcoming Math Anxiety.* New York: W. W. Norton & Co., 1978.

# Cooperative Learning in Mathematics Education

David W. Johnson
Roger T. Johnson

A FIFTH-GRADE teacher is concerned with the higher-level problem-solving skills of her students. She randomly assigns her students to groups of three, ensuring that a high-, a medium-, and a low-achieving student is in each group. She informs them that they are an engineering team being asked to submit a proposal for the development of some land into a city park. The *instructional task* is to plan a city park that includes a playground. The students are to (1) plan the design of the park, specifying what materials and equipment will be needed (the total cost must be $5000 or less), (2) draw a picture of how the park will look (including a stream, several trees, and two hills), and (3) write a report describing their design and proposing that it be implemented. The park is to be suitable for all age levels, usable both day and night and in all seasons, safe, beautiful, cost-effective, and innovative. Each group is given a description of the task and a worksheet listing a variety of materials and equipment, their cost, and some basic information about their city. Each student is assigned one of three roles: *accountant* (makes sure all group members can do the mathematical computations), *architect* (ensures that all members help lay out the park on a piece of tagboard), and *elaborator* (relates what the group is doing to previous mathematics problems solved in class).

The students had three class periods to complete the tasks. While the groups worked, the teacher quietly observed the strategies they were adopting and assessed how well they were working together. At the end of each class, the teacher announced her observations and then asked the student groups to process, or assess, how effectively they worked and how they could improve in the future.

*Positive interdependence* is structured by requiring the group to make one park plan and dividing the work into different tasks. All decisions must be made by consensus. *Individual accountability* is assured by randomly picking one member to present each part of the group's plan to the class and by giving each member an essential role. The processing of how well the group was functioning increased individual accountability and social skills, since it allowed students to give each other feedback on how effectively they were working. The *social skills* of checking for understanding (ensuring that everyone can explain), encouraging participation, and elaborating were taught and processed.

## THE NATURE OF COOPERATIVE LEARNING

The teacher described above was using cooperative learning so that students worked together to accomplish shared goals. In a cooperative learning situation, students' achievements of their goals are positively correlated; students perceive that they can reach their learning goals if and only if the other students in the learning group also reach their goals. Thus, students seek outcomes that are beneficial to all group members. When students work on mathematics assignments, they discuss the material with their group, explain how to complete the work, listen to each other's explanations, encourage each other to understand the solutions, and provide academic help and assistance. When everyone in the group has mastered the material, they help another group, until everyone understands how to complete the assignments.

Cooperative learning can be contrasted with competitive and individualistic learning. When mathematics lessons are structured competitively, students work against each other to determine who is best. Students are graded on a curve, which requires them to work faster and more accurately than their peers. In an individualistic lesson, students work by themselves at their own speed to accomplish learning goals unrelated to those of their classmates. Individual goals are assigned each day, students' efforts are evaluated on a fixed set of standards, and rewards are given accordingly. Most whole-class instruction traditionally has underlying competitive elements where students try to give the "best" answer and then are expected to work individualistically on worksheets and textbook assignments.

## COOPERATIVE LEARNING AND LEARNING MATHEMATICS

If mathematics instruction is to help students think mathematically, understand the connections among various mathematical facts and procedures, and be able to apply formal mathematical knowledge flexibly and meaningfully, cooperative learning must be employed in mathematics classes, for several reasons (Johnson and Johnson 1983; Johnson and Johnson forthcoming (a); Johnson, Johnson, and Maruyama 1983; Johnson et al. 1981).

*First, mathematical concepts and skills are best learned as a dynamic process with the active engagement of students.* Mathematical learning should be active rather than passive. Traditional mathematics instruction has been based on the assumption that students are passive absorbers of information who, as a result of repeated practice and reinforcement, store what they know in easily retrievable fragments. Active learning requires intellectual challenge and curiosity, which are best aroused in discussions with other students.

*Second, mathematical problem solving is an interpersonal enterprise.* Talking through mathematics problems with classmates helps students understand how to solve the problems correctly. Explaining reasoning strategies and analyses of problems to classmates often results in new insights and the use of higher-level reasoning strategies and metacognitive thought. Students are also required to use the language of mathematics. Having to explain one's reasoning allows classmates (and the teacher) to check assumptions, clarify misconceptions, and correct errors in understanding and applying mathematical principles. Students have more chances to explain their reasoning and are more comfortable doing so in small groups than in whole-class discussions.

*Third, mathematics learning groups have to be structured cooperatively* to communicate effectively. Within competitive and individualistic structures, students will not engage in the intellectual interchange required for learning mathematics. Their tendency is to cut off communication, to avoid sharing analyses and strategies with each other, and even to deliberately communicate false information to each other.

*Fourth, cooperation promotes higher achievement in mathematics than competitive and individualistic efforts.* In our meta-analyses (Johnson and Johnson forthcoming (b); Johnson et al. 1981), we found a number of studies comparing the effects of cooperative, competitive, and individualistic learning experiences on achievement in mathematics classes. Seventeen studies comparing cooperative and competitive learning contained enough data to compute effect sizes (average effect size = 0.55), and thirty-one studies comparing cooperative and individualistic learning contained enough data to compute effect sizes (average effect size = 0.68). These results indicated that students at the 50th percentile in the cooperative condition would perform at the 71st percentile in the competitive condition and at the 75th percentile in the individualistic condition. In addition, cooperative learning promotes more frequent discovery, the use of higher-quality reasoning strategies, the generation of new ideas and solutions (i.e., *process gain*), and the transfer of the mathematical strategies and facts to subsequent problems considered individually (i.e., *group-to-individual transfer*).

*Fifth, by working cooperatively, students gain confidence in their individual mathematical abilities.* They receive encouragement and support in their efforts to learn mathematical processes, strategies, and concepts. Furthermore, students in cooperative groups tend to like and value each other and see each other as able to solve mathematics problems. These positive peer relationships and perceptions result in higher levels of self-esteem and a sense of self-efficacy in approaching mathematics problems.

*Sixth, choices of which mathematics courses to take and what careers to consider are heavily influenced by peers.* If one's peers perceive certain classes as being inappropriate, then considerable resistance to taking them develops. Within cooperative learning situations, students tend to like and enjoy mathematics more and to be more intrinsically motivated to continue learning about it. This is especially important for female and minority students—if they are to take advanced mathematics courses and enter mathematics-related careers, their classmates must encourage and support them.

The data indicate that to become confident and successful mathematical problem solvers, students need to work cooperatively. Not only are problem-solving success and individual achievement higher in cooperative groups than in competitive or individualistic situations, but the more conceptual the learning and the more analysis required, the greater is the necessity to discuss, explain, and elaborate what is being learned, all of which increase students' ability to communicate mathematically. The support, assistance, and liking found within cooperative groups, results in more positive attitudes toward mathematics and greater self-confidence.

## BASIC ELEMENTS OF COOPERATIVE LEARNING

Simply placing students in groups and telling them to work together does not promote greater understanding of mathematical principles or the ability to communicate mathematical reasoning to others. Group efforts can go wrong in many ways. Less able members might "leave it to George" to complete the group's tasks (i.e., *free-rider effect*); more able group members might expend less effort to avoid the *sucker effect* or they might do all the explanations and elaborations themselves (i.e., *the rich-get-richer effect*) (Johnson and Johnson forthcoming (a)). Group efforts can be handicapped by self-induced helplessness, diffusion of responsibility, social loafing, negative reaction, an uneven division of labor, or other debilitating patterns of behavior (Johnson and Johnson, forthcoming (a)). Only under key conditions can group efforts be more productive than individual efforts:

1. *Teachers must clearly promote positive interdependence in each learning group.* Positive interdependence is the perception that one is linked with others in such a way that one cannot succeed unless the others do (and vice versa) and therefore that the work of each benefits the work of all. All cooperative efforts begin with the realizations that "we sink or swim together" and that the efforts of all group members to learn mathematics must be coordinated.

2. *Students must engage in "promotive" (face-to-face) interaction while completing mathematics assignments.* Promotive interaction includes assisting, supporting, and encouraging each other's efforts to achieve. Some cognitive processes and interpersonal dynamics occur only when students explain their mathematical reasoning to each other. These include discussing the nature of the concepts being learned, teaching one's knowledge to classmates, and connecting present with past learning.

3. *Teachers must ensure that each student is individually accountable to complete math assigments and promote the learning of other group members.* Students must know that they cannot "hitchhike" on the work of others.

4. *Students must learn and frequently use interpersonal and small-group skills.* Many students have never collaborated in learning situations and therefore lack the social skills needed for doing so. Such skills include leadership, decision making, trust building, communication, and conflict management. These skills have to be taught just as purposefully and precisely as academic skills. Procedures and strategies for teaching students social skills can be found in Johnson (1986, 1987), Johnson and F. Johnson (1987), and Johnson, Johnson, and Holubec (1986).

5. *Teachers must ensure that the learning groups engage in periodic and regular group processing.* Group processing is the discussion of how well group members are learning mathematics and maintaining effective working relationships. Group members need to reflect on how well the group is functioning, describe what member actions are helpful and unhelpful, and make decisions about what behaviors to continue or change. In essence, group processing is metacognitive thought about the functioning of the group.

## THE TEACHER'S ROLE IN IMPLEMENTING COOPERATIVE LEARNING

In a third-grade classroom, the teacher assigns students a set of mathematical story problems to solve. She divides the students into groups of three, ensuring that each group has a high-, medium-, and low-performing mathematics student and both males and females. The students' *instructional task* is to solve each story problem and understand the optimal solution strategies. Each group member is given a set of story problems, and the group receives a set of three "role" cards; each member is assigned one of the roles. The *reader* reads the problem aloud to the group. The *checker* makes sure that all members can explain how to solve each problem correctly. The *encourager* encourages all members of the group (in a friendly way) to participate in the discussion, sharing their ideas and feelings.

Within this lesson positive interdependence is accomplished by the group agreeing on the answer and the strategy for solving each problem. The group certifies that each member has the correct answer on the answer sheet and can correctly explain how to solve each problem. Thus, individual accountability is achieved by having the teacher randomly score one member's answer sheet and select group members to explain how to solve the problems. The collaborative skills learned are checking and encouraging. Finally, the groups process their functioning by answering two questions: (1) What did each member do that was helpful for the group? (2) What could each member do to make the group even better tomorrow?

In cooperative learning, the teacher functions as both an academic expert and a classroom manager (Johnson and R. T. Johnson 1987; Johnson, Johnson, and Holubec 1986, 1988). First, you specify the objectives for the lesson. Second, you make a number of preinstructional decisions. Third, after the lesson is planned, you explain the learning task, the need for positive interdependence, and related instructions for working with each other. At this point you teach the academic concepts, principles, and strategies that the students are to master and apply. Fourth, while the students work in groups, you monitor their effectiveness in completing the assignment and in working cooperatively. You provide task assistance (e.g., answering questions) and help students increase their interpersonal and small-group skills. You expect them to interact with each other, share ideas and materials, support and encourage each others' achievement, explain and elaborate the concepts and strategies, and hold each other accountable for learning. Finally, you evaluate their achievement and help them assess how well they cooperated with each other using a criteria-referenced evaluation system.

### Objectives

When you plan a cooperative lesson, you need to specify two types of objectives: (1) an academic objective matched to the level of instruction and the students' abilities, and (2) a social skills objective detailing what interpersonal and small-group skills will be emphasized. An error commonly made by many teachers is to specify only the academic objectives and ignore the social skills.

Besides these immediate objectives, long-range academic and attitudinal objectives should be specified. Long-term academic objectives include mathematical problem solving and learning to communicate and reason mathematically. The attitudinal objectives include—

- positive attitudes toward mathematics;
- confidence in one's ability to reason mathematically;
- willingness to try various strategies and risk being wrong;
- ability to accept frustration and to persevere when solutions are not immediate;
- attributing failure to not yet using the right strategy, rather than not being able.

Confidence in one's ability to reason mathematically is a prerequisite for learning. Once lost, it is difficult to restore.

### Decisions

Once your long- and short-term objectives are clear, another set of decisions has to be made. The first is to decide on the size of the learning groups. Teachers experienced in using cooperative learning groups keep them small, perhaps two, three, or sometimes four students. The more inexperienced the students are in working cooperatively and the shorter the class period, the smaller the group should be. We prefer groups of three.

The second decision involves assigning the students to groups. You can assign students to heterogeneous or homogeneous ability groups. For work on a specific skill, procedure, or set of facts, homogeneous groups can be effective. For problem-solving tasks or learning how to communicate mathematically, heterogeneous groups are most appropriate. When in doubt, assign one high-, medium-, and low-achieving student to each learning group. In addition, try to maximize heterogeneity in terms of ethnic membership, sex, and social class. Take special care in building groups in which students who have special learning problems in mathematics or who are isolated from their peers will be accepted and encouraged to achieve.

Next you need to plan how long groups will work together. Usually it is preferable to keep groups together two or three weeks, so that eventually every student works with every classmate. Some teachers, however, assign students to groups for a whole semester or even an entire academic year. In some schools student attendance is so unpredictable that teachers form new groups each day.

Your next decision is how to arrange the room. Move the furniture to the sides of the room and arrange each triad in a circle. Students should sit close enough to each other so that they can share materials, talk quietly, and maintain eye contact. The teacher should have clear access to every group. Common mistakes that teachers make are (1) to place students side by side at a rectangular table where they cannot have eye contact with all other members or (2) to have too much furniture between students, so that they are too far apart to communicate quietly and share materials.

You need to decide how instructional materials will be distributed among group members. Especially when students are inexperienced in cooperating, you will want to distribute materials so that the assignment requires a joint effort and that students are in a "sink or swim together" situation. Materials can be arranged like a jigsaw puzzle so that each student has part of the materials needed to complete the task, or one copy of the materials can be given to each group to ensure that the students will have to work together.

Finally, you should plan whether to assign students specific roles or responsibilities. To gain confidence and proficiency in mathematical problem solving, students must arrive at solutions through their own efforts. They must take an active role in solving problems and not simply observe the teacher or other students leading the way. To ensure the active involvement of each student, teachers assign each specific roles that are rotated daily. If students are young or cannot read well enough to comprehend the problems, assigning the roles of reader, explainer, and praiser can be advisable. When all group members can read well, our favorite roles for mathematics groups are the checker (who ensures that all members can explain how to arrive at an answer or conclusion), an accuracy coach (who corrects any mistakes in another member's explanations or summaries), and a relater/elaborator (who asks other members to relate current concepts and strategies to material studied previously). Assigning students such complementary and interconnected roles is an effective method of teaching them cooperative skills and fostering positive interdependence.

### Explaining the Academic Task and Cooperative Goal Structure

The academic task must be explained so that students are clear about it and understand its objectives. One assignment might be to identify all the ways to express the numbers from 1 to 15 as the sum of consecutive numbers. With the whole class, present or review the concepts, facts, principles, and strategies they are expected to learn or apply. Direct teaching can take place at this point.

Modeling problem-solving behavior is always a good idea, especially demonstrating that temporary perplexity is a natural state in problem solving. Pose a problem similar (but smaller) to the ones students are to solve, explain the steps for solving it, and check their understanding of your explanation. Make sure the students realize that ($a$) understanding the strategies for solving the problems is more important than getting the right answer and ($b$) problem solving is a process, with solutions resulting from exploring situations, stating and restating questions, and devising and testing strategies over time. Answer any questions students have about the concepts, facts, strategies, or procedures they are to learn or apply.

Second, you explain positive goal interdependence. You can ask the group to produce a single answer to a problem and arrive at a consensus concerning the optimal strategy. For example, ask how many ways the number 28 can be represented with ten-rods and unit rods. Have them do it once with physical materials and once symbolically. Positive interdependence can be strengthened by providing group rewards, such as bonus points if all members of a group reach a preset criterion of excellence; assigning complementary and interlocking roles; and dividing materials among group members.

Third, you ensure that students understand they are individually accountable for completing the assignment. This accountability can be achieved by individually testing each student, randomly choosing a student to explain the group's answers and strategies to the class, or having each student teach what they know to another student.

Next, you explain the criteria for success, ensuring that all students realize that a criterion-referenced evaluation system is being used; structure intergroup cooperation by giving bonus points if all members of the class reach a preset criterion for excellence; and specify the behaviors you expect of the learning groups. Initially, such behaviors are "stay with your group," "use quiet voices," and "take turns." As already discussed, some general roles include a summarizer, a checker, an accuracy coach, and a relater/elaborator. Other possible student roles specifically relevant for mathematics include the following:

1.  Problem restater: To get to know the problem students use their own words to describe the information provided and the information they seek.

2.  Elaborator: To relate this problem to what has already been learned, ask, "Does this problem remind us of any problem previously solved by the class?"

3.  Strategy suggester/seeker: Suggest possible alternative strategies or ask others to do so.

4.  Approximator: To have group members estimate and approximate the answer before solving it exactly, ask, "What range of answer would be reasonable?"

5.  Review/mistake manager: If a group missed the problem, ask, "What can we learn from this mistake?" If the group solved the problem correctly, ask, "How can our solution be improved?"

6.  Confidence builder: Say, "We can do it!"

## Monitoring and Intervening

After the lesson has been structured and students have their initial instructions, the teacher should observe each learning group to keep track of the students' problems (and successes) in solving the problem and working together effectively. Careful and systematic observation allows you to see if and how they might be failing and what they do not understand.

When needed, help students to work productively and independently. In essence, you become an intellectual and social skills coach. Establish the rules that (1) you will not respond to a student's question unless all group members have their hands in the air and wish to ask the same question, and (2) you will not give correct answers but rather will help students understand where they have made mistakes.

Frequently, students embark on a single strategy to solve a problem without questioning its effectiveness. This practice guarantees that they will fail. You will need a set of questions to break their fixation on the strategy they are using and to help them consider others, for example:

1. What are you doing?
2. Why are you doing it?
3. How will it help?

When helping a group, stay at its eye level by pulling up a chair or kneeling. Question the group members or assign a member to fill a missing role, and leave when the group members can function independently. Have some extensions of the problems to give to groups who finish before the rest of the class.

If you find students who do not have the necessary cooperative skills or groups where members are having problems in working together, intervene to suggest more effective procedures and student behaviors. Basic interpersonal and small-group skills can be taught directly (Johnson 1986, 1987; Johnson and F. Johnson 1987).

You will also wish to provide closure to the lesson. At the end of the lesson, conduct a whole-class discussion in which you randomly pick students (1) to summarize how they solved the problems, with emphasis on the strategy chosen and why, rather than on answers; (2) to elaborate by relating the problem to ones solved previously or by giving students similar problems to solve. Ask, "What strategy did your group use?" "Did you consider other strategies and how did you decide on this one?" and "Can you think of another problem you have solved that this one reminds you of?" At the end of the whole-class discussion, you can summarize the major points in the lesson, answer any final questions students have, and pose additional challenges for the more interested and able students. Asking students such questions ensures that they engage in metacognitive consideration of how they discovered which strategies are appropriate for solving a problem.

### Evaluation and Processing

At the end of the lesson you will evaluate students' learning and give feedback as to how their work compares with the criterion of excellence.

Qualitative as well as quantitative aspects of performance should be addressed. The learning groups then process, that is, assess, how well they worked together and how they can improve their effectiveness in the future. Our two favorite questions for doing so are "What actions helped the group work productively? What actions could make the group even more productive tomorrow?" A common error of many teachers is not giving students enough time to process the quality of their collaboration.

## GETTING STARTED

Implementing cooperative learning is a structured, but complex, process. Start small by using cooperative learning procedures for one mathematics class or unit and then expanding the procedures into other classes or units. For example, ask the class a question such as "Which is greater, 3/4 or 2/3, and why?" Tell students to turn to a partner and decide in two minutes on an answer that either student can explain. This is cooperative learning. Learning partners can check each other's homework, prepare each other for a test, contribute different steps to solving a math problem, and think up alternative strategies to use.

## PROFESSIONAL SUPPORT GROUPS

To gain and maintain expertise in using cooperative learning, you need assistance and support from colleagues. You cannot become proficient in using cooperative learning procedures by reading this article or even attending a workshop. You become proficient and competent from using cooperative learning in your classes. The sustained use of cooperative learning is ensured by a collegial support system in which you give and receive continual and immediate in-class assistance. Have frequent discussions with colleagues about cooperative learning, model its use, co-teach lessons, and help each other solve implementation problems.

## SUMMARY

Cooperative learning is essential if mathematics teachers are to promote students' problem-solving competency, ability to communicate and reason mathematically, perception of the value of mathematics, and self-confidence in their ability to apply mathematical knowledge to new situations. Although competitive and individualistic assignments should be given at times, cooperation should be the dominant learning structure in mathematics.

Cooperative learning is more than simply assigning students to groups and telling them to work together. To be cooperative, a lesson must include positive interdependence, face-to-face interaction of students, individual